THE CRITICAL LAWYERS' HANDBOOK 2

**EDITED BY PADDY IRELAND
AND PER LALENG**

D0708535

Pluto Press

LONDON • CHICAGO, IL

First published 1997 by Pluto Press
345 Archway Road, London N6 5AA
and 1436 West Randolph
Chicago, Illinois 60607, USA

British Library Cataloguing in Publication Data
A catalogue record for this book is available from the British Library

ISBN 0 7453 1087 7 hbk

Designed and Produced for Pluto Press by
Chase Production Services, Chadlington, OX7 3LN
Typeset from disk by Stanford DTP Services, Milton Keynes
Printed in Great Britain

Contents

PART FOUR – ENVIRONMENT

Table of Cases

Acknowledgements

Many people have been involved in the production of this book. Of those known to us, we would like to offer particular thanks to Donald Nicolson who was involved in the project in its early stages, to Katherine de Gama for her invaluable contribution to the chapters on gender and to Peter Fitzpatrick, our series editor, for his encouragement and (at times, sorely tested) good humour.

We would also like to thank our contributors, not least for their patience; Pluto Press, and especially Anne Beech and Robert Webb, for their assistance and efficiency; Emma Thompson for her sterling editorial work; and Joanne Conaghan, Patrick, Rosie and (latterly) Edward for, among other more important things, putting up with the domestic problems caused by books like this. Rather more than mere thanks are due to Ian Grigg-Spall for not only getting this book but the idea of critical lawyers groups off the ground.

Paddy Ireland
Per Laleng

Kent Law School,
University of Kent at Canterbury
March 1997

List of Contributors

Paddy Ireland and Per Laleng teach law at Kent Law School, Eliot College, University of Kent, Canterbury.

Roger S. Clark is Distinguished Professor of Law at Rutgers Law School, Camden, New Jersey, USA.

Joanne Conaghan teaches law at Kent Law School, Eliot College, University of Kent, Canterbury.

Katherine de Gama teaches law at the School of Law, Keele University.

Steve Emmott is a member of The Genetics Forum.

Peter Fitzpatrick is Professor of Law at the Faculty of Laws, Queen Mary and Westfield College, University of London.

Makbool Javaid, former chair of the Society of Black Lawyers, now works with the Commission for Racial Equality.

Wade Mansell teaches law at Kent Law School, Eliot College, University of Kent, Canterbury.

Donald McGillivray and John Wightman teach law at Kent Law School, Eliot College, University of Kent, Canterbury.

Werner Menski teaches law at the Department of Law, School of Oriental and African Studies, University of London.

Gillian More is a visiting fellow at the Department of Law, London School of Economics and Political Science.

Pragna Patel is a member of the Southall Black Sisters.

Aimee Paterson teaches law at the Department of Law, Birkbeck College, University of London.

Sol Picciotto is Professor of Law at the Department of Law, Lancaster University.

Sally Sheldon teaches law at the School of Law, Keele University.

Patricia Tuitt teaches law in the School of Law, University of East London.

David Wilkinson teaches economics and law in the Department of Economics, Keele University.

Introduction: Critical Legal Studies and Radical Politics

Paddy Ireland and Per Laleng

The first volume of the *Critical Lawyers Handbook*, published in 1992, offered essays on critical legal theory, critical legal education and critical legal practice. It sought to provide an introduction not only to critical legal studies in general but also to the academic and political differences which had emerged within the movement, touching on the contrasting approaches and strategies being adopted at that time by critical lawyers. This volume focuses on some (but by no means all) of the areas which have in recent years occupied the attention of critical legal scholars, offering a range of chapters on race, gender, environmental and international issues. The underlying objective remains the same, however: to try to suggest ways in which critical legal studies might become more than an academic movement and inform radical legal practice specifically and political practice more generally.

There are a number of themes running through the chapters in this volume. One of the most prominent, and one which has come to characterise much recent work by critical legal scholars, is the emphasis on, and celebration of, diversity and difference. In this context, many of the chapters examine the ways in which law operates so as to suppress diversity, excluding and silencing some voices while privileging others. In those on race, for example, Peter Fitzpatrick explores the 'New Europe' where a new culture of exclusion has emerged, based on a supranational nationalism which, he argues, is integrally racist and culturally fundamentalist; Patricia Tuitt analyses the (selectively) exclusionary way in which the idea of 'the refugee' has been constructed; and, in different ways, Werner Menski, Aimee Paterson and Makbool Javaid all chart the continuing insensitivity of British legal education to ethnic, cultural and religious diversity, with Menski questioning the the use of 'race' as an analytical category and noting the differential treatment offered by English law to different ethnic groups. The chapters on gender similarly explore the ways in which law excludes, in this case the experiences and voices of women. Joanne Conaghan, noting the poor representation of women in its case law, examines the gender bias of tort, including that embodied in the notion of the 'reasonable man' or 'person'; Sally Sheldon considers the consequences for women of the medicalisation of issues such as abortion; and both Katherine de Gama and Pragna Patel expose the continuing gender insensitivity of law in general and the criminal law in particular. In the realm of international law, the chapters by both Wade Mansell and Sol Picciotto can also be read as showing how traditional approaches to international law tend to evade questions of (economic and political) inequality and power. Picciotto, in particular, reminds us that despite the contemporary emphasis on 'globalisation' the internationalisation of markets does not necessarily entail homogeneity; that, on the contrary, despite the homogenising tendencies of consumer culture, the world is far more heterogeneous than many seem to think.

Many of the chapters also raise the recurring question of the efficacy or otherwise of law and the Rule of Law – both in pursuing the goals of multiculturalism and cosmopolitanism which have emerged in the wake of the growing focus on diversity and difference, and in dealing with the more specific and concrete problems associated with racial and sexual inequality, ecological destruction and international instability. Some of our contributors seek to show how law might be used in a progressive manner. Donald McGillivray and John Wightman, for example, argue that it may indeed be possible to mobilise private law actions such as nuisance and trespass against official definitions and assumptions of the possibilities of environmental protection. Roger Clark demonstrates how international law can be mobilised to gain, at the very least, a symbolic recognition of international human rights abuses. And Pragna Patel's stirring account of the campaign to free Kiranjit Ahluwalia shows how fighting legal battles can not only raise consciousness but also act as a springboard for campaigning on wider social and political issues. One of the themes of both her chapter and some of the others, however, is the need for more than purely legal action to achieve change. In this context, many of the contributions highlight the fact that the language and form in which social problems are framed shapes not only perceptions of them but also the solutions offered; that law in its construction of issues marginalises certain experiences and voices; and that when problems are (re-)defined in legal terms, the social structures and processes of which they are part often disappear from view. Crucially, of course, when such structures and processes are overlooked, so too are vitally important questions of power. Thus, Wade Mansell argues that where international law uses the language of formal or procedural civil and political rights (such as democratic elections, state sovereignty and so on), consideration of substantive issues such as poverty, racism or 'lifestyle' (social, economic and cultural rights) tends to be avoided, not least because they are not easily justiciable. While Western cultures often favour a legalistic, 'rule'-based approach to social problems, developing countries sometimes prefer a more elusive and inclusive 'principled' approach. And yet, as Picciotto observes, in a world characterised by growing inequality, both between and within states, power legitimated through law is far preferable to that exerted through the barrel of a gun.

Nor are these problems confined to legal discourses and interpretations. For example, in looking at abortion and battered women's syndrome respectively, both Sally Sheldon and Pragna Patel examine the disadvantages for women of framing issues in medical terms. The medicalisation of daily life in general and of abortion in particular, Sheldon argues, can operate in an exclusionary way. The regulation of abortion, for example, is now commonly constructed as a (depoliticised) medical issue confronting an individual woman – a woman who within medical discourse is commonly constructed as a biologically 'natural patient'. On this basis, law feels justified in vesting enormous power in doctors, granting them considerable discretion and autonomy. As Sheldon observes, this not only works so as to deny women participation in crucial decisions concerning their own bodies and lives; it also marginalises a whole range of vital social questions relating to abortion – lack of contraceptive advice and access, the fact that the burden of childrearing still falls squarely on the shoulders of women and so on. As a result of the medical interpretation of 'the problem', debate tends instead to centre on questions of foetal status and development; social structures and processes disappear from view. It is with similar awareness of these wider structural questions that David Wilkinson assesses the limits of public regulation of the environment and Steve Emmott draws our attention to the need for a wider debate on the appropriation of the world's genetic resources rather than expecting existing law to adequately encompass modern technological developments.

In short, then, the chapters raise many difficult questions not only about the power relations embodied in law, but about the limits to, and problems associated with, progressive legal action. Does the use of law to pursue some goals inevitably entail the reinforcement of an ideologically laden and exclusionary (legal) discourse? Is it the case, as Gillian More puts it in the conclusion of her contribution, that in order to realise our goals 'we must look further than litigation'?

THE RISE OF 'LOCAL' RESISTANCE

As this brief survey suggests, since the publication of the first volume the difficult questions concerning the role of law in progressive political movements and the meaning of 'critical' in relation to legal studies and practice have, if anything, become even more troublesome.[1] The backdrop to the debates in this area has, of course, been one of major political upheaval. We have been through, we are told, an epochal change, in some versions moving 'beyond left and right' (Giddens, 1994), in others reaching the 'end of history' (Fukuyama, 1992). Certainly, there is no longer the once clear sense of left–right political division; of parties representing the interests of different social classes; of conflict between two (or more) dramatically different and competing visions of the future. Hence the rise of what one commentator – commenting on the Clinton–Dole presidential race and, in particular, on the former's focus on issues which in the past would have been regarded as part of the humdrum minutiae of local government (school uniforms, teenage curfews, waiting periods for handgun ownership and so on) – has called 'micro-politics'. In this context, the terrain of 'radical' politics has itself been gradually redefined. Some have characterised the changes as a move from class politics to a politics of 'social movements' and 'identity' in which class is but one identity among many; others as a move from an overriding concern with the economy (and therefore with capitalism) to a concern with 'civil society' and a range of social practices previously neglected by the old left; still others as a move away from so-called totalising theories to pluralism, from Marxism to postmodernism with its emphasis on contingency and fragmentation, and its hostility to structure, totality, process, and so-called 'grand narratives'. No matter how one characterises the changes, however, what is abundantly clear is that there has been a shift in focus from an emphasis on social transformation in general towards strategies of 'local' resistance in a range of discrete areas.

There can also be little doubt, as the chapters in this volume show, that these developments have enriched both radical politics and critical legal studies. Some of the discussions found in these chapters would have been unimaginable when the banner of critical legal studies was first unfurled twenty years ago. The new pluralism, with its focus on 'civil society', has led to a much closer examination of a whole range of previously neglected institutions and relations, and this has helped to generate a range of emancipatory struggles not based on class. In turn, the recognition and celebration of diversity and difference has helped the development of new and valuable sensitivities which focus on dimensions of human experience often ignored by the old left. As the contributions to this volume demonstrate, we are now much more aware of the heterogeneity of injustice; of the gendered nature of law; and of its discriminations and racism. With this, the spaces within which it seems possible to engage in radical political and legal practice have increased and widened, with people now engaging with a range of social movements and politically self-conscious 'identity' groups. Moreover, the increased focus on more manageable, particular, 'local' issues of this sort seems to provide both the legal practitioner and the legal academic with a more prominent role to play in achieving concrete social change. In general terms, the underlying political hope seems to be that through the reform of 'civil society' citizens can be empowered by an extension of freedom and choice in ever more democratic and accountable institutions. What is required to fulfil the promise of civil society, the argument runs, is substantial *legal* reform of (and by) the state – hence the recent pressure for Bills of Rights, constitutional reform, 'democratisation', Citizen's Charters and so on. If power and coercion in their many guises can be resisted and eradicated by progressive legal change, it is argued, a better, freer world can be achieved.

But has this shift in political (and legal) focus been unequivocally beneficial? What, if any, are its drawbacks? The political theorist Ellen Meiksins Wood suggests that while 'there are strong and promising emancipatory impulses at work today', they may 'not be active at the core of social life, in the heart of capitalist society'. Is it possible that the new approach adopted by many within the critical legal studies movement itself operates so as to exclude consideration of crucial (structural) questions? That while the increased emphasis on struggles for what Wood calls extra-economic goods – gender emancipation, racial equality, peace, ecological health and so on – is healthy and desirable, in avoiding a confrontation with capitalism, it is also, at least in part, self-undermining (Wood, 1995, ch 9)? These are some of the broader theoretical questions that we wish briefly to address in this introduction. In doing so, we urge the critical legal studies movement to redirect some of its attention to the broader questions of social and economic structure which, we believe, it is increasingly neglecting.

POSTMODERNITY OR MATURE CAPITALISM?

Much has been written about the alleged historic transition from modernity to postmodernity. In many circles, modernity and what is now commonly called the 'Enlightenment project' – meaning, crudely, a belief in universal truths and values, in progress, and in reason – are frequently blamed (in the more temperate accounts) for everything from imperialism to the Holocaust, from world wars to the destruction of the environment. Associated with this postmodern view is, of course, a denial of the possibility of 'totalising' knowledges. Belief in the systematic power, unity and logic of capitalism, for example, has been replaced by a belief in multiple social realities and causalities. Indeed, some contemporary left intellectuals are reluctant to recognise the existence of capitalism, let alone analyse it, while others seek to emphasise the varied and fragmentary nature of modern capitalism*s*. Paradoxically, however, the very intellectual trends which have led to the rejection of such 'totalising' theories have been accompanied by a tendency to treat 'the market' as something akin to a law of nature, thereby linking themselves with the grandest of all grand narratives – 'the end of history'. As a result, in many postmodern accounts, capitalism becomes all but invisible, part of a seemingly unchanging and unchangeable background reality. Its social origins disappear, as does its historical specificity; it is as though capitalism has no beginning and no end, but has always been there waiting to fulfil its natural destiny (Wood, 1991). This has contributed to the contemporary feeling that there are no more 'big' issues to be resolved; that all that remains for radicals to do is to fight for a wide range of 'single' issues, a process which does not require any challenge to the basic social and economic organisation of society.

As a result, the growing tendency (often unwitting) has very much been to seek changes *within* capitalism. Hence, the aim of much contemporary radical political activity seems to be to create a 'left' culture which concentrates not on political economy, but on discourse and identity; a political culture which operates between capitalism's fragments rather than seeking directly to challenge it. To a significant extent, the terrain of politics has thus become not capitalism itself – as a systematic unity, it has to a large extent been conceptualised out of existence – but the various discourses and identities which can be found within it. The underlying assumption appears to be that the world can be changed by discursive (de- and re-)construction (we can be what we think we are), an activity which can, of course, be conducted, in the academy at least, with minimal material constraint, save those of funding cuts and the demands of the Research Assessment Exercise. The result has been the rise of something resembling a radical liberal pluralism, which does not attempt to engage in an exploration of modern capitalism and of the material constraints that it might impose on 'local' resistance. The question as to how far it is possible to fight successfully for these single issues within the capitalist system is rarely posed, let alone answered. In short, there has emerged a radical version of 'micro-politics'.

The postmodern focus on the diverse, fragmentary, heterogeneous nature of modern 'society' (the term 'capitalism' is usually avoided) is in certain respects rather curious. As Sol Picciotto points out, at a time when both markets and societies are increasingly being opened up to global competition through the elimination of barriers to economic flows, more and more aspects of social life are being exposed to the pressures of world markets. There has never been a time when capitalism's totalising power and homogenising force has been greater. What, perhaps, really marks out the modern epoch as distinctive and different is not a move from modernity to postmodernity, but the maturation of capitalism: the universalisation of capitalist social relations, of commodification, of accumulation, of profitability. Every aspect of life has become subject to the abstract requirements and imperatives of capitalist markets; capitalism is increasingly penetrating every nook and cranny of the life-world. With this has come growing legal colonisation (Habermas, 1992), growing legal regulation of social life by the state, and increasing pressure on law to provide legitimation – all things that are (and should be) of particular concern to critical legal scholars. In this context, it is clearly arguable that there has never been a time when a critical understanding of capitalism has been more urgently needed. Indeed, many of the outrages now routinely attributed to the 'Enlightenment project' and to modernity and its values might better be ascribed to capitalism as an economic and social system. Far from being the purveyor of modernity, capitalism is, perhaps, better seen as its destroyer.

Paradoxically, the contemporary response to growing capitalist totalisation (and the intellectual and political problems that accompany it) appears to be a rejection of totalising theory. The fact that forms of domination other than class domination are to be found in contemporary society – that there are a plurality of social identities and social relations – comes to be regarded as evidence, if not proof, that capitalism is not a totalising system. It might, of course, be precisely its omnipresence that renders it invisible; precisely the growing commodification of the life-world that has generated the increasing sensitivity to, and ever greater emphasis on, the lifestyle diversity celebrated by postmodernism. With true postmodern irony, the denial of capitalism's growing penetration and power might itself be a reflection of the very thing denied.

However, the reality is, surely, that the 'identities' and social spheres targeted by modern radicals are themselves increasingly subject to the determinative forces of capitalism, and for that reason alone, as well as for others, the analysis of modern capitalism ought to remain an important starting-point for a politically informed critical legal studies, if only because it is only from here that one might begin to assess both the limits and possibilities of different forms of both political and legal action. In other words, it may be that the intellectual dissolution of capitalism into an essentially unstructured plurality of social relations and practices – none of which have any general explanatory power – not only causes emancipatory projects to lose much-needed political guidance, but also causes them to underestimate and misunderstand what it is they are up against. For example, as David Wilkinson suggests, it is difficult to see how, under a capitalist system, continuing environmental damage and destruction might be averted. This is not to say that environmental protection is not itself a potentially profitable activity and that some measures cannot (and will not) therefore be taken to alleviate the devastation. It is, however, to say that, ultimately, not only does the environmental movement lack a clear political agent, but that there are good reasons for thinking that the imperative to accumulate might well impose serious structural constraints on what it can achieve in a capitalist world. Indeed, it is difficult to avoid the conclusion that if there really is a sense in which capitalism represents the end of history, it may turn out to be a product of the fact that it brings pressures on the world such as to make continued life unsustainable: the continued emphasis on accumulation and growth, on the exploitation of resources, human as well as natural; the constant competitive drive to push wages still lower, even among the already lowest paid; the constant setting of working people against one another (both nationally and internationally) as they struggle to find decently paid work; and, finally, in the West, the erosion of welfare provision.

In this respect, race, ethnicity and gender might be rather different from the environment. One of the defining characteristics of capitalist exploitation is precisely its 'purely' economic nature: it does not rely upon extra-economic, legal or political identities. In principle, capital will exploit anybody, whoever and whatever they are. Hence, as it seeks out new labour markets, capital has a tendency to treat alike all potentially exploitable workers. This tendency towards formal equality (of a sort) can be – and, of course, has been – exploited by (among others) critical legal scholars. Having said that, when it is advantageous to do so, capital has also shown itself to be very adept at taking advantage of and preserving existing gender, ethnic and cultural differentiations and oppressions. It is, then, neither surprising nor insignificant that, as Lynne Segal has pointed out, in the last twenty or so years, despite possessing the largest and most vociferous feminist movement in the world, American women have seen less change in their overall (disadvantaged) position than the women of other Western democracies. Notwithstanding the huge gains made by American women in the most lucrative and prestigious professions, nowhere has the feminisation of poverty been more apparent (Segal, 1991). This, of course, raises the question of where class identity fits into contemporary identity politics. Inequality, oppression and power, surely, go to the very heart of class identities. We may wish to encourage and celebrate a range of different cultural diversities – sexual, racial and other – but do we really want to encourage and celebrate class diversity?

In short, then, the new liberalism, with its emphasis on pluralism and diversity, needs to be wary that it doesn't come to represent a silent accommodation with capitalism. And critical legal scholars and practitioners need, in turn, to take care that the welcome emergence of a wide range of emancipatory aspirations does not become an excuse for political retreat; that the move from universalism – now reflected in the West in the shift from universal (modernist?) programmes of social security to the targeting of particular groups – does not fragment and undermine rather than consolidate any broader sense of (class) solidarity; that in encouraging us to conceptualise capitalism away and to disaggregate the world into a multiplicity of particular and separate realities, we are not also being encouraged to abandon much that is good in the Enlightenment project, notably its commitment to universal human emancipation.

At present, the evidence is that we are going backwards in a wide range of areas – poverty (national and international), education, immigration and asylum, social security, the environment, police powers, to name but a few – notwithstanding the growing legal regulation of more and more aspects of social life by the state. For the latter reason alone, it is likely that practising lawyers will continue to have an important role to play in fighting oppression in its many forms, and that academic lawyers will continue to be very well placed to plot and clarify the movements of modern capitalism, ensuring that the determinations of all relationships and institutions are fully explored. Whatever one's view, critical legal studies clearly has an important contribution to make to the crucial battles of ideas and understandings taking place across a whole range of social and political issues: as the imperatives of capitalism increasingly determine the parameters of all our lives, the urgent need is to move away from the mindset of 'there is no alternative' to one of 'things cannot go on like this'. However, while critical lawyers will be required to fight for the disadvantaged and underprivileged every inch of the way, the question remains as to whether law can provide an adequate defence against oppression, let alone help to deliver a transformed world.

In making these points, we are not proposing that critical legal studies retreat into abstract theorising. Nor do we think that critical legal studies should entirely abandon its focus on civil society. Far from it. We do, however, believe that certain difficult questions and issues need to be confronted if the movement is to fulfil its aims. Ultimately, therefore, we find it hard to resist David Harvey's conclusion that 'the mere pursuit of identity politics as an end in itself (rather than as a fundamental struggle to break with an identity which internalises oppression) may serve to perpetuate rather than to challenge the persistence of those processes which gave rise to those identities in the first place' (Harvey, 1993). Paradoxically, it may be in a critical re-engagement with political economy that similarity and solidarity between different groups will be found to reside, for it is, perhaps, in their subjection to the imperatives of capital accumulation and profitability that people increasingly find themselves in a world which, in certain respects, is homogeneous.

NOTE

1. See Kim Economides and Ole Hansen, 'Critical Legal Practice: Beyond Abstract Radicalism' and John Fitzpatrick, 'Legal Practice and Socialist Practice', both in Ian Grigg-Spall and Paddy Ireland (1992, pp 142–8, 149–57).

Part One

International

1
International Law: The Legitimation of Power in World Affairs
Sol Picciotto

International law sits very uncomfortably in the law school curriculum. For legal professional requirements, it has until recently been treated as irrelevant and is still considered to be peripheral for practising lawyers in the UK. Law is mainly taught as private law governing relationships and transactions between individuals, and even public law tends to focus on the rights of the individual. Thus, coming to international law, which deals with the regulation of world affairs, students are forced to confront much more directly questions about the relationship between law and public power. These are especially hard to resolve from the traditional perspective of legal positivism, which sees legal norms as commands issued by a superior authority, rather than as growing out of and being rooted in social relationships and institutions.

The result is that 'international law' is still commonly regarded as a contradiction in terms, and therefore not 'real law'. Its precepts are either considered to be rationalisations of the interests of the powerful; or they are seen as idealised aspirations for world peace, human rights, or saving the planet, which are flouted by the powerful. In fact, international law manages to be both of these, due to the ability of law both to articulate power and to legitimise it.

Public international law is defined as law between states. Hence it is impossible to make much headway in understanding it without grasping the nature of the state. Usually, however, both international lawyers and international relations specialists treat the state as a subject – that is to say they reify or personify the state. It is treated as a unit, and international society is referred to as a 'community of states'. Discussions about international law therefore focus on the special characteristics of this community, which are said to explain the peculiar nature of its law. Since there is no supreme authority in 'the international community', there are no compulsory procedures for law-making, dispute-settlement, or enforcement, and therefore from the viewpoint of pure legal positivism it has no 'law' at all. Others regard international law as law of a peculiar kind, generally as that of a less developed or primitive society, reliant on self-interest, reciprocity and decentralised sanctions for its enforcement. Enthusiasts for international law, on the other hand, consider that these features are in fact its strengths: the behaviour of states is said to show at least an expectation of compliance with commonly accepted rules, and these rules are argued to be effective most of the time, due to their relative determinacy and coherence, their power of symbolic validation, and general adherence to them (Franck, 1990).

The modern territorially defined state is at the intersection of the distribution of political power. Its authority to assert an internal monopoly of coercion depends upon and interacts with the international normative framework. The state consists of public bodies asserting exclusive authority over a territorially defined space, but the extent of that authority is limited by the international context. The main limitation is exerted by the existence and possibilities of international contacts, transactions and flows across state borders. In the pre-modern state, authority was personal and trade was long-distance, between communities which regarded each other as exotic. Imperial China built the Great Wall to keep out the hordes and gave European merchants special rights of access, requiring them to live in enclaves where their own laws applied (the classic system of 'extraterritoriality'). In Europe also, the political structures were vertical, built on the personal ties of allegiance of the subject to a superior 'sovereign', and not defined primarily by territory. Such sovereignties could be piled one atop the other; only gradually was the absolutist concept of the power of a liege converted into a notion of exclusive legal power. In contrast, the post-Napoleonic state claims exclusive authority over a defined territory, but that authority is not absolute, either internally or externally.[1] Internally, the exercise of the modern state's authority is legitimated through the abstract and impersonal processes and symbols of law, and this is counterpointed externally by the norms and rules of international law which regulate the interrelationships of those public sovereigns. It is this interaction of state sovereignties and the changing nature of the state that underlies the development of international law, and current debates and struggles over its transformation.

CRITIQUES OF INTERNATIONAL LAW

Significantly, the new wave of debate in the 1980s, as writers from various perspectives have sought to rethink the nature and role of law in international affairs, predated the major changes in interstate relations which occurred in the 1990s. Much of the writing on international law in the 1970s accepted a functionalist and even instrumentalist view of law, arguing for an adaptation of law to the changed 'realities' of international society, especially the creation of many new states by decolonisation. Equally major upheavals have transformed the political landscape since 1989: the collapse of state socialism in Eastern Europe, the end of the Cold War, and the disintegration of the Soviet Union and of other states created in the years following the First World War. Yet the new concern with re-evaluating international law has not been a direct response to these changes in the character and number of states, but has deeper roots in the broader global crisis. Despite immense advances in productive potential in the international economy, we still do not have minimum tolerable standards of housing, sanitation, health, education or even food for the vast majority of the world's people. Even more agonisingly, continuing violence and even desperate warfare has symptomised the continuing disintegration of the European-inspired nation-state – in many parts of Europe itself as well as in Africa and Asia. Yet the sharpening of these contradictions has generated a widespread sense of powerlessness.

It is this which is reflected in the current ferment of intellectual debates about the possibility and limits of reason, order and justice in society. In earlier periods, dissatisfaction with traditional perspectives and explanations led either to projects for a new world order, or at least to critiques of the existing bases of social power, aiming to empower the oppressed. In contrast, the postmodern pessimism of the recent period makes its challenge not just to the existing order but to the possibility of any order, or of any objective basis for universal or even generally acceptable principles of law governing conduct in international society (Carty, 1986; Kennedy, 1986; Koskenniemi, 1988, 1991a). Yet in relation to the central issue of the changing nature of the state and of the global system, some of the critical and theoretical approaches which are confined to linguistic deconstruction of the conceptual framework of international law have serious limitations. Thus, Carty refers to the state as a 'metaphysical entity'(Carty, 1991, p 94), and Allott (1990) argues for dissolving the state as an illusion preventing the proper self-awareness of individual human beings as part of world society. In contrast, Koskenniemi has pleaded that we must 'take statehood seriously' and has opted for formal statehood as a necessary (although second-best) protection from the anarchy of global diversity (Koskenniemi, 1991a, p 42; 1991b, p 397).

The new concern with the basis of normativity in international society has led to the rethinking of the conceptual structure and ideological effects of international legal rules, whether by those who wish to explain and justify their efficacy (Franck, Kratochwil), those who seek a reconceptualisation (Allott), or the deconstructionist critics (Kennedy, Koskenniemi, Carty), who reject the pretence or deception involved in maintaining the possibility of a universal system of rules. In general, however, there seems to be a large gulf between the debates within theory and any engagement with or attempt to understand the changes taking place in international society. As a first step, it is certainly important to abandon the simplistic positivist belief in law as rules, and view it as a social process which helps to structure and mediate political and economic relations. Rosalyn Higgins, recently elevated to the International Court of Justice as its first woman judge, has pointed out that, at least in this emphasis on law as process, some of the critical legal studies (cls) perspectives resemble the 'policy-science' school pioneered at Yale and of which she is an adept exponent. However, the cls writers view law as radically indeterminate and contradictory, so that international legal arguments cannot be evaluated except by going outside the law – yet the realm of politics is not one in which the postmodern critics are generally comfortable. The policy-science school, on the other hand, argues that legality entails ensuring 'that decisions are made by those authorised to do so, with important guiding reliance on past decisions, and with available choices being made on the basis of community interests and for the promotion of common values' (Higgins, 1994, p 9). However, this perspective offers little theory or analysis of society, viewing politics essentially as a process of decision-making based on values, without reference to social structure or organisation and therefore evading questions of inequality and power. Thus, especially in the hands of the dominant Yale theorists of the Lasswell–McDougall school, it tends to result in apologia for the perspectives of authoritative decision-makers, and especially of US foreign policy-makers, cloaking their policies in value-justifications based on generalised concepts of the human good.

Although traditional approaches, whether positivist or realist, can be criticised for treating international politics merely as an objective realm of 'pure facts' which can be quarried to provide evidence of the observance or non-observance of international law (Koskenniemi, 1991a, pp 37–9), not all sociology or social inquiry is positivist. Theoretical reflection can provide a basis not only for understanding but also for committed interventions in social practices; while a critical interpretation of these practices should in turn contribute to the construction of a reflexive theoretical standpoint. No individual can claim to have privileged knowledge of the truth, but social inquiry takes place as a process of interaction, which is also bound up with broader social and political processes. Thus, a social-science methodology based on a reflexive perspective and self-aware political practice must take into account that necessary interaction, and help the intended audience make its own intersubjective evaluation.

'GLOBALISATION'

Our objective should be to seek a better understanding of the role of law in the global political economy, and especially its relation to power. This is especially so now, in the closing decade of this century, with major changes and conflicts in the global system, in which international law is being revamped and pressed into playing an increasingly important role. These changes are often summarised by reference to the much-contested concepts of 'globalisation', and the 'new world order'. The terms are misleading, since a glance at the daily news shows that the world is not moving either towards a stable order or increased global unity. These are also ideologically loaded terms, often used to present a particular vision as inevitable.

Nevertheless, there have undoubtedly been major transformations in the global political economy, especially since the disintegration of the Soviet bloc and of state socialism. A major feature has been the opening up of markets and societies to global competition, through the drive to eliminate all barriers to economic flows and to give market access for all kinds of trade and investment. While this has increased the potential for such international flows, and their volume has increased in absolute terms, they are not generally greater when considered as a proportion to internal flows within national socioeconomic space (Thomson and Krasner, 1989). The effect has rather been to increase competitive strains, so that every aspect of social life is now more exposed to pressures from world markets. This inter-nationalisation of markets does not create an inevitable trend to global homogeneity, but fosters a greater awareness of diversity and difference, and a tension between the tendencies and strategies towards homogeneity and those towards heterogeneity. There are certainly manifestations of the same consumer culture everywhere from Birmingham to Beijing, symbolised by the arrival of McDonald's in Red Square. At the same time, there is greater awareness and appreciation of cultural diversity, for example in world music or cuisine, as well as a resurgence of local pride and often aggressive nationalism or sectarianism, from Belfast to Bosnia.

The crises of identity resulting from these tensions are widely familiar, but less discussed is their very unequal impact. Certainly, people everywhere are being increasingly exposed to the possibilities of international flows and contacts, but for most they are mainly a threat. A coffee grower in Colombia, a tuna fisher in Peru, or textile worker in the Philippines are vulnerable to globally interconnected forces over which they have little control. Only for a relatively small elite does 'globalisation' create improved opportunities, greater choice, and more control based on improved information. Yet even these are only possibilities, offering challenges: for example, the availability of a wide range of global information sources from TV, newspapers or the Internet does not necessarily improve its quality. The ease with which the attention of millions can quickly be focused on a global drama such as an oil spill, a famine, or a civil war, does not necessarily facilitate a sustained and profound understanding of global issues – on the contrary, it can foster soundbite politics. It certainly increases the political importance of control of access to information-diffusion networks: the first action taken by the French military when they boarded the Greenpeace ship taking action against the Mururoa nuclear tests was to disable its satellite-transmission equipment.

In many ways such changes, now described as 'globalisation', are a heightening of contradictory tendencies present in the international system for the past hundred years or more. Although they are often said to herald the demise of the nation-state, as its capacities for effective action are undermined by the pressures of global forces, it can equally justifiably be said that control and regulation of global market forces still essentially depend on states. However, the very character of the state, and in particular of the international states system, are undergoing some major transformations, as part of the changing pattern of local–global links.

UNIVERSALIST AND STATIST VIEWS OF INTERNATIONAL LAW

The underlying concern in contemporary debates about international law is what sort of legality is possible or appropriate in a world which has become increasingly diverse, complex and conflictual, and at the same time increasingly interdependent. Although this dual centripetal and centrifugal process has become increasingly acute in the past decade, it has marked the history of this century. The attempt to grasp the tensions created by this dialectic of increased diversity and interdependence has also polarised international relations theorists. This relatively new discipline has, virtually since its inception, been broadly split between the realists or neo-realists who, continuing the tradition of diplomatic history, have focused primarily on interstate (meaning essentially intergovernmental) relations, and on the other hand a variety of neo-functionalists, who have preferred to emphasise the 'spider's web' of social relations in 'world society' which cut across the 'billiard balls' of the territorially defined nation-states (Burton, 1972). This latter approach has appeared in successive manifestations as interdependence theory, transnational relations, regime theory (Krasner et al., 1982; Levy et al., 1995), and currently 'policy networks', 'epistemic communities' (Haas et al., 1992) and 'global civil society' (Lipschutz, 1992; see generally Groom and Taylor, 1990). They have recently been reinforced by sociologists and social theorists generally, who have discovered the issue of 'globalisation' (see, for example, Sklair, 1991), discussed in the previous section.

For international lawyers these debates strike a familiar chord, since for most of this century they have been wrestling between statist and universalist conceptions. On the one hand, the state-centred view has retained its power, emphasising the autonomy and sovereignty of the nation-state, and therefore a strict dualism between international and municipal law and a reluctance to accept that international legal obligations restrict state autonomy unless very clearly accepted through the 'consent' of sovereign states. Against this there has been a pull towards a new universalism, involving a close interaction or symbiosis between international and national law, accepting that international law can create rights and duties not only for states but also for individuals and transnational corporations, and arguing for global legal regimes covering matters as diverse as human rights, the protection of the natural environment, and international business or commercial transactions.[2] The tension between these two perspectives underlies much of the theory and practice of contemporary international law. It also cuts across jurisprudential divisions such as divide positivists and naturalists, as well as the different political standpoints and economic interests of rich and poor, developed and underdeveloped countries. Thus, in Britain there has been a neo-Grotian revival, initiated by figures such as Hersch Lauterpacht and Wilfred Jenks, who wrote of the Common Law of Mankind; while in the United States, teachers in the major law schools from the 1950s began to combine elements of private and public international law, together with comparative, constitutional, but most importantly corporate and commercial law, into what Philip Jessup as long ago as 1956 named Transnational Law. It was this approach that helped revive US international law from a neglected subfield to an important place in their law schools, nearly all of which now have their own journal of the law/politics/economics of inter- or transnational transactions. This combination of international and business law has also helped equip US corporate lawyers to play a major role in building the new fields of international legality (Dezalay and Garth, 1995; Trubek et al., 1994).

By contrast, in Africa, Asia and Latin America, where so many new states had been formed during the postwar process of decolonisation, the politics of nationalism led to a strong emphasis on state sovereignty. Although during the independence movements and in the first flush of the post-colonial dawn, the principle of self-determination was seen by some to entail the rejection of imposed colonial boundaries, it quickly became apparent that the political basis of the nation-state owed more to the lengthy historical experience of administration of territorially defined entities than it did to ethnic ties. Thus, the African states quickly followed the historical precedent of Latin America in adopting the *uti possidetis* principle,[3] and the grander projects of overcoming these divisions through a process of African unification were rapidly eclipsed by the consolidation of a nationalism which was both quick-growing and tenacious. The more recent experience of Eastern Europe again emphasises that viable statehood requires a delicate combination of a culturally constructed national identity linked to a territorially defined unit, even if this be an administrative unit of a previously federal or unitary state.[4] The long agony of the former Yugoslavia shows the damage which can result from ethnic, racial or linguistic consciousness alone.

However, the granting of independent statehood to peoples who had been colonised and dispossessed also implied the creation of a more egalitarian international society and the ending of historical injustices which had been fostered or tolerated by a Eurocentric legal order. It also soon became clear that this was not simply a case of rewriting legal rules to catch up with social changes, but involved complex interactions between the law and political and economic power. The drive towards political self-determination was quickly reinforced or complemented by pressures for economic self-determination, which mainly took the form of the assertion of a right to sovereignty over natural resources, and then the broader programme for a New International Economic Order. Thus, the very strength of the pressures for national political sovereignty nevertheless engendered the paradoxical effect of a heightened awareness of international interdependence. Nevertheless, the political elites in poorer and weaker states, both those in power and the oppositional currents, have generally continued to stress the formalist legal concept of the sovereign equality of states. In a world in which social and political inequalities are also expressed as inequalities between states, national sovereignty is seen as a bulwark against the threat of political intervention from more powerful states. At the same time, the poorer states can try to rely on their numerical strength within international institutions to attempt to bring about the transformations in the international system which could overcome the massive international disparities and inequalities which were the heritage of colonialism.

The difficulty is that formal legal sovereignty without economic or political strength is an empty vessel, as is shown by the experience of over three decades of negotiations between the Group of 77 countries and the developed states in various forums. For example, while the latter have been stubborn in protecting their markets against imports of manufactured goods in which poorer countries are competitive, notably textiles, they have insisted on liberalisation and removal of barriers even where there is total lack of reciprocity – for example, patents and other intellectual property rights. The setting up of the World Trade Organisation brings this to its logical conclusion, by tying together many of the key issues of international economic relations within an institutional framework dominated by the bargaining of market access, which creates a ratchet effect in favour of the rich. States now find themselves very directly subject to the pressures exerted from the world economy, or 'market forces', and even the most powerful sovereigns find themselves unable to impose national political controls which can stand up to the relentless pressures of global competition.

THE NATION-STATE, SOVEREIGNTY, AND JURISDICTION

Much of the confusion about the implications of globalisation for the nation-state is due, as already mentioned above, to the reification of the state, reinforced by the concept of 'sovereignty'. The modern form of state, which emerged in the post-Napoleonic period, is a particular form of governance, in which the overt elements of coercive power are removed from personal relations and vested in autonomised institutions with a public character. The scope of the formal power of these institutions is defined in terms of territory, as opposed to the personal ties of allegiance which delimited the powers of the feudal and absolutist sovereigns. However, the foundation of modern states took place through political processes central to which was the cultural conception of the national community. Thus, the 'nation' of the nation-state is not a natural, predefined ethnicity but a powerful ideological construct, an 'imagined community'(Anderson, 1991).

The notion of supreme or untrammelled power embodied in the concept of sovereignty has two aspects, internal and external. Internally it legitimises the assertion of the state's monopoly of coercive force. A key prop in this legitimation is a particular form of legality, based on abstract and universalist principles, which claims to underpin and guarantee the formal equality and freedom of legal subjects facilitating capitalist economic exchange. Externally, it is the states themselves that are free and equal legal subjects, interacting in a community of a different order and on a higher plane, with no overarching authority but God.

Thus, the concept and discourse of sovereignty functions as a particular way of legitimating the distribution of political power. The exercise of power is legitimated within the state by the generation of consensus around the national common interest through the institutions and processes of political participation involving all citizens on a basis of formal equality. Some restrictions on the apparently unlimited power to adopt national policies in the common interest are accepted as resulting from the need to bargain with other formally equal sovereigns on the basis of the national interest of each for reciprocal benefits or to secure mutual or common interests. The fiction of unlimited internal sovereignty is complemented and sustained by its corollary, the sovereign equality of states.

The concept of state sovereignty, the unlimited and exclusive powers of the public authorities within the state's territorial boundaries, appears to be fixed and unchanging. Looked at more closely, however, its content and character are highly flexible, and have changed and developed together with the very form of the state as well as the changing nature of social relations. This can be seen very clearly when one focuses on the functional content of sovereignty – state jurisdiction. Jurisdiction may be defined as the scope within which the power of public or state authorities can *effectively* and *acceptably* be exercised. The emphasis on effectiveness and acceptability, usually ignored by formalist perspectives, is essential for an understanding of the limits of jurisdiction and therefore of sovereignty. In the modern state, the scope of sovereignty is said to be territorial: 'the right to exercise (in regard to a portion of the globe) to the exclusion of any other state the functions of a state' (Judge Huber, *Island of Palmas case* (1928) p 92).

However, this exclusivity can only be fully effective if the state prohibits all transborder interactions. Since transborder social and economic activities entail multiple geographic contacts, even if states exercise their powers purely territorially there will be considerable overlapping and interaction in states' exercise of jurisdiction. The identification of the state with the 'nation' further transforms the basis of the exercise of state sovereignty into the more flexible and elusive notion of national jurisdiction. While the state has generally imposed obligations on all those resident within its borders, the privileges of citizenship have been bestowed on a more restricted category, its nationals. Nationality, again, is a variable concept, so that different national cultures have given varying importance to ties of blood, birthplace, or loyalty, in the conditions for grant of nationality or of discretionary 'naturalisation'. These bonds between its nationals and the state have also been used to justify the extension of state jurisdiction, as citizenship is considered to carry a nexus of obligation, by most states in some degree, to their nationals' activities abroad.

It can be seen, therefore, that far from being circumscribed in precise and mutually exclusive terms, the scope of exercise of states' powers defined by their jurisdiction, which is the substance of 'sovereignty', is flexible, overlapping, and negotiable. This is especially so in relation to jurisdiction to regulate business activities, since the claim to jurisdiction over nationals has been extended to the fictitious legal personality bestowed on the business unit, in particular the company or corporation. Jurisdiction over a corporation can be based on the fictions either of its nationality or residence, and can vary for different purposes, using as criteria either the law under which it is formed, the location of its 'seat' or head office, or the place from which central management or control is exercised. A 'control' test may be used to justify a claim to jurisdiction over the worldwide activities of transnational corporate groups or transnational corporations (TNCs), on the grounds that foreign subsidiaries are subject to ultimate control by their dominant shareholders or parent company, and states have increasingly asserted such jurisdiction over 'foreign' companies especially to defeat or prevent regulatory avoidance by the use of 'foreign' subsidiaries incorporated in jurisdictions of convenience.

Thus, it is not surprising that the dual pressures on the state discussed above have increasingly brought to the fore the problem of jurisdiction. The overlap of jurisdictions has become greater with the interpenetration and globalisation of markets, while the increased regulatory role of the state has rendered ineffective the traditional mode of accommodating jurisdictional interaction based on 'comity' (Picciotto, 1983). Initially this led to jurisdictional conflicts and accusations of 'extraterritoriality', followed by attempts to moderate the exercise of jurisdiction (OECD, 1987), and the growth of arrangements for coordination or cooperation in the exercise of jurisdiction. More recently, the pressures towards global market liberalisation have virtually created a market in state regulation, as states compete to attract investment by offering the most advantageous regulatory regime (Bratton et al., 1996).

CHANGING FORMS OF INTERNATIONAL LAW

International law was born as a form of regulating relationships between sovereignties which were both autonomous and interacting. Hence, the tensions traced in the earlier section in the postwar representations of international law between statism and universalism merely rearticulate in new forms issues and themes which go back to the very origins of the system. However, the personification of the state and the emphasis on a unitary concept of sovereignty have helped to conceal the very major changes that have taken place in the nature of states, and therefore in the character of their interaction and the role of law within and between states. The procedures, institutions and concepts of international law have undoubtedly become far more complex and diverse over the past few decades, as the expectations and demands on states have grown, while at the same time the range and variety of issues identified as global or international have also increased exponentially.

Probably the most significant change, but one strangely neglected by international lawyers, is the development of a vast international institutional framework for international relations. Certainly, lawyers acknowledge the centrality of the United Nations system, but this is usually presented in the curious form of the debate about whether General Assembly resolutions are a 'source' of international law. Beyond that, and a chapter on the 'peaceful resolution of disputes', many international law books do not venture, although the practice of the discipline, certainly by state officials, now largely takes place in and through such organisations. This means not only the major and relatively visible intergovernmental organisations, of which there are now estimated to be many hundreds, but an even larger network of bodies ranging from relatively formalised institutions with written constitutions and a permanent secretariat, to committees of diplomats or officials meeting when required.

Such bodies now deal with matters involving a vast range of state functions, and their importance often varies inversely with their visibility or degree of formalisation. For example, in 1950 an informal Consultative Group was set up at the initiative of the US, which operated for several decades as a means of coordinating the embargoes on trade in military items and related technology by its members, consisting of representatives of the NATO countries with the exception of Iceland and the addition of Japan. The Group has apparently met rarely at Ministerial level, but functioned continuously through the so-called Coordinating Committee, or CoCom, consisting of midlevel diplomats and technical military specialists, whose task was to establish and then revise and review the comprehensive lists of embargoed items. CoCom was apparently not based on any treaty or other formal legal instrument, operating as a 'gentlemen's agreement', yet was nonetheless effective. Although it was wound up in 1994, after the end of the Cold War, it is being reborn in a similar form to coordinate trade in militarily sensitive technology to destinations deemed to be politically undesirable. An equally important and informal body is the so-called 'Paris Club', which is simply a procedure for the multilateral renegotiation of government debt by creditor countries when they are in a situation of 'imminent default'. It has no fixed members, but consists of meetings convened and chaired by a French finance ministry official on the request of a debtor country and involving all its official creditors. As with the CoCom, agreements under its auspices are not considered to be legally binding, but establish a framework for formal bilateral pacts. Just as CoCom operated in the shadow of NATO, the Paris Club depends on the IMF, since its participants reschedule their bilateral debt only after a creditor state's acceptance of the 'conditionality' terms laid down by the IMF for its credits. Both bodies coordinate international negotiations on important issues of power (the one military-industrial, the other economic-financial), and utilise primarily technicist and bureaucratic techniques. Yet, although their formal status is quasi-legal at best, law also plays a part: there is precedent and reasoning by analogy, there are documents and rules and agreements to be drafted, and above all they deal with legal concepts and ideas such as liability, prohibition, obligation and sanction.

Thus, behind or below the highly visible and formal structures of the major intergovernmental organisations, the United Nations and its specialised agencies, the IMF, World Bank and others, there is a much denser network of less formal but in many ways more functional arrangements for coordinating state policies and actions. Their ambiguous status in international law arises because they are established or operate essentially as an arena for the interaction, below the level of foreign offices and diplomacy, of officials or a more general policy community concerned with specific areas of state or quasi-state activity. Even Interpol, which facilitates international cooperation in a function as central to state sovereignty as policing, has long tried to resist formalisation as a treaty-based intergovernmental organisation, preferring to operate as a club for policemen without political 'interference' (Anderson, 1989, esp. ch 3). More easily accepted as a nongovernmental organisation is IOSCO (the International Organisation of Securities Commissions): although its members are the official regulators of securities markets, in many cases from national finance ministries, they also include designated self-regulatory associations such as stock exchanges, which are not direct branches of the state.

Such bodies in any case often act not as a means of achieving formal international agreement but as a stage or arena for multilateral negotiation of standards or arrangements, perhaps supplementing or reinforcing networks of bilateral contacts and agreements. Thus, a working group of IOSCO's key body, the Technical Committee, produced two detailed reports in 1990 analysing the problems (mainly legal) experienced in developing international exchanges of information by the regulators on the basis of MOUs or Memorandums of Understanding. These arrangements are examples of the growth of international administrative cooperation involving officials, regulators, and policy communities of many kinds. Since they involve the interaction of national systems of law and administration, they attempt to resolve the often complex problems of conflict and coordination of national laws as applied to transnational transactions: for example, whether the enforcement powers of a national regulator may be used to collect evidence of breach of another state's laws. As international agreements, they are certainly drafted using legal form and terminology, but explicitly disavow an intention to create legal obligations between the signatories, let alone their states.

Nevertheless, these MOUs illustrate very clearly that international agreements are today not merely pacts between rulers, but increasingly establish systems of coordination between national legal regimes. Due to the very wide range of state functions and activities with which they deal, international agreements can take a wide variety of forms, ranging from these MOUs establishing administrative cooperation among national regulators, to the comprehensiveness of the multilateral framework established to coordinate regulation of the uses of the world's seas by the 1982 UN Convention on the Law of the Sea (UNCLOS III). Indeed, the UNCLOS diverges from the standard image of a treaty as much, although in different ways, as the MOUs. UNCLOS does not establish a set of rules merely to be obeyed by states, but a framework of principles which have evolved over the 15 years it took to negotiate the Convention, as well as in the further dozen years until it entered into force in 1994. Indeed, the post-signature period was one of continued negotiation, mainly due to the USA reopening the compromises embodied in the text, due to the Reagan government's opposition to the deep-seabed mining regime provided for in Part XI. Although this conflict was resolved by the adoption of an Agreement on Implementation of Part XI which effectively modifies UNCLOS,[5] many of the principles both of the modified Part XI as well as of UNCLOS as a whole, will provide a focus for continued debate and bargaining. Thus, the requirement that the Enterprise set up under Part XI to conduct deep-seabed mining operations should do so in accordance with 'sound commercial principles', or that the transfer of technology to it should be 'on fair and reasonable commercial terms',[6] may establish some parameters but clearly still leave considerable scope for discussion and negotiation. This is even more obviously the case for other important issues, notably the delimitation of international maritime boundaries, which has exercised negotiators and adjudicators for several decades, especially since the rejection by the International Court of Justice of the equidistance rule and its affirmation that delimitation is based on 'a rule of law which itself requires the application of equitable principles'.[7]

LAW, POWER AND LEGITIMATION

This imprecision or indeterminacy of legal rules creates unease, especially among positivists,[8] for whom legal rules must be capable of clear and logical application to fulfil their function of providing certainty and predictability. On the other hand, it is the focus of critical legal scholars, who from their various perspectives seek to demonstrate that the indeterminacy of law means that the substantive content of legal rules is supplied from politics,[9] and hence law's autonomy is a sham. As mentioned in the opening paragraph of this chapter, international law is especially vulnerable to this charge, since the lack of compulsory adjudication leaves it without guaranteed procedures for the authoritative interpretation of its rules.

My own view is that it is important to understand and appreciate the relationship of law to politics and economics, and the particular role it plays in mediating social relationships. To say that those relationships are relations of power and often of exploitation, and that law generally helps to legitimise them, is neither to denounce law as illusory nor to deny its civilising role. After all, relations of power are of many sorts, and involve degrees of consent and coercion, and power legitimised through law is far better than that exerted by the barrel of a gun. It is nevertheless also important to probe and expose the limits of law's capacity to legitimise, and to see how this can be strengthened, as part of a more general process of achieving social and economic justice. In particular, merely to denounce liberal legal principles for their indeterminacy is perhaps to overlook that it is precisely this fluidity and flexibility that enables them to fulfil their role of mediating social relations of power.

The main problem for international law is the extremely weak nature of the international political system, which creates a great burden or dilemma for international law. If sovereignty, or political legitimacy, resides only in nation-states, then the content of international law can only be supplied by the reciprocal bargaining of 'national interests' between government representatives. If, however, there are higher global interests at stake, in peace, in the preservation of the ecological balance, in economic development or at least the satisfaction of basic needs for the world's population, then how and by whom are those interests to be expressed? This, surely, is the dilemma of the international lawyer, which Koskenniemi has articulated as the alternative of becoming the apologist for diplomacy or power politics, or of projecting utopian designs for world order. What needs to be recognised is that this is not a dilemma the international lawyer can solve alone, although there are certainly important contributions to be made from that perspective. A major step is to look behind the distorted or partial legalistic perspective, to try to understand law's relationship to broader social changes.

As I have tried to indicate in this chapter, the central limitation of international law lies in the personification of the state, which draws a veil over the very real contradictions and changes that have been taking place in the nature of the state and the international system. What is more, it impedes an adequate appreciation of international law itself. I have argued that the main feature of the past few decades has been the increasing demands made on the state, while at the same time states have become increasingly interdependent. As a result, it is hardly surprising that there has been a process of fragmentation of the state, both internally and internationally. This can be seen also in the many changes that have been taking place in the role of law in international relations and activities. The horizontal and vertical axes of law have become intermingled, so that new categories of transnational and supranational law have been devised. Perhaps less often noticed, the very category of law itself has become more diffuse, and forms of quasi-law or 'soft' law have come to play a part in mediating different aspects of international relations. However, underlying all these changes in the forms and functions of international law are the increasing pressures under which it has come in attempting to provide legitimation for the acute tensions in a world community characterised primarily by the very great inequalities within and between states.

NOTES

1. An excellent account of the simultaneously national and international nature of the modern states system, combining a theoretical analysis with a historical account, has recently been provided by Joshua Rosenberg (1994).

2. David Kennedy, in his re-evaluation of the writings of the 'primitives', from Vitoria to Grotius, contrasts them with the 'traditional' international legal scholarship of the post-Westphalia period, and the 'modernists' of the twentieth century. Indeed, although he is scrupulous to read the primitives on their own terms, his interest is to contrast their ideas with the subsequent perspectives: in his reading, the traditional scholars emphasise state sovereignty and make a sharp distinction between international and national law, while the 'modernists' attempt in various ways to overcome this, without returning to the naive universalism of the 'primitives'. His essay (Kennedy, 1986) itself thus attempts to chart modern concerns by re-reading the past.

3. Benedict Anderson has stressed the historical significance of the fragmentation of the Spanish empire into 18 states at the end of the eighteenth century. Although the geographical and economic factors which moulded Spanish policies helped turn the arbitrarily defined territorial units into economic zones, Anderson argues that the decisive force was the generation of a national consciousness involved in the formation of a specific creole culture (Anderson, 1991, ch 5). Although the twentieth-century nationalisms of the Asian and African colonies had their own distinct social roots (and the fact that, following a century of state formation, there was an established model for their aspirations), Anderson argues that the cultural patterns which formed the key strata of nationalist intellectuals were again rooted in the fatal racism of colonialism, which offered those intellectuals access to metropolitan civilisation, but only to a limited and circumscribed extent (Ibid, ch 7).

4. The principle of self-determination has operated most strongly to legitimise the independence of colonial dependencies, but the breakup of the USSR, Yugoslavia and Czechoslovakia show that it has broader application. Although the people of Eritrea had a longer struggle they also vindicated a right which was based on their long independent history, and the same claim can surely be made for others such as the people of West Sahara and East Timor. The detailed statement of the principle of self-determination contained in the 1970 Declaration on Principles of International Law Concerning Friendly Relations and Co-operation Among States strongly opposed 'any action which would dismember or impair, totally or in part, the territorial integrity or political unity of

sovereign and independent states'; however, this was subject to the important qualification, 'conducting themselves in compliance with the principle of equal rights and self-determination of peoples as described above and thus possessed of a government representing the whole people belonging to the territory without distinction as to race, creed or colour'. This recognised a link between internal human rights and the right to self-determination as a separate state, and this has been more explicitly stated in the EU's Guidelines on the Recognition of New States in Eastern Europe and in the Soviet Union of 1991. However, the Yugoslav experience also shows that unless the claim to self-determination can be identified with an existing territorially defined administrative unit, it is likely to spark off the vicious circle of interethnic conflict seen not only in Bosnia but also in Cyprus, Northern Ireland and elsewhere.

5. Annex to UN General Assembly resolution 48/263 of 28 July 1994.
6. Agreement Relating to Implementation of Part XI, sec 2.2 and sec 5.1.
7. *North Sea Continental Shelf Cases* (1969) ICJ Reports 3, at 46–7; see generally Charney, 1994.
8. See the discussion by R. Higgins of the ICJ's use of the doctrine of equity especially in the maritime boundary cases (Higgins, 1994, pp 219–28); despite her orientation towards policy jurisprudence, Higgins is also uneasy about the uncertainty produced by the ICJ's use of a notion of equitable principles, on the grounds that only a series of disparate criteria have been enunciated, with no evaluation of their relative weight (Ibid, p 227).
9. See, for example, Koskenniemi, 1990, p 28, where he specifically refers to UNCLOS as having no real rules but allocating decision-making power elsewhere by the use of equitable principles. For a discussion of cls views on indeterminacy, see Kelman, 1987.

2
Pure Law in an Impure World
Wade Mansell

Students new to international law studies are often surprised by its content. Those who come from an international relations background are often astounded. If they come to the study with an initial assumption that international law is intimately involved with current international affairs, they will usually be quickly disabused. British international law textbooks, at least, seem to deny any such involvement. The inference to be deduced from the content of such books is that a study of international law can be a very pure one indeed without any necessity for reference to the rather sordid contemporary political world about which international law is supposedly concerned. The political world as it appears in the texts is not only merely historical, it is history without context and without emotion. For such texts the greatest international events of the twentieth century appear only as desiccated legal decisions or opinions.

There is, furthermore, a remarkably standard content to the texts with the main differences to be found in the depth of detail. This suggests either that there is an agenda for the study of international law which is accepted and noncontroversial, or that such has been the consistency in the way in which international law is taught in British universities that it is almost impossible to provide a critique of the subject without giving universal offence to the authors of such texts and thus making oneself available to ridicule. In this chapter I will suggest that we should be suspicious of such orthodoxy and that a critique of international law must necessarily consider the politics which underlie it and with which it is inextricably interlinked. The intention is not, however, to denigrate international law as such but rather to provide ways of considering its ideological assumptions, assumptions which are not only to be found in the content but in the very process and procedures of international law.

Among the exceptions to my typification of British international law texts is Antonio Cassese's *International Law in a Divided World.*[1] He at least addresses, albeit perhaps with excessive generalisation, the lack of a common agreement on international law method (Cassese, 1986). His argument with regard to 'developing countries' and the 'socialist states' (which were extant at the time of his writing) is that there are crucial differences in perceptions of international law. I shall mention only his assessment of the ideological perception of various African countries. It does not take a genius to understand that given the very different cultural traditions of these states, with emphases upon family, lineage, and tribe, a different conception of international law is not unlikely. Cassese suggests that for such states international law cannot be seen as an abstract problem-solver (as it often appears in texts), but that 'rather [to them international law is relevant to the extent] that it protects them from undue influence by powerful states and is instrumental in bringing about social change with more equitable conditions stimulating equitable development' (Ibid, p 249).

To this end Cassese sees many developing states very much preferring 'to elaborate general principles as opposed to detailed and precise legal rules' (Ibid, p 119) and he uses a telling quotation from an Egyptian international lawyer (G. Abi Saab) upon which I wish to elaborate:

> ... in dealing especially with the Western countries, anything which could be formulated in the very precise terms of an operational rule was considered nonsense [by developing countries], while Third World representatives in general attached great weight to general principles which sometimes could not be refined into operational rules. If we look at the same thing from a different point of view I would say that in most cases the attitude of the Third World was defined by the total effect of a proposed solution ... I think that the Western powers put too much emphasis on the mechanistic elements [of law] while for Third World countries if by going through all the motions and respecting all the procedural rules you end up with an unjust solution, this would be bad law. And if you have a general directive, even if you cannot reduce it to very precise procedural rules, it is still good law, though it may be imperfect in terms of application. (Cassese, 1980, p 249)

In many ways that quotation summarises a fundamental distinction in the perception of law, both international and domestic. I have argued elsewhere that what distinguishes the Rule of Law way of viewing the world is that the Rule of Law gains its effect and authority through its ability to translate social problems into legal questions, but this is both a strength and a limitation in that the question which is resolved through law is the legal question rather than the social problem (Mansell, 1991; Mansell, Meteyard and Thomson, 1995). Often this will not matter, but equally, particularly in the case of international disputes, it may on occasions matter a great deal. If the effect of a legal answer is not to resolve the social problem (as I argued it did not in the case of Third World 'debt') then the problem may be aggravated rather than resolved. Nevertheless, two further comments must be made. Because the West sees such 'principles' as not truly justiciable they are often regarded as of no real legal value and while the West has acceded to such General Assembly resolutions as that concerning a right to development, it has done little to give the right content. Secondly, theoretically at least, the West claims to uphold the Rule of Law in international law and to be bound by it even when this is inconvenient or worse. We will consider this claim a little later.

The difference of approach in international law is nowhere more clearly exemplified than in the area of international human rights. Exemplifying the Western approach is a study by Charles Humana, an earlier edition of which received the stamp of approval of the United Nations in its 1991 Development Report (Humana, 1992). The *Sunday Times* in London described the study as 'useful and telling ... [showing] in the clearest possible way, how the world is divided at present between the free and the unfree'.[2] Humana's methodology was to ask each of the 104 countries 40 questions which elicit answers which allow him, in the space of a mere four pages, to make a comprehensive human rights assessment for each of the chosen countries. Before these questions are posed Humana summarises for each country, population, life expectancy, infant mortality, United Nations Covenants ratified, form of government, gross national product per capita, and the percentage of GNP spent on health, military and education. The results are fascinating. The average human rights 'rating' for the 104 countries is 62 per cent.

Western readers may not be surprised to discover that not one Muslim country or Islamic state reaches that average. Malaysia manages 61 per cent and Bangladesh 50 per cent, while all the rest hover between the 17 per cent of Iraq and the 33 per cent awarded to Kuwait, (apart from Turkey at 44 per cent). In Humana's assessment, whatever else they might excel at, Muslim governments are rotten at protecting human rights. Also lurking down with the human rights pariahs are states (of which there are very few left now) which purported to pursue socialist goals. Cuba receives a dismal 30 per cent, with Humana summarising the position as follows:

> For over thirty years the country has been a one-party Communist state under the leadership of President Fidel Castro. All aspects of government, political life, and society are directed toward the perpetuation of the system and its ideology. Although there is less overt brutality than in previous years, human rights relating to political opposition, a free press, the independence of the courts, trade unions and seats of learning are severely circumscribed. With the end of communism in the Soviet Union, the economic aid and

international support given by that country to Cuba are being terminated, and new austerity measures are being adopted. Human rights improvements are unlikely until the regime is deposed. (Humana, 1992, p 83)

By contrast Guatemala received a human rights rating of 62 per cent with Humana disingenuously commenting that:

The holding of multi-party democratic elections regarded by foreign monitors as genuine and equitable, contrasts with the reality of one of the most violent societies in the world. As well as conducting operations against guerilla groups, the army and security forces follow a policy of arbitrary killings of many of those opposed to their right wing dogmas. Their victims therefore include human rights monitors, academics, students, trade unionists, liberal politicians, and journalists who risk criticizing them. The death toll exceeded 5,000 in 1990, a proportion being victims of the guerillas. Attempts by the government to control its own forces are usually ineffective, partly from the fear of the consequences and partly because the military and the police seem to be above the law. (Ibid, p 122)

To those of us who know anything of the conditions in Cuba and Guatemala in 1990 those ratings must surely come as a surprise. The surprise is aggravated when one contrasts not the answers to the questions Humana posed but the preliminary information he provides. Cubans had a life expectancy of 75.4 years, Guatemalans, 63.4 years. The infant mortality rate per thousand live births was 14 in Cuba and 97 in Guatemala. Cuba spent 3.2 per cent of its GNP on health, Guatemala 0.7 per cent. Guatemala devoted 1.8 per cent of its GNP to education and Cuba 6.2 per cent. This is undoubtedly an extreme example, but it is not atypical. El Salvador, at that time still in the grip of the death squads, rated 53 per cent, Honduras 65 per cent and Costa Rica 90 per cent! Even Rwanda in 1991, which has since seen a massacre of a million or so of its people, rated 48 per cent as did Kenya, though not surprisingly the rating for Africa as a whole, with one or two exceptions, was dismal. South Africa, still pursuing a policy of apartheid, nevertheless managed a 50 per cent rating.

Of course the obvious response for Humana and his defenders is to state that the concern of the human rights rating scale is with civil and political rights rather than economic, social and cultural rights (though how well he does even this is open to question). Coincidentally, these civil and political rights are the very rights at which the rich and 'developed' world excels. With some notable Islamic exceptions there is a close correlation in Humana's tables between not only wealth and rating, but between the pursuit of liberal capitalist goals and human rights rating. Even so, it might be thought unjust in judging Humana not for what he did but for what he did not do. This is certainly an argument, but on another level what Humana has done is not simply partial in the sense of only looking at civil and political rights, it is also partial in its ethnocentricity – in its continuing emphasis upon one aspect of human rights at the expense of others no less important. Humana continues the Western tradition of regarding rights which are not clearly justiciable as children of a lesser god. His work also exemplifies dramatically the politics of human rights language and theory, and it also has wider implications in international law.

It is not coincidental that the International Covenant on Civil and Political Rights of 1966 is so differently expressed from the International Covenant on Economic, Social and Cultural Rights of the same year. Nor is it surprising that the level of implementation is so different. The former draws upon the 'Rule of Law' tradition while the latter is much more of the non-Western tradition of normative and flexible declarations of principle. One can make any of several inferences from this. Firstly, that the difference in tone reflects a difference in the type of goals pursued, in that civil and political rights should be immediately realisable regardless of economic, social and cultural problems; whereas economic, social and cultural rights must be considered in the light of existing realities. Secondly, that the West has a much greater commitment to civil and political rights which it generally grants without problem or expense, than to economic, social and cultural rights which it could, though only with financial commitment, greatly advance. And thirdly, that the interests of Western and 'developing' countries coincide in this division in that prioritising the alleviation of poverty is certainly not made mandatory for either.

Moving away from the human rights example, we see a continuing tension in the way international law is expressed and indeed even a serious debate about what amounts to international law. 'Developing' countries have often sought to use General Assembly resolutions (often expressed in the broadest language) as principles with legal content.[3] Western countries, even when they have been prepared not to obstruct the adoption of resolutions with which they have little sympathy, deny the legal content of such resolutions. Nowhere is this more clearly to be seen than in the General Assembly resolution on a Right to Development passed with only one state (the United States) opposing, 9 abstentions and with 156 votes in favour (Mansell and Scott, 1994).

From this it might seem that I am suggesting that the Western tradition is to accept international law in the spirit of the idea of the Rule of Law, whereas for other states, notwithstanding international law, resolution to conflicts remains negotiable. This is misleading for two reasons. The first is that it puts undue emphasis upon the 'gone wrong' problem case in international law whereas the 'gone right' is infinitely more frequent if very much less visible. As in domestic legal subjects, we tend to gain a misleading understanding of international law because of the emphasis in legal education upon the pathological case. The second is that although it might be denied, when a powerful state (actually the leaders of that state) decide that international law compliance is contrary to its interest it is disingenuous to suggest that it will feel the same attachment to the Rule of Law. To illustrate that proposition I want to use the example of the United States, partly because it is the world's most powerful state and partly, and almost paradoxically, because its discussions and decisions are so transparent.

At first sight it may seem that the subsequent discussion is confused because I am attempting to make two points which may initially seem incompatible. The first is the exemplification of the United States' willingness to ignore international law and the unfortunate consequences that follow, and the second concerns the relationship between this and the non-Western states' emphasis upon international law as principle rather than rule of law. I hope to remove any confusion a little later.

The easiest source for material evidencing the United States' position with regard to international law which its leaders think inimical to its interests might be thought to be Noam Chomsky, whose writings[4] continue to provide a cynical and well-documented interpretation of United States' motives which is difficult to refute. But in order to appeal to those for whom Chomsky is anathema, it is less controversial to refer to the writings of D.P. Moynihan who has also written about United States foreign policy in the 1980s. Moynihan's background is less controversial than that of Chomsky. He was for some time US ambassador to the United Nations, has been a US senator for New York, and has also been a professor of Government at Harvard University. In 1990 he published a revolutionary book entitled *On the Law of Nations* (Moynihan, 1990). The thesis of the book is that in the 1980s, particularly under President Reagan, the United States treated international law with something approaching contempt – 'approaching contempt' in the sense that it was in some ways less than contempt in that the United States simply ignored legal dimensions of their foreign policy. Moynihan is incensed by this and argues cogently not only that this was an immense break with the past (the most doubtful piece of this thesis!) but also that in pragmatic terms, and with hindsight, this ignoring of international law was dysfunctional to United States foreign policy. Given Moynihan's conservative background, what are we to make of this thesis?[5] Why and under what circumstances does Moynihan wish to uphold the rule of law in international law?

Political explanations are perhaps threefold. Firstly, the lack of compliance with international law might have meant that goals could be pursued which ought not to be pursued. Secondly, to ignore international law had the potential to rebound against the United States if other states were to follow suit – that is, the United States' self-interest might best be served by upholding international law. Thirdly, any lack of legitimacy in international policies could in turn corrupt the Rule of Law within the United States' domestic legal system. To some extent the three are interrelated, but significantly they are not co-extensive. Generally speaking, Moynihan does not seem to oppose the policy goals pursued by the United States in the 1980s. His real complaint is that in ignoring international law, the goals become *more* difficult to accomplish rather than less. When we realise what these goals were, the fact that they might have been more acceptably and efficiently achieved in conformity with law rather than in contravention of it is important. The particular goal of the Reagan foreign policy, of course, was to overcome 'the evil empire' of the Soviet Union and all of its clients, friends and collaborators – or, in the words of Billy Bragg, 'making the world safe for capital*ism*'. Before giving examples of what Moynihan sees as US conduct incompatible with international law, it is worth quoting Louis Henkin's summary of the Reagan administration's apparent understanding of international law.[6] The United States appears to have adopted the view that under international law a state may use force in and against another country for the following reasons:

   to overthrow the government of that country in order to protect lives there;
   to counter intervention there by another state and carry the attack to the territory of the intervening state;
   to overthrow the government of that country on the grounds that it is helping to undermine another friendly government;
   in reprisal for that country's suspected responsibility for terrorist activities in the hope of deterring such acts in the future;
   to overthrow a communist (or 'procommunist') government from assuming power even if it was popularly elected or emerged as a result of internal forces;

Professor Henkin, for some time Professor of International Law and Diplomacy at Columbia University, and co-editor in chief of the prestigious *American Journal of International Law* was neither joking nor approving; he was indignant.

To some extent I find the indignation a little belated because I am not at all sure that those of us who remember the Bay of Pigs invasion of Cuba in 1961 or the invasion of the Dominican Republic in 1965 (or indeed the Vietnam War) would detect quite such a change in foreign policy and method as Moynihan has suggested. This, however, is not essential to the core argument and I want to provide one or two examples by Moynihan of the lawless American foreign policy and its inherent dangers, remembering always that this was pre-Gulf War, and there was effective (if temporary) US control of the Security Council. Perhaps the most blatant example in his thesis is the invasion of Grenada in October 1983, a remarkable international event by any standards. Chomsky's description of the event in a single sentence scarcely needs elaboration:

> [America's] 'sickly inhibitions against the use of military force' as the symptoms were described by Reaganite intellectual Norman Podhoretz, were thought to have been cured by the glorious triumph over Grenada when the United States was once again 'standing tall' in the words of the president, after six thousand elite troops succeeded in overcoming the resistance of several dozen Cuban construction workers whom they had attacked and a few Grenadian militiamen, winning eight thousand medals of honour. (Chomsky, 1994, p 94)

It is clear that this invasion was irrefutably in contravention of international law though of course it comes within the Henkin summation of the US assertion of rights. It was the clearest possible violation of both the United Nations Charter and Article 18 of the Organisation of American States Charter. Moynihan reports a *Wall Street Journal* editorial which began by quoting a dinner table conversation in which a guest declared 'we are only going to be able to talk sensibly about [the invasion of] Grenada if anyone who is an international lawyer agrees to keep his mouth shut'. Diplomatic attempts at legal justification were scarcely bothered with. It was suggested that the invasion had been intended to secure the safety of US or Grenadian citizens, or that the invasion was at the behest of neighbouring states. Neither defence is impressive and Moynihan fears that the use of such lame excuses suddenly makes events such as the seizing of the US hostages by Iran much less unimaginably abhorrent – certainly in treating international law with such contempt the US loses its moral superiority *and* its ability to use law to resolve its own disputes. In his view, having trusted the World Court to rule (as it did) in favour of the US on the issue, it should have been trusted with other US international complaints.

This view is not simply altruistic then – it is the view that the US has more to gain from compliance with international law than in ignoring it. As to Grenada itself, it was his view that an internal change of government was inevitable anyway, but even if this did not eventuate the principle of sovereignty had to prevail over intervention, whether humanitarian or otherwise, except, as we shall see later, pursuant to decisions of the United Nations.

Another episode which rendered Moynihan almost speechless was the mining of Nicaraguan ports in 1983 in an attempt to aid the overthrow of the Nicaraguan Sandinista government. With Moynihan's agreement, Senator Barry Goldwater, a conservative Republican, wrote to William Carey, Director of the Central Intelligence Agency in the following (remarkable!) terms:

> All this past weekend I've been trying to figure out how I can most easily tell you my feelings about the discovery of the President having approved mining some of the harbours of Central America. It gets down to one little, simple phrase: I am pissed off! ... This is an act violating international law. It is an act of war. For the life of me I don't see how we are going to explain it. (Ibid, p 14)

Again it was not that Moynihan was unsympathetic to the removal of the Sandinista government but that this goal had to be achieved, if at all, in conformity with international law – seemingly by a refusal to trade and by patience in the 'knowledge' that such 'lawful' pressure must finally succeed. Only after the US invasion of Panama and the kidnapping of General Noriega under President Bush in 1989 (an event with the Orwellian US code-name 'Operation Just Cause') was there any attempt to justify the action in international law. The attempt was not impressive. President Bush did assert that:

> The deployment of US forces is an exercise of the right of self-defence recognised in Article 51 of the United Nations Charter and was necessary to protect American lives in imminent danger and to fulfil our responsibilities under the Panama Canal Treaties.[7]

There was also the suggestion that the Panamanian government had requested intervention, but this was not known to the Panamanian representative at the United Nations. There were suggestions that the terms of the 1977 Treaty covering the Permanent Neutrality of Operation of the Panama Canal, known as the Neutrality Treaty, could justify the intervention, but this only gave either party the right to use force to maintain the neutrality of the canal. The United States, with the help of the United Kingdom, managed to prevent the Security Council resolutions condemning its aggression, but there was a UN General Assembly resolution that condemned the invasion as a 'flagrant violation of international law and of the independence, sovereignty, and territorial integrity of states' and called for the withdrawal of the 'US armed invasion forces from Panama'. The United States even suggested that it had a right in international law to pursue fugitives from US justice within the fugitive's own state! Moynihan at least was not surprised when shortly after this assertion the Iranian Majlis (parliament) approved a bill allowing Iranian officials to arrest US citizens anywhere in the world should they violate Iranian law.

The Moynihan argument is, then, not that US foreign policy goals are wrong or immoral but that unless they are pursued in conformity with international law the United States may finally lose more than it gains. The United States has a vested interest in a world system of international law which should have precluded its violations generally, and its withdrawal from the World Court when challenged by Nicaragua in particular.

To those readers familiar with E P Thompson's agonising over the efficacy and place of the Rule of Law in democratic government, the Moynihan position will have a familiar ring. In *Whigs and Hunters* Thompson argued that although the Rule of Law did in some ways operate to disguise the exercise of power by and for the powerful, at the same time so coercive did the rhetoric become that in due course the concept inhibited the actions of the powerful themselves and prevented the arbitrary exercise of force which was always detrimental to the powerless (Thompson, 1985). Thus, the worst excesses were prevented, but paradoxically the Rule of Law made more difficult the resistance of those subject to the powerful. It has been forcefully argued that Thompson's view that the Rule of Law has to be considered 'an unqualified good' must at least be open to challenge. Very much the sort of argument that might be made by such opponents is in fact made in the US over Moynihan's position. Interestingly and significantly, the argument here comes from the political right rather than the left.

Robert Bork, an unsuccessful appointee of President Reagan to the US Supreme Court, published an article entitled 'The Limits of "International Law"' which (and not only in its quotation marks around 'international law') really challenged the whole basis of international law in terms of sovereign equality (Bork, 1989). Just before the invasion of Panama, Bork wrote:

... by eliminating morality from its calculus, international law actually makes moral action appear immoral. It can hardly be doubted that, in the American view, it would be a moral act to help a people overthrow a dictatorship that had replaced a democratic government by force, and to restore democracy and freedom to such people. Yet when our leaders act for such moral reasons, they are forced into contrived explanations. The implausibility of such explanations then reverses the moral stance of the parties.

International law thus serves, both internationally and domestically, as a basis for a rhetoric of recrimination directed at the United States. Those who disapprove of a President's action on the merits, but who fear that they may prove popular, can transform the dispute from one about substance to one about legality. The President can be painted as a law breaker and perhaps drawn into a legalistic defence of his actions. The effect is to raise doubts and lower

American morale. The Soviets and other nations have no such problem.

As currently defined, then, international law about the use of force is not even a piety; it is a net loss for Western democracies. Senator Moynihan, speaking of international violations in Woodrow Wilson's time, said, approvingly, that the 'idea of law persisted, even when it did not prevail'. That is precisely the problem. Since it does not prevail the persistence of the idea that it exists can be pernicious. There can be no authentic rule of law among nations until nations have a common political morality or are under a common sovereignty. A glance at the real world suggests we have a while to wait. (Bork, 1989, p 10)[8]

The response of those who were sympathetic to the Moynihan view was astonishment that the very subject of international law was being called into question. The questioning of treaty law, which is part of the supreme law of the US, threatened the very basis upon which nations relate. The system has always been based upon sovereign equality and *pacta sunt servanda,* and if this was to be challenged the world would quickly become anarchic.

Since the Panamanian invasion, the US has been able to resile from the position adopted then. The reason for this, however, has not been a sudden realisation of the worth of international law, but rather because the US, through its effective control of the Security Council, has been able to achieve its aims in accordance with some interpretations of international law rather than against all. I shall consider this shortly. Before doing so I want to make some comments about the US position with regard to international law in the 1980s. It has first to be said that its contempt for international law was very much restricted to constraints upon direct US intervention in the territory of other states. This is of course fundamental, but it did not mean that the US was not otherwise continuing to act in conformity with international law when it was in its interests to do so. What was different though, was that in intervention, particularly under the Reagan presidency, the US no longer felt constrained to mount legal arguments which purported to justify its action in the language of international law. When Rosalyn Higgins describes international law not as rules but as process, her argument is that international law cannot, and will not, ever resolve issues in isolation from political facts and realities, and that this will almost always make the outcome arguable (Higgins, 1994). Law will not be able to dictate the result simply on the basis of treaty and precedent because the political realities of each new international law case will differ. This does not, however, make law irrelevant. There will be some conduct it simply never countenances (genocide, for instance), even if it may be powerless to prevent or punish. There will be other conduct which (as in the US in the 1980s) even though an argument might be made (as by Judge Bork) that the 'socially desirable' goals were vital, is most unlikely to lead to any conclusion other than that the actions were unlawful. International law, in other issues, provides a way of *structuring* arguments so that the debate is joined on specific issues around a specific agenda. While it is difficult to take issue with this analysis, it does seem to me to leave unmentioned one phenomenon without which the discussion is necessarily misleading, and that is power.

The United States has, almost without sanction, been able to deal as it would towards international law even to the point of breaking the Charter of the United Nations and breaking a treaty to which it was party, in withdrawing from the World Court. It is not entirely (though partly) facile to repeat Chomsky's suggestion that the number of civilian casualties in the US invasion of Panama was comparable to the number of civilian casualties in Kuwait in the invasion by Iraq – at least before international reaction; nor yet to suggest that the aims of Iraq in Kuwait and of the US in Panama were not as different as often portrayed. Chomsky quotes Friedman and Karsh's *The Gulf Conflict 1990–1991: Diplomacy and War in the New World Order* with whom he generally disagrees, as stating:

> Saddam apparently intended neither officially to annex the tiny emirate nor to maintain a permanent military presence there. Instead he sought to establish hegemony over Kuwait ensuring its complete financial, political and strategic subservience to his wishes. (Friedman and Karsh, 1992, pp 67–8)

Even for those who find this analogy difficult to accept, the fact is that Indonesia was permitted to invade and annex East Timor, Turkey to invade Cyprus, and Israel to invade Lebanon, all without severe sanction because of the power of the states who lent their support. This perhaps in itself provides some reason for the developing world's different preferences in international law creation. The 'developing' world's numerical strength, in a world of stated sovereign equality, has not been reflected in its capacity to create treaties, particularly economic treaties, to its advantage. And given the strength of the United States and its allies, not only does this show little sign of changing, but power also seems to bring the ability to favourably interpret international law. Thus beside Cassese's reasons must be placed the reality that the only real way in which the numerical strength of the developing world can be illustrated is through the realm of General Assembly resolutions. Sovereign equality does not bring equality in formulating international law.

What I have argued, then, is that the different perspectives of developed and developing countries in fact coincide much more than they might seem to. In particular, the idea that the West is content to be bound by international law in a way in which developing states are not is very misleading indeed, both because, in general, international law is better seen as process rather than rules and so results are almost always negotiable, and because also as has been shown, it is possible, with sufficient power, to override even clear international law rules.

The power dimension has become even more pertinent since the demise of the Soviet Union and the East European 'communist' states. Until that time the United Nations, had, by and large and for better or for worse, been little more than a diplomatic forum. Its direct intervention in conflicts had, with the notable but extraordinary exception of Korea in the 1950s, been largely confined to peace monitoring and keeping, and comparatively uncontroversial activities concerned with refugees, education and so on. The major reason for this stasis was, of course, the Cold War and the global rivalry of the participants. Because there were no common goals, there were no unanimous Security Council resolutions permitting the use of force under the banner of the United Nations. Thus, when it came to forcible intervention, the United Nations was effectively impotent. This was both a matter of regret and a cause for some celebration. It did mean that atrocious regimes survived to the great harm of their people in countries as desperate as Haiti, Chile, Ethiopia and Sudan. It has meant that sovereignty remained a basic principle of international law, although it was under constant stress because of increasing arguments about the compatibility of the paragraphs of Article 2 of the United Nations charter with other considerations. While Article 2(1) provided that the Organisation was based on the principle of sovereign equality of all members and Article 2(7) provided that the UN was not to intervene in matters which were essentially within the domestic jurisdiction of any state, the question of human rights, in particular, came to be accepted as not essentially within domestic jurisdiction. The cause for celebration was to be found among those who argued that sovereignty was more important than any right of intervention, if only because intervention was very seldom for totally pure motives anyway, and experience suggested that direct intervention generally gave rise to more problems and instability than were resolved.

Outside the UN this did not mean that direct intervention was unknown but it was seldom more than condoned. There were many examples, some with more merit than others, including the Indian intervention in what was East Pakistan in 1971 which led to the creation of Bangladesh, the Indonesian 'intervention' in East Timor in 1975, the Tanzanian removal of Idi Amin from power in Uganda in 1979, Vietnam's overthrow of the Khmer Rouge in Cambodia in 1978–9, and the various mentioned efforts of the US in the 1980s. The

United Nations proved itself not only unable to intervene militarily but also incapable of responding to intervention until the end of the Cold War.

Since then there have of course been two cases when the United Nations has authorised the use of force, on both occasions under the leadership of the US: the Gulf War and the Somalia intervention. The change is redolent of nothing so much as Fukuyama's *The End of History and The Last Man* for it seems that those actions were the result of a new international consensus reflecting the triumph of liberal capitalist values (Fukuyama, 1992). This is not irrelevant, but it was the power of the US (military power) combined with Arab and Western money in the first instance, and US power and domestic political considerations in the case of Somalia, which was crucial. Even in the peaceful but forceful intervention in Haiti this too was administered by the US.

It is impossible not to be a little cynical about the change in the US attitude to international law since it found itself with new power in the United Nations. Following the World Court judgment against the US, Nicaragua brought the matter to the Security Council in a resolution calling on all states to observe international law. The US vetoed the resolution. The General Assembly passed a similar resolution by 94 votes to 3 calling for compliance with the World Court ruling – only Israel and El Salvador voted with the US. Consistently when the Security Council has sought to condemn Israel for flagrant breaches of international law, the US has vetoed such resolutions.

What is the significance of this for a critical understanding of international law? The conclusions seem threefold. First, the most powerful states tend to use international law when it is (as it usually is, given its origins) in their interests so to do. Not only the US but the United Kingdom and France (as, for example, in Suez in 1956 or in the French bombing of the *Rainbow Warrior*), the Soviet Union (in its invasions of Hungary and Czechoslovakia and Afghanistan), and other powerful states have all on occasions spurned international law without sanction following directly. Client states of powerful states have been able to do likewise and of this Israel is the clearest example. For states without such allies life may be much more difficult as both Libya and Iraq evidence. Second, because international law is *not* a pure subject but inevitably involved with social and political realities, in *most* disputes the position of international law itself will be arguable. This in turn acts to the advantage of the powerful unless they have accepted the authority of a body such as the International Court of Justice. Understandably but sadly, the majority of states do not accept compulsory jurisdiction and certainly not unequivocally. When the United States sought to have the question of intervention in Nicaragua made a Security Council matter its motives were all too clear – in the Security Council sovereign equality, extant in the court, is replaced by considerations of power and with the power to veto provided for five. Thirdly, there is little likelihood that the consensus in the Security Council will continue unless this is dictated by economic considerations. The global ambitions of China, the US, Russia, Europe and Asia are unlikely to remain compatible. They remain so only so long as trade and economic benefit dictate consensus. When these ambitions conflict we can anticipate seeing the US denied once more the cloak of legitimacy to place over its activities, but one can also anticipate that the US will continue to defend its perceived material interests, whether in Kuwait, Haiti or Cuba.

This excursion seems to take us back to my initial comments about texts and international law teaching in the United Kingdom. It might be that some will argue that the recognition that international law is better understood as process rather than rules provides some justification for the pure approach to the subject. This presupposes, however, that the process is objective and this, I have suggested, is manifestly not the case. Unless it is appreciated that it is not only how the process is used, but by whom it is devised that is important, the very discussion which ensures that international law is dynamic will be missing. It can only be through constant emphasis on the interrelationship between internal law, power and politics that the possibilities and limitations of the legal way of pursuing international issues can be appreciated.

NOTES

1. Significantly, this work is by an Italian scholar.
2. Quoted on the cover of the book.
3. This statement oversimplifies a complex question but the complexities are not relevant for this discussion. For further information, see Shaw, 1991, pp 93–6.
4. See most recently Chomsky, 1994.
5. Or, to quote a story told by Moynihan of Count Metternich who in response, when told of the death of the Russian Ambassador, is supposed to have asked 'What *can* have been his motive?'.
6. 'Use of Force: Law and US Policy' in Council on Foreign Relations, *Right v Might: International Law and the Use of Force* (1989) at p 53.
7. Letter to the Speaker of the House and the President *Pro Tempore* of the Senate on United States Military Action in Panama, 21 December 1989.
8. Readers would be well advised to read Robert H. Bork generally. His book *The Tempting of America: The Political Seduction of the Law* is both gripping and encouraging. Bork takes the US critical legal studies

movement (which he describes as 'a nihilistic, neo-Marxist movement that views all law as oppressive and political. It is nihilistic because its members typically demand the destruction of current doctrine and hierarchies as illegitimate, but they acknowledge that they have no notion of what is to replace this society') extremely seriously and for that alone we should be grateful! Coming in for particular opprobrium is Professor Duncan Kennedy. See his contribution to *The Critical Lawyers' Handbook* (Grigg-Spall and Ireland, 1992).

3
Public International Law and Private Enterprise: Damages for a Killing in East Timor

Roger S. Clark

DEATH IN DILI

This is about a successful private effort to use the United States' legal system in Massachusetts to vindicate a breach of public international law in East Timor. On 12 November 1991, the Indonesian occupying forces carried out a massacre in East Timor in which several hundred people died or 'disappeared'. Largely because of the presence of international media, the event caught public attention in a way that the earlier deaths of perhaps 200,000 members of the pre-invasion population of the Portuguese colony had not. Among the dead in November 1991 was a 20-year-old New Zealander, Kamal Bamadhaj. A student in Australia at the time, he was travelling in Indonesia and East Timor before his death. Generally supportive of pro-democracy efforts in Indonesia and East Timor, he had offered his assistance to various groups and individuals as a translator. With the aid of the United Nations, tortuous negotiations had resulted in a planned visit to Timor of a Portuguese parliamentary delegation which would be accompanied by diplomats and journalists from various nations. The approach of the time for this delegation led to considerable ferment among the populace and to preparations among many to make sure that the facts would be properly presented. Responding, the Indonesian military increased its efforts at repression. At the last moment, the delegation was cancelled when the Indonesian side refused to accept the presence with the delegation of a Lisbon-based Australian journalist (an expert on East Timor) whom the Portuguese insisted on including.

On 28 October 1991, Indonesian forces stormed the Motael Catholic Church in the capital, Dili, and killed a young man, Sebastiao Gomes, who had taken refuge there. A mass was scheduled at the church two weeks after Gomes's death. This mass would become a highly political event. Kamal Bamadhaj went to the church to record the mass and to take photographs of the subsequent procession from the church to the cemetery where the young man was buried. He and other Westerners present in Dili had apparently met the night before and, as his mother, Helen Todd, put it in a declaration filed in support of the legal proceedings she later brought in Massachusetts, 'decided that it was important that they attend ... They hoped that the obvious presence of Westerners and media would deter the Indonesian military from further violent action.' When the peaceful crowd reached the cemetery, the Indonesian soldiers opened fire for five to ten minutes.

Bamadhaj may have been hit for the first time at this point. He was seen shortly afterwards, walking alone about half a kilometre from the site. In his mother's words:

> Witnesses saw a military vehicle approach him; an argument ensued – apparently over his camera; shots rang out. Kamal fell and was left bleeding by the side of the road. The autopsy showed that he had been shot once in the arm and once at close range in the chest, by different calibre weapons.
>
> Anton Marti, a representative of the International Red Cross, found Kamal bleeding by the side of the road, still conscious, waving his New Zealand passport. He no longer had the camera. Marti placed Kamal in his Red Cross vehicle and attempted to deliver him to the nearest general hospital. (He was delayed by the military for a considerable period of time and finally directed to a military hospital.) The delay was fatal. Kamal died of loss of blood.

Initial reports were that Kamal had been injured only. His mother immediately endeavoured to fly to Dili. By the time Ms Todd reached Denpasar in Bali, it was clear that her son was dead. She then sought to continue her flight to recover the body but was prevented by Indonesian military officials from boarding a plane from Denpasar to Dili.

Some of the New Zealand diplomatic traffic relating to the incident has been released to a member of Parliament, Phil Goff, under New Zealand's Official Information legislation. The tone of much of the correspondence – a mixture of distress and a desire to assist the Indonesians in damage control – is captured by the following report of a dressing-down received by the Indonesian *chargé* in Wellington on 15 November 1991, as recorded in foreign affairs correspondence between Wellington and Jakarta:

> We are seriously concerned at events in Bali when the parents of Kamal were not allowed on the plane by military personnel ... It is particularly unfortunate ... Indonesian authorities gave assurances that all assistance would be given to the parents in going to Dili and making arrangements for the body ... We had been assured that

Indonesian authorities wished to contain the consequences of this tragedy and that Indonesian authorities accepted that the best way was to facilitate the visit of the parents ... We now have very grave doubts about the sincerity of the Indonesian authorities ... When the media learn of this, there will be greater pressure on the [Prime Minister] ... Indonesian Ministers must get involved ... We need to get the situation back on track.

Further released documents suggest continuing efforts for at least a few weeks on the part of the New Zealand authorities to obtain a full explanation of Kamal's death, but there is nothing to indicate that any such explanation was forthcoming. In a letter dated 28 July 1992, the New Zealand Prime Minister forwarded to Ms Todd what seems to be the most detailed, but hardly informative, response from the Indonesians. It claimed that Kamal 'was seen to be actively engaged in fomenting and encouraging the demonstrators to be defiant to the security officers'. Ms Todd, not surprisingly, regarded the response as inaccurate and quite inadequate.

One thing the New Zealand Government did not do was make a claim for reparation in respect of Kamal's death, as it would be entitled to do under the international law on state responsibility for injuries to aliens. That was left to private enterprise.

THE SUIT IN BOSTON

Sintong Panjaitan was, at the time of the Dili massacre, the Indonesian military commander of the region which includes East Timor. He was 'punished' for his part in the massacre by being sent to management school at Harvard University in Cambridge, Massachusetts. It was here that representatives of Kamal's mother discovered him in August 1992 and filed suit in the United States Federal District Court in nearby Boston. The Complaint described the suit as being for 'summary execution, wrongful death, assault and battery and intentional infliction of emotional distress'. The summary execution claim relied on international human rights law; the other claims appealed to basic notions of the common law and statutory law on personal injury resulting in wrongful death that are part of the body of law in Massachusetts and other states. According to a definition of summary execution provided for the plaintiff in an affidavit by professors of international law:

An act constitutes summary execution if it (1) intentionally results in the proximate death of an individual; (2) is not the result of a fairly and publicly constituted tribunal based on the existing law of the state, and (3) is caused by or at the instigation of a public official.

Upon receipt of the Complaint, Panjaitan returned to Indonesia where he now advises the government on the environment. On 26 October 1994, Judge Patti B. Saris entered a default judgment in Boston, the essence of which was (in the judge's words):

(1) An award of compensatory damages to Helen Todd as administratrix of the estate of her son Kamal Bamadhaj for the conscious mental and physical pain and suffering of Kamal Bamadhaj in the amount of two million dollars ($2,000,000), plus interest.
(2) An award of compensatory damages to plaintiff Helen Todd for her pain and suffering and loss of companionship of her son in the amount of two million dollars ($2,000,000), plus interest.
(3) An award of punitive damages to plaintiff Helen Todd in the amount of ten million dollars ($10,000,000).

JURISDICTION

The federal courts of the United States are courts of limited jurisdiction. A plaintiff must show that there is personal jurisdiction over the defendant, typically by showing that the defendant is present in the area. More significantly, a plaintiff must also point to some statutory basis under federal law on which the court has jurisdiction over the subject-matter. The Plaintiff's initial Complaint and later Memorandum of Law in Support of Motion for Default Judgment in the Todd case relied on various theories of subject-matter jurisdiction, only two of which are relevant here, the Alien Tort Claims Act and the Torture Victim Protection Act. Only the first of these is mentioned in the judge's brief one-and-a-half page default judgment. Apparently she regarded it as sufficient. Both grounds are of interest in the present context of private actions for an international law claim and will therefore be discussed in the paragraphs that follow.

The Alien Tort Claims Act of 1789
The Alien Tort Claims Act (also known as 28 United States Code, Section 1350) was enacted in 1789 by the First Congress. It provides that: 'The district courts shall have original jurisdiction of any civil action by an alien for a tort only, committed in violation of the law of nations or a treaty of the United States.'

The potential of the statute in a modern human rights context became apparent in 1980 in *Filartiga* v. *Peña-Irala* where the Police Chief of Asuncion, Paraguay, was sued in federal court in New York for torture committed in Paraguay. Plaintiffs were the father and sister of the victim, a 17-year-old tortured to death. The trial judge initially dismissed the suit on the ground that violations of the law of nations do not occur when the aggrieved parties are nationals of the acting state. He believed that he was bound to so interpret the Alien Tort Claims Act on the basis of existing authority. He was reversed on appeal to the Second Circuit Court of Appeals. In the catchy words of the Court, 'for the purposes of civil liability, the torturer has become – like the pirate and the slave trader before him – *hostis humani generis*, an enemy of all mankind'. It followed that there was jurisdiction under the Alien Tort Claims Act. The Filartigas were represented by the same public interest group that would later represent Ms Todd, the New York-based Center for Constitutional Rights.

What exactly is included in the concept of a 'tort' which is 'in violation of the law of nations' is far from obvious – the term is hardly in general usage and the original understanding of the drafters is at best murky! *Filartiga* merely decided that torture at least was included. There are, however, some fairly well-established international law categories that can be used by analogy to suggest what must be a significant part of the field, including the following.

The Restatement of the Foreign Relations Law of the United States, Section 702, has a category of 'customary international law of human rights'. It provides that

> A state violates international law if, as a matter of state policy, it practices, encourages, or condones (a) genocide; (b) slavery or slave trade; (c) the murder or causing the disappearance of individuals; (d) torture or other cruel, inhuman, or degrading treatment or punishment; (e) a consistent pattern of gross violations of internationally recognized human rights.

The American Law Institute's Restatement of Foreign Relations Law seeks, in provisions like these and others to be mentioned shortly, to go beyond 'American' law and capture the current state of public international law. Section 702 is concerned specifically with state responsibility. In order to utilise it to flesh out the Alien Tort Claims Act, it is necessary to make the evidently sensible step to individual tort responsibility for these acts. We are talking here of the tort equivalent of the Nuremberg Tribunal's proposition that '[crimes] against international law are committed by men, not by abstract entities, and only by punishing individuals who commit such crimes can the provisions of international law be enforced'.

Another provision of the Restatement, Section 404, does, moreover, deal specifically with individual responsibility, albeit criminal responsibility. It concerns 'Universal Jurisdiction to Define and Punish Certain Offenses'. It posits the existence of a category of criminal offences 'recognized by the community of nations as of universal concern, such as piracy, slave trade, attacks on or hijacking of aircraft, genocide, war crime and perhaps certain acts of terrorism ...'. A Comment by the Reporter of the Restatement suggests that tort liability is acceptable here too: 'In general, jurisdiction on the basis of universal interests has been exercised in the form of criminal law, but international law does not preclude the application of non-criminal law on this basis, for example by providing a remedy in tort or restitution for victims of piracy.'

Then there is the International Law Commission's project for a Draft Code of Crimes Against the Peace and Security of Mankind. The successor to the Nuremberg Charter's Crimes Against Peace, War Crimes and Crimes Against Humanity, the list of horrors includes aggression, genocide, apartheid, systematic or mass violations of human rights, exceptionally serious war crimes, international terrorism, illicit traffic in narcotic drugs and wilful and severe damage to the environment. If there is international criminal responsibility for individuals in such cases, which may be adjudicated either by an international tribunal or by states on a universal jurisdiction basis, it is surely plausible that tort liability is acceptable on a similar basis.

Other possible 'sources' of what might amount to a tort in violation of the law of nations include the categories of *jus cogens* (or peremptory norms), obligations *erga omnes*, and the various items that the International Law Commission in its work on state responsibility regards as state crimes. But it is unnecessary to elaborate further. Enough has been said to indicate that there are several possible analogies. None of these classifications was created with the Alien Tort Claims Act in mind. But then the founders of the American republic did not explain what they had in mind, so some analogies must be found from other parts of general international law.

The Center for Constitutional Rights and the Lowenstein International Human Rights Project have developed a law professors' brief on the issues, which was filed, *inter alia*, in the Todd case. In this brief, more than 25 leading United States professors of international law argue that 'summary execution, torture, disappearance, cruel, inhuman, or degrading treatment, and arbitrary detention violate universal, obligatory, and definable norms of international law'. Most of this package has some support in the case-law. There are, in short, several areas of breaches of public international law in which the kind of litigation carried out in the Todd case might also be promising. One matter that is not yet resolved in an appellate court is whether the Alien Tort Claims Act defines the parameters of the cause of action as well as being jurisdictional, or whether it is merely jurisdictional. We shall return to that question once the Torture Victim Protection Act has been described.

The Torture Victim Protection Act of 1992

In spite of its more limited title, the Torture Victim Protection Act deals with civil actions both for torture and for extrajudicial killings. This statute was adopted at least partly to dispel doubts that had been raised about whether *Filartiga* was good law. Section 2(a) of the 1992 Act provides:

> An individual who, under actual or apparent authority, or under color of law, of any foreign nation – (1) subjects an individual to torture shall, in a civil action, be liable in damages to that individual; or (2) subjects an individual to extrajudicial killing shall, in a civil action, be liable for damages to that individual's legal representative, or to any person who may be a claimant in an action for wrongful death.

'Extrajudicial killing' (apparently synonymous with summary execution) is defined in Section 3(a) of the Act as a deliberate killing not authorised by a previous judgment pronounced by a regularly constituted court affording all the judicial guarantees which are recognised as indispensable by civilised peoples. This act, more clearly than the Alien Tort Claims Act, is both jurisdictional and defining of a federal (statutory) cause of action. It also (unlike the Alien Tort Claims Act) contains a provision requiring the exhaustion of 'adequate and available remedies in the place in which the conduct giving rise to the claim occurred'. Given that the Indonesian legal system is not responsive in such cases (to say nothing of its dubious applicability in East Timor) the exhaustion clause presented no problem in *Todd*. The difficulty with applying the Torture Victim Protection Act was that it had not been enacted at the time the killing occurred in Dili. The theory presented in the Plaintiff's Memorandum of Law to overcome this was that there was no problem with any presumption against retroactivity since 'it is clear that the statute does not affect substantive rights, but merely clarifies pre-existing law'.

Evidently the judge did not think it necessary to pursue this line of reasoning in *Todd* v. *Panjaitan*, since she was persuaded that the Alien Tort Claims Act provided an adequate basis for decision in the case of Kamal. Nevertheless, the Torture Victim Protection statute will be available in future appropriate cases. (It has, for example, been strongly relied upon in cases arising out of the struggle in the former Yugoslavia.)

CHOICE OF LAW ON SUBSTANCE AND DAMAGES

The Alien Tort Claims Act is jurisdictional. One question, however, that was not fully explored by the Second Circuit Court of Appeals in *Filartiga*, nor resolved in subsequent cases, was whether it is *merely* jurisdictional. That is to say, as to the substance of the cause of action (including liability and the measure of damages), does the 'law of nations' provide the basis? Or is it necessary to refer out to some state's body of substantive rules in accordance with some of the principles of choice of law found in doctrines of private international law? ('State' is used here with deliberate ambiguity to include both a constituent entity of a federal country like the United States, and a 'state' in the international sense. Either 'federal' or 'local' law may be relevant.) Which law is chosen may well affect the existence of a cause of action or particular categories of damages.

On remand in *Filartiga*, the trial judge took the view that since the 'tort' to which the statute refers was a wrong 'in violation of the law of nations' rather than 'a wrong actionable under the law of the appropriate sovereign state', the court should determine the substantive principles to be applied by looking to international law, which, as the Court of Appeals stated, 'became a part of the common law *of the United States* upon the adoption of the Constitution'. Nevertheless, the judge hedged a little by placing partial reliance on Paraguayan law in assessing damages. (The plaintiffs had provided a careful expert analysis of potentially applicable Paraguayan law.) An initial assessment of damages had been made by a federal Magistrate who had concluded that the plaintiffs were entitled to receive only those damages payable under Paraguayan law. This did not include punitive damages. Paraguayan law did, however, forbid torture and provide for 'moral damages' in such cases, which would include emotional pain and suffering, loss of companionship and disruption of family life.

In the Court's view, it was 'essential and proper [to go further and] to grant the remedy of punitive damages in order to give effect to the manifest objectives of the international prohibition against torture'. Since international law did not itself spell out the details, the Court saw itself in this connection as a kind of delegate of the international community:

> The international law prohibiting torture established the standard and referred to the national states the task of enforcing it. By enacting Section 1350, Congress entrusted that task to the federal courts and gave them power to choose and develop federal remedies to effectuate the purposes of the international law incorporated into the United States common law.

Punitive damages, the 'federal remedy' chosen to effectuate the purposes of international law, had, at least in the magnitude of the awards contemplated, a somewhat American cast to it. Subsequent cases under Section 1350 have followed a similar approach, including substantial punitive awards. In *Todd* v. *Panjaitan* the Center for Constitutional Rights argued along similar lines, emphasising an international standard bolstered by an award of punitive damages to vindicate the international interests involved.

In its argument concerning the international law standard, the Center referred to the much-cited decision of the Permanent Court of International Justice in the *Case Concerning the Chorzow Factory (Germany v Poland)* which came before the Permanent Court of International Justice in 1928. There the Court took the position that reparation must, so far as possible, wipe out all the consequences of the illegal act and re-establish the situation which would, in all probability, have existed if that act had not been committed. As applied to injuries to individuals, the argument for *Todd* was that the injured person is, under the rules of international law, entitled to be compensated for such items as mental suffering, injury to his feelings, humiliation, shame, degradation, or loss of social position. Such principles had been applied in 1989 by the Inter-American Court of Human Rights in the *Velasquez Rodriguez Case*, in which the Court awarded damages against Honduras for loss of earnings and psychological injuries to the family of a disappeared person.

If the substance of the action depended in whole or in part on some domestic rule or decision, there were at least several possibilities in *Todd*: the reference might be to the law of the forum (probably Massachusetts law in accordance with the normal federal rule which sends the court to state law in such cases), the law of East Timor (that is to say Portuguese law), or the law of Indonesia. In view of the limited connection of Massachusetts with the events giving rise to the cause of action, it seemed unlikely that Massachusetts law would be applied. It was argued strongly that it would be utterly inappropriate to apply Indonesian law, the law of an illegal occupier. This was especially so in light of the 1976 decision by the United Nations General Assembly which rejected the Indonesian claim of annexation of East Timor, inasmuch as the people of the territory have been prevented from freely exercising their right to self-determination. The United Nations continues to treat Portugal as the administering power of the territory.

This left Portuguese law. Careful lawyering (bearing in mind the way in which the trial judge had proceeded using Paraguayan law in part in *Filartiga*) suggested that Portuguese law of wrongful death ought to be explored in *Todd*. Three members of the faculty of Coimbra University were asked to do this. Their analysis, like that of the Paraguayan expert in *Filartiga*, is particularly interesting to a common law lawyer who is more used to the way in which the Anglo-American law approaches the question of damages. They concluded that under the Portuguese civil law system (notably the Constitution and the Civil Code) the wrongful acts alleged against Panjaitan would give rise to an enforceable obligation to compensate. Under Portuguese law, moreover, public employees and members of the armed forces are liable for torts committed in the course of their employment. An action for wrongful death in Portugal belongs to the heirs of the victim. The mother of the victim has standing to sue if there is no spouse or children. The measure of damages in such a case was said to include 'damage for death, non-patrimonial damages (pain and suffering) as well as emergent patrimonial losses and lost earnings'. 'Emergent patrimonial damages' would include such expenses as medical care before death and the funeral. The study indicates typical figures that are awarded in Portugal for death and for pain and suffering. An award for lost wages is normally based on an estimate of future earnings to age 65 less 25 per cent of that sum that the deceased might reasonably be expected to spend on himself. The experts noted that 'although Portuguese law does not provide for punitive damages *per se*, our concept of compensatory damages does include some of the factors classified as "punitive" in the United States, such as the brutality of the defendant's conduct and the correspondent suffering of the victim and the defendant's ability to pay'.

In the event, Judge Saris did not find it necessary in her default judgment to explain the basis of her damage award. The difficult choice of law issues were thus left unresolved. Moreover, while the plaintiff's lawyers had generated projections of Kamal's future earnings and tax liabilities as an Australian academic, Judge Saris did not make an award under this head of damages; instead she contented herself with making hefty awards for pain and suffering and punitives.

COLLECTING ON THE JUDGMENT

The odds of collecting the money from Panjaitan are fairly low. He left no obvious assets in Massachusetts, and the Indonesian legal system is unlikely to be helpful. Nonetheless, the whole exercise must give him pause. It is probable that he will not wish to return to the United States; certainly he will not want to move assets there. In accordance with rules in various jurisdictions about the enforcement of foreign judgments, it may be possible to take the American judgment and seek to execute it elsewhere. Some jurisdictions do this on a statutory or common law basis; in others there are treaties on the reciprocal enforcement of judgments. If nothing else, the prospects of attempts to execute might make Panjaitan feel like a pariah and inhibit his future freedom of movement to travel internationally.

There is also the question of whether it might be possible to collect from Indonesia itself at the international level, rather than in some domestic court. It must be emphasised that the United States judgment is against Panjaitan, not against Indonesia. There are serious foreign sovereign immunity problems in most domestic legal systems with suing (or trying to collect from) the state, even in cases where there are egregious human rights violations. But on the international scene, there is no reason why an effort could not be made to collect sovereign to sovereign. That is to say, there is nothing to prevent the New Zealand Government, armed with the judgment, from finally espousing the claim of its citizen, Kamal, and suggesting to Indonesia that it might discharge the obligations of *its* citizen – or its own responsibilities in turning Panjaitan and his troops loose to behave in the way they did. Panjaitan was, after all, acting on its behalf at the relevant time. There are some analogies. For example, it is not uncommon in domestic legal practice for governments whose employees have been sued personally for torts committed in the general scope of their employment to indemnify them and pay any judgment.

The New Zealand Government has apparently given some thought to this kind of issue of state responsibility. On 16 October 1975, another New Zealand citizen, Gary Cunningham, was killed near the Indonesian border with East Timor by Indonesian forces who were already encroaching on Timorese territory. He was one of five journalists for a Melbourne TV station covering Indonesian border incursions. The Australian Journalists Association pressed the Australian Government to seek compensation. The New Zealand Secretary of Foreign Affairs hoped (according to the material released under the Official Information Act) that New Zealand would not need to get involved although there might be some 'demands' in that direction. The hope was that Australia – whose television coverage was involved – would deal with it. As the Secretary put it, '[w]e can expect that to do so [seek compensation] would harm our own relations with Indonesia'. The matter was not pursued by New Zealand (or Australia for that matter).

The New Zealand Government has, however, been more forceful on at least one other occasion and was then successful in encouraging the payment of compensation. When French agents sank the Greenpeace ship, *Rainbow Warrior*, in Auckland harbour, the Government, in spite of its lack of formal standing, encouraged the French to compensate the dependents of the photographer killed in the incident (a Dutch citizen) and Greenpeace itself (the vessel was registered in the United Kingdom). France did so. As the New Zealand Minister of Justice at the time put it, 'what New Zealand was saying to France on this matter was, in effect, that it was a *political* imperative that decent arrangements be made for compensation for damage suffered in New Zealand but not by New Zealand' (Palmer, 1989, p 594). One might have thought that there was more than a political imperative where one's own citizen was involved!

Perhaps collecting the money is not what is significant. An important feature of such a lawsuit is the catharsis it entails for those who remain. There is also some political pressure and some measure of accountability for the perpetrators. Kamal's mother put it eloquently:

22. I bring this case because those who killed him and those in power who set the policies that killed him have not even acknowledged that a crime has been committed. They lead privileged lives. The policy of repression continues. The military culture that systematically tramples on human rights still flourishes.

23. I bring this case not only as Kamal's mother but on behalf of the hundreds of East Timor mothers who are forced to grieve in silence for their dead children. Our grief and anger is the same, but, unlike them, I can bring a case against a military officer without putting the rest of my family in danger. Whatever compensation is awarded by the court in this case will belong to the mothers of all the victims of the Dili massacre, and I will find a way to get it into their hands.

24. There must be some accounting for the unarmed young people shot to death by the military in Dili that morning simply because they dared to raise their voices against sixteen years of organized military brutality against the people of East Timor.

CONCLUSION

One should perhaps avoid overstating the novelty of the United States' approach in the Alien Tort Claims and Torture Victim Protection Acts. After all, as the court pointed out in *Filartiga*: 'Common law courts of general jurisdiction regularly adjudicate transitory tort claims between individuals over whom they exercise personal jurisdiction, wherever the tort occurred.' Turning the latter into a federal case, however, entails a measure of uniformity and demonstrates the extent to which 'the United States' as an entity takes the matter seriously. The challenge we are left with is whether the legal systems of other countries can be used in the same creative way.

NOTE ON SOURCES

The factual material herein is based on news reports; on material filed with the United States District Court for the District of Massachusetts, Boston, in *Todd* v. *Panjaitan*, Civil Action No. 92-12255-PBS; on material from the files of the New Zealand Ministry of Foreign Affairs and Trade released in July 1994 to Phil Goff, MP, under the (New Zealand) Official Information Act; and on a Report by the United Nations Special Rapporteur on Extrajudicial, Summary or Arbitrary Executions, Mr Bacre Waly Ndiaye, on his mission to Indonesia and East Timor from 3 to 13 July 1994, UN Doc. E/CN.4/1995/61/Add.1 (1995).

Part Two

Race and Ethnicity

4
Race and Law
Werner Menski

A CRITICAL APPROACH TO 'RACE' AND LAW

In this field, two simplistic assumptions, brought together, have wreaked conceptual havoc and continue to obstruct critical legal studies. They are, in a nutshell, that skin pigment or phenotype and state law constitute central factors in the interaction of legal systems with various ethnic minority groups. Accepting the challenge to write about 'race and law', therefore, offers a chance to question the simplicity underlying this prominent binary combination, which encapsulates the legal problems that white-dominated Britain continues to have with the presence of large and growing ethnic minority communities.

I teach one of the very few law courses in the country which attempts to address such issues, but there are powerful disincentives: teaching and writing about 'the other' in a legal context not only turns oneself into 'the other' by association, irrespective of phenotype; it also continues to be dismissed as irrelevant, extra-legal, sociological waffle. Even within the protective and legitimising framework of critical legal studies, apprehensions about describing one's interests as anything other than 'mainstream' and 'white' reflect a fear of being sidelined which goes much beyond 'race'. Just as in daily life, problematic questions may be left undiscussed because one would rather not have the answers, legal research frequently avoids critical key issues such as 'race' and law.

Writing critically about law from within the profession in such a context also means that one cannot avoid unearthing imbalances of academic coverage and the persistence of remarkably undemocratic positions in the official law itself, statute as well as case-law. Much has happened since Lester and Bindman (1972) analysed British race relations law, yet the writer's task in this field is still more political than most legal scholars seem willing to bear. It has always been easy for timid lawyers to seek refuge in the 'black letter' approach. However, when even technical legal substance has now become 'tainted' with sociological matters such as 'race' and 'ethnicity', the view that it is better not to touch some subjects at all acquires added force. For legal scholarship today, it has become impossible to deal narrowly with 'race' without opening several cans of worms about the predicaments lawyers face in conceptualising law, and in understanding and operationalising diversity and pluralism.

I am not suggesting, therefore, that the dearth of analytical writing on race and law in Britain is only due to the traditional lawyer's abhorrence of sociology or to establishment cowardice. No part of the field of 'race and law' is emotionally neutral and there are many other reasons for status quoist approaches. Black law students have said to me, in all seriousness, that they could not bear studying a course on Ethnic Minorities and the Law, because it involved them in too painful self-questioning. In the long run, this could have the effect that non-white law lecturers, if we shall ever see them in significant numbers, will also find it convenient to hide behind colour-blind black-letter approaches.

The fact that English criminal law continues to be taught in most law schools as though black and Asian British people did not exist, reflects not only an unwillingness to address real legal problems but also compliance with the dominant view that law teaching is a form of training in and for subordination (Grigg-Spall and Ireland, 1992, p x). Similarly, the absence of immigration law coverage in most British law degrees, despite the fact that immigration-related case-law has long constituted an ever-growing segment of legal work, reflects an unwillingness to address certain core issues in modern public law. I would not call this ethnophobia as yet, but the reproduction of legal education as an exercise of oppressive power is clearly flourishing and, with regard to ethnic minority issues, legal education in Britain has remained much more self-censoring than necessary.

To follow well-trodden paths and to deviate just a little may still qualify as critical scholarship, but it does not go far enough and is, moreover, highly selective. The first volume of the *Critical Lawyers' Handbook* duly mentioned 'race' in a number of places but otherwise merely appears to challenge the idea that law could be politically netural. That was hardly a great revelation, although it remains a premise of immensely wide import. My point is that the task of being critical is much more demanding: writing from within law, criticising the inadequacies of official legal systems as justice-oriented regulators of human life, uncovering the insufficient depth of analysis that clouds the standard perceptions of legal centralism, demands a full scale critique of Western 'model jurisprudence' with its inattention to so-called extra-legal factors (Chiba, 1986, 1989). This goes much beyond a narrow critical analysis of 'race' or a critique of certain phenomena in a particular common law or civil law jurisdiction. It also extends to the sphere of international law with its manifold layers of dramatised lip-service to universal standards which, from a critical perspective, may be seen to mask continued Western hegemony of legal analysis and law-making processes. Much of the discourse about international law is as premised on assimilationist ideas and on ideologies of 'racial' or cultural superiority as similar debates at domestic level.

If one comes to this discussion as a specialist in non-Western legal traditions, particularly in Asian law, one's perspective is bound to be different, and to be seen as somewhat idiosyncratic. But in an increasingly globalised world, in which long-distance migration and therefore diversified ethnic coexistence have become almost the norm, narrow nationalistic perspectives repress legal analysis and impede more holistic approaches to legal studies. The entrenched presence in Europe today of large and increasingly vocal groups of migrants from non-European backgrounds and their descendants contains important lessons about comparative jurisprudence which legal education and training appear unwilling to learn. Observing such phenomena confirms for me, as a specialist on South Asian laws and an analyst of 'ethnic minority laws', that the principles of non-Western laws continue to claim the same universality as Western legal systems and that at least two forms of 'model jurisprudence'[1] are, therefore, bound to clash in very interesting ways. Indeed, recent research is beginning to show in more detail that various forms of Asian laws have been reconstructed in Britain (Menski, 1987, 1993) and elsewhere in Europe (Bistolfi and Zabbal, 1995; King, 1995). How do we prepare Europe's young lawyers for an understanding of such phenomena? And how do we assist the growing number of young ethnic minority lawyers within Western jurisdictions to find their own rightful place in this ever-changing world of legal analysis and practice?

It is an undeniable fact, now increasingly recognised, that progress in this area has been immensely slow and that the academic discourse about such processes has been subject to various political interferences which impede rational analysis. Nobody would argue today that 'race relations' is not an emotive subject. Leading British politicians continue to exploit such emotions to try to win elections, playing the race card, portraying themselves as saviours of the nation and manipulating legal rules whose primary purpose is to further marginalise anyone who does not look white enough. In Britain, it remains an uncomfortable fact that immigration rules, for example, can be changed overnight with little parliamentary scrutiny, making a farce of much-heralded basic principles of law-making. The resulting cynicism, on both sides, appears to be getting worse, while critical legal analysis largely ignores such developments, seeking refuge in the more fashionable activity of theorising.

By dragging such loaded non-discourses away from the prominent label of 'race', as I intend to do here, one does not make them less controversial, but one may achieve a healthier distance from emotional involvements of the primordial type. This may facilitate a rephrasing of the conceptual difficulties encountered by Western laws and their analysts, in terms of diversity and non-Western concepts and ways of life; in short, with 'the other' in all kinds of manifestations. Race, in other words, is only one of many factors relevant to the present debate, which is in fact an ancient one: 'the other' has always taken many forms.

Putting race and the law together channels one's mind into certain well-trodden avenues in the recent history of sociolegal writing. There is, indeed, a huge literature on racial issues, in the United States as well as in the UK; one must note immediately that the legal input into that discourse has been minimal. While race and ethnicity are now given full recognition as a key issue in sociology (Mason, 1995), their legal analysis remains undeveloped. Obviously, any meaningful legal debate would now need to take pointers from the existing non-legal scholarship.[2] However, quite apart from legalistic aversions to sociology, what if tackling the issue in this way still represents a start on the wrong foot? What if the critical element in the legal analysis of race is not in fact 'race', as much of Britain's sociological writing continues to argue,[3] but rather something like 'ethnicity' or 'culture'? These are complex terms in themselves, broadly indicating the 'otherness' of ethnic minorities; they complicate legal analysis, but that is hardly a valid reason not to use them. Especially in the discourse on race and crime in Britain today, it is increasingly obvious that monocausal racial arguments are by no means sufficient to explain differential legal reactions, such as targeted implementation of stop-and-search laws and disproportionate incarceration patterns.

When one thinks about race and law, besides the issues of power and control, a more or less immediate focus today is the theme of exclusion and its manifold implications. Social as well as legal dimensions of exclusion have historically been studied in terms of racial distinctions, predominantly in the context of colonialism and apartheid, or racial segregation under more democratic systems such as the United States. All of this has shown that discrimination and democracy are not incompatible. Over time, to follow the cherished axioms of a modernising world, race, class and disadvantage should all have withered away, but law manifestly continues to be an instrument of exploitation and of allocating power and status, both in a positive and negative sense. Whether one looks at those who exclude, those who are being (or simply feel) excluded, or at the implications for a particular society as a whole, complex sociolegal issues continue to arise today within a historically loaded network of parameters. The earlier focus on biological criteria and class structures has now given way to intricate differentiations of ethnicity. Thus the analytical problem today, rather simply stated, is that ethnic minorities anywhere in the world no longer form some uniform class of underlings who are content to occupy the niches allocated to them. They are split into mobile elites who generate enormous jealousies, by no means a new phenomenon, while other segments continue to display the multiple effects of deprivation. Law, being intricately linked with power, is bound to face, and in fact itself generates, severe conflicts if it continues to be based on convenient fictions of immigrant disadvantage rather than fuller, more realistic analysis.

All the contributions in Part Two focus on exclusionary mechanisms and their implications while using 'race' as a given major constitutent. I am not convinced that this is the only possible way of writing about the subject. Putting it this way is less a critique of my fellow critical writers than a reiteration of the protest about being asked to write on 'race and law', when 'ethnicity and law' would now appear to be a more appropriate heading.

After the present section, a brief overview of the existing writing on race and the law in Britain is provided before we proceed to an analysis of the conceptualisation of 'race' in English law. This uncovers what one can only see as uncomfortable evidence, to the effect that even the race relations law of the UK itself discriminates between different ethnic minorities. Far from preventing discrimination, it has turned into an intricate science of differential treatment, with multiple players and disturbing results. The problems uncovered are then further analysed by questioning the assimilationist underpinnings of English law as inherently racist and suggesting a wider conceptualisation of law, which makes more allowances for social plurality and legal pluralism. The final section of this chapter discusses how legal education in the UK may be reformed to take more explicit account of ethnoplurality.

THE EXISTING WRITING

It is immediately obvious that race-related writing in Britain has been dominated by sociologists, anthropologists and political scientists.[4] The strong emphasis on pigment, predominantly marked as 'race', is widely reflected in the titles of leading studies (see Benedict, 1983; Miles, 1989), including those which focus on social policy and discrimination (see Rose, 1969; Smith, 1977). Very recent titles (for example, Mason, 1995) clearly reflect growing recognition of ethnic as opposed to 'racial' factors and emphasise that everybody is ethnic (Ballard and Kalra, 1993, p 9). Lawyers have hardly contributed to these debates. Legal writing, in turn, does not appear to have been systematically absorbed by writers from other disciplines.[5] Legal scholarship, while not entirely absent,[6] has tended to become narrowly specialised and thus less accessible and somewhat detached from wider policy debates. For example, the earlier close link of immigration and discrimination law (see Macdonald, 1969) was largely broken by the phenomenal growth of the former as a separate branch of law, with its own textbooks (Macdonald and Blake, 1991), looseleaf collection, law reports and journal.

Discrimination law, too, has been developing in the same way. In fact, the most fertile area of scholarly activity related to 'race' is found in anti-discrimination law. Some challenging early work focused on economics (Pascal, 1972), industrial relations (Rimmer, 1972), or politics (Edwards and Batley, 1978). While the more specifically legal input has continued to become stronger over time, it seems that economists, in particular, have lost interest in the subject, whereas sociologists and political scientists, rather than lawyers, now dominate the field. Following the early warning that the common law was not sufficient to tackle racial disadvantage (Lester and Bindman, 1972), important studies have focused on discrimination, particularly employment (see Lustgarten, 1980; Jenkins, 1986; McCrudden et al., 1991; Palmer, 1992), but here, too, growing legal specialisation has created its own problems: anti-discrimination law today is divided between gender and racial issues and it is well known that the concerns of the former match quite uneasily with the agenda of the latter (see Hepple and Szyszczak, 1992). Some feminists argue, for example, that legal recognition of Muslim demands would contradict and undermine axioms of gender equality. Further, this kind of writing has often become quite technical (see McCrudden et al., 1991; Lockton, 1993), based as it is on complicated statute and case-law. Thus again, technical legal analysis, which tends to ignore policy issues and demands different skills from its authors, has distracted attention from the ethnic dimensions. At the same time, complex new issues, such as racial harassment (Forbes, 1988, 1995; Bridges and Forbes, 1990) have continued to arise and there has been much recent writing on race and crime.[7]

Some non-white, non-law authors, such as Cashmore and Troyna (1990), Solomos (1993) and Modood (1992, 1993), have contributed much to the debate on race and culture, while a group of 'white' academics, trained in non-Western legal systems, have been interested in various questions around pluralism.[8] It would appear that most English lawyers are not in fact academically prepared for tackling critical questions of race and law.[9]

It is pertinent to point out, finally, that a good number of standard English textbooks on public law contain some coverage of anti-discrimination law and racial issues.[10] Whether such textbooks are actually widely used to teach public law seems quite a different matter. Overall, it appears that such new topics are not being absorbed sufficiently well into general public law teaching. This helps to explain why the academic coverage of such issues has remained segmental, underdeveloped and Euro-focused, while leading writers (see Poulter, 1994) appear reluctant to acknowledge diversified perspectives. In other words, there has been no real, meaningful legal debate, so that stereotyped, outdated conceptualisations continue to be reflected in the unsatisfactory analysis of current law.

THE DEFICIENT CONCEPTUALISATION OF 'RACE' AND ETHNICITY IN ENGLISH LAW

Since the presence of 'new' ethnic minority communities has become a more prominent feature of life in most Western societies, the social, political and legal systems of such countries have more visibly been expected to take account of, and even formally recognise, various forms of multiculturalisation.[11] This process does not stop before the portal of law, yet the various facets of sociolegal change in this context have excited sociologists, anthropologists and political scientists rather than legal scholars. Perhaps this is so because the law continues to view itself as a controlling mechanism rather than a factor subject to social changes brought about by migration. If this is correct, we see here again a negative impact of legal centralism (Griffith, 1986) and assimilationist ideologies, reflected in an unwillingness to grasp the enormity of recent changes in multiethnic modern societies. The current reversal of colonialism, as it were, demands that legal systems in the receiving countries should explicitly take account of the new structural realities created by migration processes.

A closer analysis of the legal changes in relation to ethnic minority presence shows that most non-Western legal systems have developed a framework of so-called personal laws, to the effect that members of different (mainly religious or ethnic) communities are governed by their own laws, which are recognised as part of the official law. This model inherently respects diversity and pluralism, but not of a narrowly racial kind. It is quite wrong to assume that this pattern is a colonial by-product (Hooker, 1975) or a British invention; such recognition of ethnic diversity existed, certainly in India, the Middle East and Africa, long before colonial intervention. While current debates in developing countries are often focused on plans for legal uniformisation,[12] the Western ideology of legal uniformity resists official recognition of ethnic diversity, responding as though law and culture could be neatly separated and race was legally neutral within a secular egalitarian framework.

In reality, however, Western legal systems have long operated a pattern of selective toleration and recognition of 'ethnic' needs and claims.[13] This approach is problematic, since recognition of diversity has tended to be viewed as a favour which may be withheld by those in authority, not as an integral structural element. Such strategies of selective recognition inevitably produce conflicts. In fact, they end up discriminating: not only in Britain does 'ethnic' recognition by the official law clearly discriminate between different claimant groups. Although we cannot explore this in detail here, while various forms of Asian ethnicity are widely accepted in English law, those of African and Afro-Caribbean groups have tended to be dismissed, probably because they were assumed to be racial rather than cultural.

The underlying argument against the recognition of racial diversities, that colour is only socially but not legally relevant, and that at any rate uniformity is best, so that diversities and pluralisms should be ignored as far as possible, has landed English race relations law in a conceptual mess: while the purpose of the law would appear to be protection against discrimination, the case-law shows that even when racial discrimination admittedly took place, the law as it stands now will not protect victims of discrimination unless they can bring themselves under the increasingly arbitrary judicial definition of 'racial group' in s 3 of the Race Relations Act, 1976. The case-law confirms this: Trevor Dawkins,[14] a Rastafarian driver told to cut his hair if he wanted a job, found that the decision in his case contrasted somewhat illogically with the leading case of *Mandla*,[15] in which a Sikh schoolboy had been told to cut his hair if he wanted admission to a particular school. The Sikh boy achieved the full protection of English law, but not the Rastafarian appellant. Thus, in virtually identical factual situations, English law today protects only members of certain 'racial groups', and on the basis of heavily contested criteria.

While principled arguments against the recognition of diversity appear rather too defensive at the end of the twentieth century, they do not take into account the apparent fact that even codified Western legal systems have been making all kinds of allowances for various forms of diversity. Presumably guided by sociological and 'race relations' expertise, the historical development of English law in this regard has relied on extra-legal expertise and political pressure rather than legal analysis. The law has been reactive, rather than proactive. The results seem deeply unsatisfactory in terms of intellectual clarity and cohesiveness. They are also politically insensitive, to say the least: the very legal framework which is supposed to improve 'race relations' actually does the reverse.[16] Curiously, the general public in Britain as well as many lawyers remain unaware that the law has been protecting only certain 'racial groups', so that it remains perfectly possible to discriminate against the majority of non-white citizens and co-residents. Leading judges, in critical moments, have been looking for general dictionaries rather than specialist legal analysis. Such simplistic techniques of law-making, almost inevitably, lead to strange mistakes which then have to be rectified.[17]

Lack of research and of clarity about 'race' and ethnicity' have been coupled with an aversion to address religious issues in legal contexts, especially in Parliament (see Robilliard, 1983), granting privileged status to the Sikhs as a 'racial group' under the Race Relations Act. But the Court of Appeal in 1993, faced with a claim by Rastafarians to the same effect, and in almost identical circumstances, refused them recognition as a 'racial group', sidelining the questions of religion and ethnic identity. Yet what distinguished the Sikhs from other Punjabis other than their religion? Clearly, the liberal dreams of a progressive, protective evolution of the relevant definitions in the 1976 Act have been shattered.[18]

Evidence of black disadvantage perpetrated by the law, past and present, is ubiquitous. I have tended to argue that one cannot realistically turn a law course on ethnic minorities into a module on slavery and colonial history. Can lawyers not simply take it as a fact that racial discrimination and legal favouritism have a long legacy and that Africans tend to be ranked lower (see, for example, Chamberlain, 1974, p 23)? Such racial stereotyping has obviously survived into our time and permeates the current law, providing simple associations of dark pigment with 'mugging', generally unruly behaviour and all kinds of criminality. There should be no need to prove the existence of such stereotypes, but serious legal literature has continued to prevaricate. After Hood's detailed study (1992b), there should be no need for authors to engage in such ideological juggling. Of course, the assertion that there is no conclusive evidence of discrimination against blacks nurtures the assumption that blackness is (or at least may be) criminogenic and that incomplete assimilation might be responsible for criminality. Obviously, it remains easy to blame the victims of discrimination for their own predicament.

How does one fit into this picture the fact that criminal justice agencies may refuse to pursue the murder of a black youth, in the very recent case of the fatal stabbing of a young white boy, the verdict was that one of the defendants must be made to 'carry the can', never mind niceties of evidence? We do not, apparently, need American legal scholarship to tell us that British justice is not colour-blind. Legal analysis in this field throws up many disappointments (Boothman, 1994). A policy of pigmentocracy is obviously being observed in Britain, too, where blacks – the darkest – must always come last; there is no real will to change that.

Apart from the absence of systematic sociolegal analysis, the adversarial orientation of English law continues to be a drawback; it is not conducive to public interest-oriented (and thus to some extent disinterested) legal development. If it becomes more important to win a case than to produce analytically sound rationales for a particular decision, the function of at least one branch of the divided profession, namely to guide the judges, has been given a partisan character. Over time, the result can be very unsatisfactory law.

ASSIMILATIONIST UNDERPINNINGS AND LEGAL RACISM

It should already be clear from the above that legalised racism is actually an integral structural element of legal centralism. This section briefly suggests ways of opening up a wider conceptualisation of law, making more room for social plurality and legal pluralism. With reference to international law, we saw already that the historically sanctioned, systematic disadvantaging of minorities in many jurisdictions results in selective non-protection of human rights irrespective of international guarantees, even in the supposedly most advanced jurisdictions.[19] Thus, the Western-dominated agendas for the international protection of human rights have inherent in them the potential to deny such rights to those who refuse to give up being 'the other'. This means that powerful extra-legal considerations – that is predominantly questions of politics and economics – tend to be crucial; these have not been addressed in systematic depth by legal analysts of minority studies.

Now, if 'the other' is merely perceived as racially constituted, assimi-lationist legal policy overlooks that it is not in the power of the bearers of black or brown faces to hide their otherness. Nor will members of different religions convert to the majority faith or holders of a different citizenship, such as Turks in Germany, flock to acquire the domestic one. The common (wo)man is curiously aware that (s)he will stay 'the other' in some form. Thus, within an assimilationist framework of reasoning, the onus to reduce diversity and differences is always thrown back to the minorities themselves, although this is hardly rational and does not work in practice, because one can never fully protect oneself against being defined as 'the other'. Indeed, it appears to be an inevitable consequence of minority existence, over time, that new ethnicities are being created.

Still, the same legal system which appears to promise rewards to 'conformers' continues to condone racial and ethnic disadvantaging. This is so precisely because 'race', and more so 'ethnicity', are not only a matter of defining oneself but also of being defined. Hence, the 'official' law with its centralist assumptions posits simplistic equality premises, but these are not operative in social reality: ethnicity has always been situational and thus, by definition, legal and extra-legal at the same time. No wonder, then, that most lawyers have difficulties with this concept, even though it is exceedingly simple to grasp if one accepts that everyone is ethnic.

What if a better solution were the abandonment of assimilationist assumptions and the unconditional recognition of ethnic plurality or diversity? Asian philosphies excel in such matters: let the equality of difference be our axiom! It is significant that such basic concepts have not played much of a role in debates about race and law. It seems we are afraid of this kind of equality. A recent example of such ethnophobia is found in the minutes of the 1994 Home Affairs Committee on Racial Attacks and Harassment, when the Home Secretary denies the relevance of ethnic/racial factors for crime control and draws attention to technical issues of evidence rather than substantive evidence of racial harassment. The problem here appears to be that the official law has also allocated to itself the prerogative of determining what constitutes relevant evidence. Subordination-oriented legal education would, like the Home Secretary, ignore evidence of legal discrimination, while critical legal studies, to deserve this catchy name, could not really look the other way.

Not surprisingly, in this conceptual muddle, official bodies like the Commission for Racial Equality, whose statutory duty (one must assume) is to protect ethnic minorities, have come in for severe criticism from all sides. The CRE, it seems, has an impossible brief. If the vast majority of minority groups in Britain continue to be unprotected by anti-discrimination law, it is still legitimate to ask today why we should have such a law in the first place.

Any discussion of ethnicity and the law, thus, wakes the sleeping lions of so-called uniformity and white superiority and triggers off protective mechanisms at subconscious levels which bar critical analysis. The mainstream approach to law protects 'us' from 'them', using labels like 'ethnic' and 'race' for the dangerous, unacceptable 'other'. A particular form of ethnic hegemony and the purported uniformity of the 'white' majority are guarded by the law, even if this makes a nonsense of race relations. Ballard and Kalra (1993) have rightly argued that it is a major problem in Britain today that we refuse to acknowledge that everyone, black or white, is some form of 'hyphenated Briton' now. This, precisely, marks the equality of diversity of which we are so afraid.

TEACHING 'ETHNIC' DIVERSITY AND THE LAW

How does one teach about this complexity within a legal framework? In my experience, if the ultimate aim is to enable students to become competent analysts of legal arguments and developments, a modicum of sociological input is inevitable. This can be stringently streamlined, identifying a selective range of relevant reading. Much, in fact far too much, useful material is easily available. I have found it therapeutic to use recent but outdated or insufficiently analysed material to empower the students to grasp the limits of our understanding, as well as the limits of law in this field.

Returning to the legacy of slavery and colonialism and their contested place in a law course, I would say that key concepts like 'race' and 'ethnicity', slavery and colonialism must be addressed, however briefly, since they relate directly to how the law treats certain ethnic groups today. Any teaching of such extra-legal input needs to be relevant to the subject taught. This may demand a lot of a law tutor, but it is actually quite simple to show how racial stereotyping, manifested in racial attacks or discretionary sentencing patterns, reflects the tenacity of Victorian cultural and racial images.

I am aware that two particular concerns are constantly raised by some black law students. The first point reflects my own reservations about the uncritical use of 'race': Africans and Caribbean people should not just be regarded as 'black' but otherwise culturally non-distinct. Although some assimilation-minded black students may object, competent teaching needs to demonstrate the internal diversity of all ethnic minorities (as well as the majority) and it makes sense to link this with some hard thinking about the potential for disagreement over assimilation strategies within any ethnic group.

The second concern relates to the potential for stereotyping through teaching, however well-meaning. This is a real danger when one identifies specific minority groups with certain legal topics in such a way that it reflects the differential legal treatment of blacks and Asians. While it makes sense to discuss family law questions as Asian-related, the repercussions of linking Africans and Afro-Caribbeans with topics like race and crime are alarming. The uncritical reproduction of official stereotypes is certainly problematic; it seems essential to discuss why the law has specific problems with certain groups. In the context of a course of study which reassesses the role of law as a tool for allocating power, as well as preparing students for real practice, it seems illusory and irrelevant to strive for ideological agreement, but inadvertent racism remains a professional hazard constantly shared by all participants.

An important organisational question would appear to be whether one teaches a special course on Ethnic Minorities and the Law, or whether one integrates the subject into so-called 'core' teaching, which is itself an 'ethnic' term. Both methods appear to have their advantages, while limited resources and flexibility on the part of law teachers will determine what is realistic. This, incidentally, mirrors debates about multicultural education at school level, where multiculturalism has been limited by the constraints of relevant teacher training. Arguably, a more integrated approach would encourage 'us' and 'them' thinking. At the same time, there is also a powerful argument against the spraycan principle: mere tokenism in this field of legal education will not do. Anyway, where are the teachers who could handle such a subject? If the experience of schools is a pointer, it could be disastrous to expect non-white colleagues to shoulder 'ethnic' subjects – the point of education is precisely that ethnic minority legal issues concern us all.

Without a doubt, the vast majority of law departments in the country would struggle if they were suddenly expected to incorporate teaching about ethnic minority issues. Of course, the establishment argument will be that legal education should focus on what is important, so out go ethnic studies and other peripherals for which there is no space in our timetables. Still, where such courses are being taught, the student response appears to have been enthusiastic. Nobody could deny the practical relevance of legal training at the academic stage in areas such as employment law, discrimination, immigration, and family law issues involving ethnic minority customs. In my experience, students who can neatly explain the difference between direct and indirect discrimination in a job interview have an edge over others today. It is not new that lawyers in practice want to know what the new generation of students has been learning about today's society and the legal issues it creates.

Such new forms of legal education, to be really effective, would need to become an integral part of legal training, which would therefore extend beyond law schools. However, the reduction of stupid and unthinking racism is not a specific job for legal education alone – it should be a brief for the entire educational system today. So far, relevant law courses seem to teach the converted: those students who are afraid of true equality will seek to avoid such courses and I doubt whether teaching lawyers about ethnic minorities will brainwash them into non-discriminating individuals. For this reason, I have never been surprised that confrontational race relations courses should be seen as counterproductive. Devoid of conceptual depth and critical analysis, a narrow focus on race relations simply cannot do justice to the complex web of interactions between official law and ethnicity.

NOTES

1. Chiba uses this term for the dominant analytical school of Western jurisprudence.
2. In the field of criminal law, see, for example, the excellent US study of Mann (1993), which relies heavily on sociological research.
3. See the complaint, to this effect, in Mason (1995, p 8). The other dominant factor in British discourses on race is, of course, class, with equally misleading consequences.
4. The voluminous work of Michael Banton and John Rex may serve as a prominent point of reference. For details, see Banton (1988), Rex (1983) and the excellent recent overview in Mason (1995). For bibliographical details, see Gordon and Klug (1984), Amin et al. (1988) and Ballard (1994), the latter with a South Asian bias. For a history of race relations research, see Stanfield (1993).

5. *New Community* must be credited with having made a systematic attempt to record debates about legal issues for a wider readership in a series of articles entitled 'Legal decisions affecting ethnic minorities and discrimination'. Many of these were written by David Pearl, now a judge, during the 1970s and 1980s. It appears that more recently the legal input has been reduced to occasional coverage.

6. Pearl (1986) remains important, while Poulter (1986) is more detailed, but now out of print and largely out of date. Poulter (1994) restates the earlier premises, emphasising still more the human rights dimension, but fails to take into account more recent writing of a critical nature (see especially Bradney, 1993).

7. The most important study is certainly Hood (1992b), but see Vol. 16 No. 1 (1989) of *New Community* for a collection of older articles, as well as Jefferson and Walker (1992).

8. In particular Hooker (1975), Pearl (1986), Poulter (1986, 1994), Woodman (1983) and Menski (1987, 1993).

9. This raises questions about training future law teachers. Growing awareness of this gap, from within the professions, can now have the result that law students who specialise in 'ethnic' issues are perceived as having an edge over mainstream applicants.

10. See, for example, Bailey et al. (1995). A systematic study of such writing and its impact on law teaching is being conducted at the School of Oriental and African Studies, University of London. It is too early to talk about results, but it is significant that many English law textbooks continue to ignore the presence of large ethnic minority communities.

11. Whether a country defines itself as an immigration country or not seems largely immaterial in this context.

12. Prominent examples have been India and Tanzania, more recently Bangladesh.

13. For early evidence of the English legal system's toleration of 'white' religious minorities and Jewish concerns see Hamilton (1995, pp 4 and 9). On later developments see Poulter (1986, especially pp 206–41).

14. See *Dawkins* v. *Department of the Environment* [1993] IRLR 284.

15. *Mandla* v. *Dowell Lee* HL [1983] 1 All ER 1062.

16. The same has recently been said of British immigration law and its impact on race relations. For a powerful critique, see Spencer (1994).

17. The prime example here is *Mandla* v. *Dowell Lee* CA [1982] 3 All ER 1108. Lord Denning's race-based verdict was overturned by the

House of Lords, using a wider, ethnic and cultural meaning of 'racial group' (see note 15).

18. Poulter (1990, p 14) wrote optimistically of a society where 'a Rastafarian cannot be refused employment merely because he is unwilling to cut off his dreadlocks'. As we saw, the Court of Appeal put an end to such dreams in 1993.

19. The most prominent example was Gunnar Myrdal's analysis of the 'American dilemma'.

5
The Racial, Ethnic and Cultural Values Underpinning Current Legal Education

Aimee Paterson

INTRODUCTION

This chapter offers a critical analysis of the current state of legal education in Britain in the context of the contemporary politics of race. Within traditional, established educational ideologies, many important issues are simply not addressed. For instance, are the values which currently underpin legal education, derived mainly from a European Christian discourse, shaped by cultures of exclusion? Is legal education, both in terms of its content and delivery, therefore Eurocentric and culturally insular? In advocating a democratic and pluralist enrichment of British legal education, this chapter identifies a number of fundamental questions:

1. Who are the new 'consumers'[1] of legal education today? How diverse are their ethnic, racial and cultural backgrounds?
2. Who are the deliverers, the architects, and the policy-makers of legal education? Why are there so few ethnic minority staff, and fewer still in managerial roles able to influence policy?
3. Given the character of these consumers, is there a case for cross-cultural values in legal education; that is for the adoption of an ideology in which no one culture has overall hegemony or control?

THE NEW CONSUMERS OF LEGAL EDUCATION: IS BRITISH LEGAL EDUCATION EUROCENTRIC?

The legal profession in Britain is notorious for its conservatism. It is ritualistic and unnecessarily traditional. The insistence on things such as dining, required as a formal part of a barrister's training, have long been subject to well-founded criticisms of valueless time-wasting and value-laden induction into arcane and discriminatory practices.[2] It is, therefore, no surprise that legal education has largely developed in a way that mirrors and fosters these traditions. However, recent years have seen radical changes in the composition of the law student body in Britain. These changes have been due to a number of factors. Firstly, of course, Britain has become a multicultural and multiracial society, with ethnic minorities now forming 6 per cent of the population. Secondly, higher (including legal) education has become more accessible to a wider cross-section of society. Thirdly, and perhaps most significantly, some law schools have actively recruited international students from overseas (that is, from non-EU countries).

Before putting a case for the need to diversify, it is important to explore the changing character of the new consumers of legal education. Who are today's consumers of legal education? From recent research, a very clear picture has emerged. A study by the Policy Studies Institute found that 'ethnic minority applicants are proportionately more likely to apply to study law than are white applicants' (Modood and Shiner, 1994). The popularity of legal study among ethnic minorities is also reflected in the proportion of ethnic minority students actually studying law (Ibid, p 18). Figures indicate that 18 per cent of all law students nationally are from ethnic minority backgrounds, a figure which rises to a 50 per cent average in the London area. Clearly, then, the nature of the consumers of legal education is continuing to change, increasingly reflecting the diverse cultural and ethnic make-up of contemporary British society today. So, as the consumers of legal education inevitably change from predominantly white Anglo-Saxon to multicultural in character, what of the content and delivery of legal education? To what extent have these developed so as to reflect this growing multiculturalism?

THE CONTENT OF LEGAL EDUCATION – THE NEED TO DIVERSIFY

An exploration of the courses taught within UK law schools reveals the persisting conservative traditions of the British legal profession. Very few law schools have expanded their curriculum beyond the narrow confines of traditional law courses. It is, surely, important to recognise that 'straight' law courses alone are no longer (if ever they were) sufficient to meet the needs of a multicultural society. Law schools need to adopt a more progressive stance. There is an urgent need for greater academic appreciation of the value of multicultural-ism in legal education. Legal education needs to embrace a wider range of disciplines in order to properly inform and serve its new consumers. Equally important, law schools, responsible for producing future lawyers, need to ensure they have the ability to relate to clients of diverse ethnic, cultural and religious backgrounds.

Multiculturalism in legal education would provide a platform for informing and educating students about key race relations issues where ignorance and misconception currently prevail. Training in race relations would help lawyers respond to the needs of contemporary British society. Indeed, this is vitally important if persistent allegations of injustice are seriously to be addressed and eradicated. The value of this policy has been recently emphasised by the Judicial Studies Board, when it noted that it is 'essential to equip all judges and magistrates with a basic amount of knowledge and understanding if they are to be seen to be administering justice fairly to people with whom they have little in common in terms of upbringing, culture and experience' (Shaw, 1991). In reaffirming his commitment to this ethos, Mr Justice Brooke, chair of the Ethnic Minorities Advisory Committee (EMAC),[3] noted in the eighth Kapila Fellowship Lecture that he had identified what he termed 'three great risks' caused by ignorance of race relations issues:

1. The risk of causing individual offence and hurt through ignorance of things of personal importance to people.
2. The risks associated with ignorance of other people's cultures.
3. The risk of doing injustice through ignorance of the potency of subconscious discrimination.

A policy of multiculturalism would, if implemented, not only inform and educate judges and magistrates; it would also highlight the experiences of ethnic minorities in British society. In line with this philosophy, in November 1994 the Lord Chancellor, Lord Mackay, introduced a project whereby circuit judges, part-time recorders and assistant recorders attend a one-and-a-half day seminar on race awareness. All of these initiatives strongly indicate a new realisation and recognition of the value of incorporating multiculturalism as part of legal training. However, despite these most welcome developments (and in particular Mr Justice Brooke's unwavering commitment), by introducing multiculturalism at the end rather than at the beginning of legal education – that is, in training judges rather than law students in race awareness – are we not in danger of 'putting the cart before the horse'? Of course, there is always value in education whenever it takes place, but should we not be looking to avoid judicial problems by making multiculturalism part of the ethos of all modern legal education? Given the cultural and ethnic diversity of both British society and law students, is there not a case for 'a wholesale permeation of virtually the entire curriculum with multiracial, multicultural themes' (Poulter, 1986, p 197)?[4]

THE 'UNMET NEED' IN LEGAL EDUCATION

Undoubtedly, the education and training of lawyers in and for today's culturally and ethnically pluralist British society leaves a lot to be desired. There is a clear need which is not being met. Recent problems experienced by ethnic minority students at the Inns of Court School of Law, highlighted in the Report of The Committee of Inquiry Into Equal Opportunities On The Bar Vocational Course, 1994 (The Barrow Report), are a fall-out from a system of legal education that is deficient in its approach to multiculturalism. In seeking possible explanations for the marked difference in the pass rates between ethnic groups, the Barrow Report concluded that a number of factors were relevant, including 'aspects of the design and delivery of the course that might be less successful in meeting the needs of black and ethnic minority students than of white students' (Barrow 1994, p 20). While the Barrow Report further concluded that there was no 'direct discrimination and ... indirect discrimination as defined by the terms of the Race Relations Act 1976' (Ibid, p 100), it noted that 'nevertheless, there was a form of discrimination in the year of the Bar Vocational Course. It is present in the impression that the school and the course were designed to reproduce the model English barrister, who is white, male and upper class' (Ibid, p 99).

A strong institutional resistance to multicultural education has emerged for a number of reasons. For instance, because this philosophy was a politically popular policy with the Greater London Council and the Labour Party in the 1970s and 1980s, it has tended to be associated with radical left ideology and seen as a watering down of so-called 'traditional' educational values. Be that as it may, the Labour government in its *Education in Schools* Green Paper of 1977, was forward-thinking in its response to the needs of a culturally pluralist society when it stated: 'Our society is a multicultural, multiracial one and the curriculum should reflect a sympathetic understanding of the different cultures and races that now make up our society. ... We also live in a complex, interdependent world, and many of our problems in Britain require international solutions. The curriculum should therefore reflect our need to know about and understand other countries' (Poulter, 1986, p 196). Secondly, multiculturalism in education has been rejected for leading 'to a lowering of standards' (Ibid, p 197). One can only assume that this view has arisen from a total misunderstanding and misinterpretation of what the concept involves. Multicultural education advocates an expansion and development of the curriculum to include new and broader disciplines relevant to the issues of contemporary British society. In the context of legal education, it would mean better trained and more effective lawyers, more able to meet the needs of a culturally pluralist society. It would also mean supplementing the initiatives implemented by Lord Mackay and Mr Justice Brooke for judges and magistrates, for these reforms cannot work in isolation. The idea of the proposed policy is to give academics a proactive role in the development of the profession; the types of lawyers and future judges produced would have been specifically trained to recognise and accommodate the multidimensionality of modern British society.

In seeking to achieve these objectives, there are a number of different models that might be adopted. The easiest, perhaps, would simply be to expand the curriculum to include some non-traditional courses with critical dimensions, such as, for instance, Discrimination and the Law, Immigration Law, Equality Before the Law, Refugee Law and so on. Under this model, the traditional core subjects remain untouched. This approach, however, is problematic in that the main body of students might tend to boycott or reject such subjects as not necessary or important for them. The very marginalisation of these ('non-core') courses would probably shape the student response to them. Certainly, within the profession itself, these areas of law are marginalised and, consequently, not given sufficiently high status. On the bright side, my own personal experience shows that student responses to subjects with crosscultural themes can sometimes be very positive.[5] A worrying development in this context, however, is the consequences of Britain's increasingly strong political and economic links with Europe. As European countries open internal borders and close external ones – in Britain's case, mainly to predominantly black Commonwealth nations – will the view taken of the need for multicultural legal education itself change? Although it is perhaps too early to judge what the full effect is likely to be, it appears that the immediate consequence might be that some law schools will urge the replacement of those (few) subjects with cross-racial themes by those with a more European dimension. One way of pre-empting this might be for law schools in Britain to establish more formal and informal study links and exchange programmes with universities in black Commonwealth countries. The mutual educational benefits of such programmes are limitless. Study links are now almost standard practice for many law schools, but the links tend to be limited to mainly white European countries. A further development in course reform would be to introduce a new subject which makes race relations issues a compulsory core subject for every law undergraduate, with the same status as the other core subjects. This would ensure that every lawyer has, at least, a basic working knowledge of race equality.

A more radical model would require a reconsideration of the traditional 'core' law courses, which remain a font of conservatism, exploring the extent to which it is possible and practicable to incorporate local customs and practices within English legal principles without, in the process, infringing human rights. An area where this is already happening is Family Law where English courts have adopted a broader, multiculturally aware approach in dealing with marriage and divorce matters. Admittedly, this has not been so much the product of deliberate policy on the part of the courts, or of academic pressure, but has, rather, come about as a result of the need to resolve difficulties arising out of conflicts of laws. Nevertheless, it has been a welcome development with positive human rights benefits for the groups concerned, and points to the need for academic lawyers to pose questions about other less obvious areas where culturally exclusionary frameworks prevail.

COLONIAL ATTITUDES AND THEIR INFLUENCE ON LEGAL EDUCATION

A full analysis of the current normative framework of British legal education would need to consider the relationship between Britain's imperial past, the defining moment for much of its legal culture, and the culture of its legal education. Does Britain's imperial heritage play a role in shaping the values which underpin its legal education? The formative statement of the British Critical Legal Conference noted that 'legal education and the practices of legal institutions work to buttress and support a pervasive system of oppressive non-egalitarian relations' (Grigg-Spall and Ireland, 1992, p ix). The culture of legal education and training certainly seems to be that of producing a 'model' of lawyering that continues the tradition of what a perceived lawyer should be.

Legal education appears to be structured to create and produce a stereotyped ideal lawyer. Both the content and delivery of courses, consciously or otherwise, seem designed to persuade its consumers to adopt a certain image. As noted by the Barrow Report, 'anyone who does not conform and has no wish to, or is unable to, may feel uncomfortable. This is equally so of pupillage, tenancy and further eminence at the Bar ...' although '... it is less noticeable then because those who have reached the later stages will already have successfully conformed' (The Barrow Report, 1994, p 99). But perhaps legal educators and trainers are merely responding to an agenda set by the profession itself. It is certainly the case that law firms in recruiting trainee solicitors, and barristers' chambers in selecting pupils and tenants, are more likely to prefer a white candidate. Studies consistently show that ethnic minorities find it almost three times as difficult to secure articles and pupillage as their white conterparts. The Barrow Report confirms this in its conclusion that 'white students were more likely to have been offered a pupillage than similarly qualified students belonging to ethnic minority groups' (Ibid, p 37). In 1994, the PSI Report concluded that 'well qualified ethnic minority students were much less successful than their equally – and in some cases less – qualified white counterparts in obtaining training contracts (the success rates for black students at that stage in the study being only 7% against 47% for white students)' (pp 76–7). It is against this background that the Law Society, in an attempt to reaffirm its commitment to the elimination of race discrimination, has recently introduced new anti-discrimination measures including a 'good recruitment practice' guide for law firms. But these measures, although welcome, would serve only to supplement and update race relations awareness if legal education and training was effective. As it is, available evidence suggests that such measures are very welcome by those already committed to these equal opportunities practices while they breed resentment amongst, rather than educating and informing, those opposed. It must be stressed, however, that whatever their practical impact, such schemes should continue to inform the philosophy of the profession and clearly have a policy role.

AVOIDING THE CRUSOE/FRIDAY SYNDROME

The primary objective of imperialism was economic power, but there was, arguably, another hidden and more subtle agenda – the subjugation of other racial and cultural identities. The wider implication of this imperialist culture is what I term the Crusoe/Friday syndrome, where what is gained is greatly mitigated by what has been lost in the process. For a development of this theory, it is useful to consider Toni Morrison's analysis of Robinson Crusoe's encounter with 'Friday'.

In *Robinson Crusoe*, Daniel Defoe tells the story of Alexander Selkirk's experiences on an island where he had been shipwrecked in 1709. One Friday, he comes across 'an almost drowned Indian'. The man is in fact a refugee fleeing for his life. Crusoe assumes the man has no name, or if he has, it is presumably of little importance, because 'he does not ask the refugee what his name is; instead, Crusoe names him' (Morrison (ed.), 1992, p xxiv). Crusoe's account of the story further suggests the presumption that the refugee had no language or culture of his own prior to his 'rescue', so he (Crusoe) begins a process of 'educating' him in the language and cultures of the 'rescuer'. According to Morrison, the exercise, from Crusoe's point of view, is a successful one. 'Crusoe's narrative is a success story, one in which a socially, culturally, and biologically handicapped black man is civilized and Christianized – taught, in other words, to be like a white one' (Ibid, p xxiii).

Given the current disaffection amongst ethnic minorities within the profession, and the evidence of the various reports, is there a danger that British legal education and training might be exhibiting similar traits?

WHO ARE THE DELIVERERS AND POLICY-MAKERS OF LEGAL EDUCATION?

The responsibilty for the content and delivery of legal education and training must inevitably rest with two groups of people: law lecturers of various sorts and those within both the professions and academia who formulate policy and set the agenda for legal education. An examination of the profile of these groups suggests that law lecturers are themselves recruited from a culturally narrow pool. Figures indicate that an overwhelming number of them are white, with very few coming from ethnic minority backgrounds. Significantly, of the few lecturers from an ethnic minority background, hardly any seem to be in a position to influence policy – in other words, occupying managerial roles. This is a cause for concern for a number of reasons. It has already been established that the contemporary character of consumers of legal education is multicultural and multiracial, so why are there so few ethnic minority law lecturers? Surely it is important that, in order effectively to service multiracial consumers and a multiracial society, the deliverers of legal education should themselves be drawn from culturally diverse groups? One would have thought that the positive potential of this would be self-evident. In his study on 'The Role Of Affirmative Action Officers In North American Universities', Townsend-Smith found that this policy forms the ethos for recruiting in universities for academic staff mainly because it recognises that it is important 'to provide diversity among the faculty in order to increase the quality and variety of the teaching and research' (*Anglo-American Law Review*, 1990, vol 19 p 328). A further reason for the adoption of this recruitment philosophy in North American universities is that it is accepted that 'racial distribution of ... university jobs sends an unspoken message to students which either reinforces or challenges existing assumptions' (Ibid, p 328).

What is clearly evident is that the values which currently influence legal education are traditional, white and European, clearly symbolising and reflecting those of the people who control the agenda. What is equally evident is that the Eurocentricity of contemporary legal education is failing to meet the needs of a culturally plural society. It is obvious, therefore, that in order to develop a culturally diverse legal education, those delivering and developing courses must be drawn from a much more diverse cultural pool.

While it is conceded that it does not necessarily follow that increasing the number of ethnic minority law teachers would automatically result in the introduction of multiculturalism into legal education, it is suggested that it is much more likely to do so than a policy of no change. While there is no evidence to suggest that discrimination exists in recruitment practices for academic staff at universities (such as that uncovered in the Bar by the Barrow Report and by the PSI Report on the solicitors' branch of the profession), the question as to why there are so few ethnic minorities staff members remains. Of course, it is recognised that both academic freedom and the need for quality assurance means that employers must select their workforce on merit. However, it is perhaps important to explore more carefully what is meant by 'merit'. Merit should mean objectively assessing each applicant on the basis of his or her qualifications, relevant experience and future potential. Crucially, this means trying to preclude the possibility that prejudices, stereotyping and preconceived ideas about peoples and races form, consciously or unconsciously, part of the selection criteria. This requires an effective and well-monitored equal opportunities policy which actively encourages a culturally diverse workforce.

CONCLUSION AND PROPOSALS FOR REFORM

This chapter has considered the cultural, ethnic and racial values which currently underpin legal education and training – values which are predominantly Eurocentric and conservative. Despite the changing and racially diverse character of the consumers of legal education, its content and delivery has changed little and increasingly fails to meet the needs of a multicultural society. Teachers and policy-makers continue to be drawn from a culturally narrow pool and they continue to set a tone for legal education within which traditional, conservative ideas inherited from a different era predominate. What emerges is a system of legal education and training that is culturally insular, fostering a culture of exclusion. The profession's desire (and determination) to retain a particular sense of group cohesion appears to override considerations of justice.

There is a very strong case for legal education and training shedding its traditional cultural insularity. The profession should embrace an ethos of multiculturalism as part of its policy, not only for its judges and magistrates but as a central theme in all its educational and training processes. As a basis for a popular movement for change, we could try to devise a package of practical measures to reform and develop the legal educational process which acknowledges the cultural pluralism of contemporary British society. These might include:

1. The establishment of a Centre for Multicultural Legal Studies with a view to offering:
    (i) course modules which critically appraise the legal framework;
    (ii) a new culture for textbooks.
2. The introduction of multicultural themes into mainstream courses.
3. Increasing the cultural, ethnic and racial diversity of academic staff. In this context, we might consider the value of the practice initiated by North American universities (which some British universities have already adopted) of appointing affirmative action officers (AAOs).[6]
4. Setting up mentor schemes at universities (a practice which my own institution has already introduced and which has proved invaluable), which encourages established academics and practitioners to give

practical and moral support in career development to undergraduates.[7]

We must not make the mistake of assuming that law transcends prejudices and injustices. It is indeed acknowledged amongst critical legal writers that the opposite is in fact the case. As Grigg-Spall and Ireland have pointed out, 'law generally acts to consolidate and maintain an extensive system of class, gender and racial oppression' (Grigg-Spall and Ireland, 1992, p ix). We are products of processes of education and socialisation. If legal education in Britain continues to ignore the changing character of society and remains culturally insular, this malaise will result in ever more detrimental consequences for the profession and its perceived legitimacy. The whole legal educational community has a duty to address these issues now and try to provide solutions adequate to the times.

NOTES

1. The term 'consumer' is used here to denote the idea of education as a commodity and the students as consumers. This is not a view necessarily shared by the editors.
2. The practice epitomises middle-class, Eurocentric traditions.
3. The new chair of EMAC is Mr Justice Dyson.
4. The author was writing here on multiculturalism in the context of primary education; but the issues and debates remain the same. For a full discussion, see Milner (1981, p 290); and the Swan Committee Report pp 323, 327 (as cited in Poulter (1986)).
5. 'Equality Before The Law?', a course jointly devised and taught by Aimee Paterson and Jane Pickford. There has been increasing demand for this course with over half of Year I students opting for it. It has proved the most popular first year option on the Options Programme. This year the number taking the course has had to be limited to 75.
6. For a detailed study of the work done by AAOs in North American universities, see Townsend-Smith (1990, pp 325–44).
7. For details of The Mentor Scheme at the University of East London contact the office of Norman McClean, The Director of the Mentor Unit – 0181 590 7722.

6
New Europe, Old Story: Racism, Law and the European Community
Peter Fitzpatrick

INTRODUCTION

Part of the story has already been told, well told (see, for example, Paliwala, 1995). As such the story is one of the European Community as the affirmation of a distinct European identity, of a 'Fortress Europe' consolidated in the Maastricht Treaty on European Union.[1] The story unfolds in the joining of two momentous effects: the progressive elimination of internal or national boundaries within the European Community and the increasingly draconic enunciation of an 'external' boundary within which the Community is set against certain excluded 'others'. Hence, accompanying the Maastricht Treaty there is the proliferation of shadowy but potent Community regimes evasively identified by place or code – Schengen, Trevi, D.4, and so on – all refining and heightening the exclusion of the refugee and the would-be immigrant. These regimes of exclusion do not simply operate at some putative external border of the Community. The excluded are also within. Maastricht thrusts a thin citizenship on nationals of the Community's member states, and even if this adds little to rights those nationals already had under the EC Treaty, it does focus those rights on a distinct identity, one privileged above the identity of resident non-nationals. These residents are variously estimated to number between 10 and 15 million and are most often seen as racially 'other'. So, in these accounts of 'Fortress Europe', race is the ultimate criterion of exclusion, and the included, the true Europeans, are in turn constituted in racial terms.

Yet the story can also be told in another way. And it has to be told in another way if liberal notions of universality and equality, including equality before the law, are going to be upheld. Exclusion, then, is not properly put in racial terms. True, it can come close to being so. The so-called 'blacklist' of countries whose nationals now need a visa to enter the European Community is not conspicuous for the number of 'white' countries on it. And the provisions of the Maastricht Treaty predispose 'asylum', 'immigration', and 'nationals of third countries' to the negative connotations of race by dealing with all these in conjunction with 'combating unauthorized immigration, residence and work ... terrorism, unlawful drug trafficking and other serious forms of international crime' (Article K.1). But the governing texts are not racial and, as for their application, there is the ready point that an enormous number of 'nationals of third countries' and illegal immigrants are 'white'. Add to this the academic confirmation that race has been superseded in European demonologies by notions of culture (see Stolcke, 1995), and that would appear to be the end of the matter.

The response of this chapter is one of 'Yes, but ... .' It looks initially at the 'new' cultural fundamentalism in Europe and extracts from it the lineaments of racism. It then traces these in the generation of European culture and identity within and around institutions of the European Community, including the contributions of lawyers and the European Court of Justice. In all this, the persistence of nationalism emerges as pivotal. This nationalism, however, also presents dissonances or contradictions which could impel change through law and legal practice.

CULTURAL RACISM

That there is a growing xenophobia throughout Europe is broadly agreed upon but there is less agreement as to its nature (see Hobsbawm, 1992a). At least in its more public and official guises, this xenophobia is no longer able, so as is often said, to take the form of an explicit racism. It now takes distinct form as 'culture'. But is this culture fundamentally different to racism? Gilroy, among others, would see it as 'cultural racism', wherein 'biological hierarchy' may seem in a way to be displaced but there is instead 'new, cultural definitions of "race" which are just as intractable' (Gilroy, 1987, pp 60–1). The contrary case has been influentially put by Verena Stolcke: she finds that there are in Europe 'new rhetorics of exclusion' founded in a 'cultural fundamentalism' which is distinct from and even displaces a politically discredited racism, and nation thence becomes the locus of culture (Stolcke, 1995).

Whilst it can be readily agreed that 'culture' has become the predominant idiom of exclusion, it may be doubted whether this displaces or even derogates from racism. As Stolcke recognises, not all 'strangers' (borrowing from the cultural idiom) are equally strange. Indeed, the proponents of cultural fundamentalism have little or no trouble accepting the denizens of some cultures. Yet in Stolcke's argument, the xenophobia that founds cultural fundamentalism is, unlike racism, uniform and comprehensive in its opposition to all other cultures. In this scheme, cultures relate to each other in ways that are non-hierarchical or simply spatial. Contrast this with the first slice of cultural fundamentalism that Stolcke provides, Thatcher's evocation to such political effect in 1978 of the threat of 'swamping' by 'people with a different culture' (Stolcke, 1995, p 3). What seems crucial here is the exactitude, the territorial precision with which such people are designated in Thatcher's speech just before the part used by Stolcke: these potential swampers are 'people of the New Commonwealth' (that is, 'black' people) 'or Pakistan' – which country had to be specifically added because it had left the Commonwealth. Such people so carefully specified are then counterposed to 'the British character' which 'has done so much for democracy, for law and done so much throughout the world'. Divisions of this kind, as Stolcke so aptly notes, provide the 'cultural' unity and uniformity of the nation, a nation which in reality contains a diversity of cultures. Those divisions 'reterritorialise cultures' (Stolcke, 1995, p 8). Such divisions are racist rather than non-hierarchical or simply spatial. It may help to note, with Bhabha, that 'etymologically ... "territory" derives from both *terra* (earth) and *terrere* (to frighten) whence *territorium* "a place from which people are frightened off"' (Bhabha, 1994, pp 99–100). Only some are ostracised, degraded, murdered or, in short, terrorised.

The cultural constitution of Europe is primally effected in opposition to the racially conceived 'non-European'. And that which is 'non-European' is, as Chris Shore says, 'being defined with increasing precision and thus, as if by default, an "official" definition of Europe is being constructed' – as he also says, 'the new European order ... is coming to mean a sharper boundary between "European" and "non-European"' (Shore, 1993, pp 786 and 793). This, in turn, accompanies that parallel development between integration within the Community and the increasing rigidification of what are called its external boundaries.

The negative and racial constitution of the European necessarily compensates for the failure of positive definition. In a piece plangently, not to say plaintively, titled 'What is Europe, Where is Europe?', Seton-Watson found that: 'The word "Europe" has been used and misused, interpreted and misinterpreted, in as many different meanings as almost any work of any language. There have been and are many Europes' (Seton-Watson, 1985, p 9).

He considers several contenders – such as the bounds of Charlemagne's Empire and the bounds of Christendom – but is convinced by none. The usual effort at positive definition takes the form of the list. These are collections of the vacuous, the incidental and the institutional. Take Duroselle's collection of cultural artefacts:

> ... we have been influenced by ancient Greece, by Judaism, and by Christianity, Megaliths, Roman roads and monuments, local autonomy, Romanesque art, the cathedrals, the universities, the

explorers, the Industrial Revolution, human rights: these and many more elements are of the essence of Europe. (Duroselle, 1990, p 413)

The lists can be more economical. The following from the Netherlands Ambassador for International Cultural Cooperation is close to standard:

> What determines and characterises European culture? ... Europe is formed by the ... community of nations which are largely characterised by the inherited civilisation whose most important sources are: the Judaeo-Christian religion, the Greek-Hellenistic ideas in the fields of government, philosophy, arts and science, and finally, the Roman views concerning law. (See Pieterse, 1991, p 3)

In a similar vein, the 'Declaration on the European Identity', agreed by the members of the Community in 1973, revealed that they were distinguished by 'the same attitudes to life', a commitment to the 'individual', and a determination 'to defend the principles of representative democracy [and] the rule of law' (see Shore, 1993, p 787).

Engagement with the more palpable limits of Europe are, however, less robust. The Commission of the European Community recently found 'that it is neither possible nor opportune' to locate the frontiers of the Community beyond 'the shared experience of proximity, ideas, values and historical interaction' (see Shore, 1993, p 786). The main treaty, although establishing an 'European Economic Community', betrays no interest in the nature of this Europe. And although the preamble to the Maastricht Treaty on European Union is replete with the by now standard invocation of, to quote, 'liberty, democracy, and respect for human rights and fundamental freedoms and the rule of law', nowhere is the explicit nature of this union confronted. Palpability is found, rather, in the conjunction of supposed European qualities with their non-European opposite. Thatcher, again, obliges with a telling example. She notoriously set Britain apart from the European project in her Bruges speech of September 1989, but nonetheless affirmed a common European commitment to 'the rule of law which marks out a civilized society from barbarism', and recollected a common heritage in which 'Europeans explored and colonised and – yes, without apology – civilised much of the world' (*Guardian*, 21 September 1989).

LAW AND THE EUROPEAN NATION

Not the least congenial habitat for this chilling cosiness is European Community law. The connection between this hallowed realm and the murkier world of Schengen, Trevi and the rest is the protean ambivalence of nation. Nation is the acceptable face of negation in community discourse. The savagery that it imports is rarely, however, far from its surface. Delors, for example, frequently saw a supposedly renascent nationalism as the return of malign 'phantoms' (see Grant, 1994, p 223). This is no more than the standard and simplistic conception of nationalism as importing barely suppressed primordial and atavistic urges constantly attending the precarious achievements of civilisation. In like vein, the Commission's information booklet *A Citizen's Europe* sees the Community as 'an attempt to establish between States, the same rules and codes of behaviour that enabled primitive societies to become peaceful and civilized' – the nation-states, in other words, are the new primitives (see Shore, 1993, p 793). The Community is, of course, something different. Within official discourses, Shore reveals:

> The EC is typically portrayed as a logical development of the enlightenment: a force for progress inspired by science, reason, rationality and humanism ... These discourses also tend to portray the European Parliament and Commission as heroic agents of change, on the side of history, leading Europe forward in search of its supposed 'federal destiny'. (Shore, 1995, p 11)

For Delors, the Community provides a model for a universal fraternity (see Grant, 1994, p 163). And so, considerably, on.

Such surpassing virtues of the Community are adroitly located by Schepel and Wesseling in their close observation of 'the mindset' of European lawyers (Schepel and Wesseling, 1995). This cultural construct encompasses judges, practising lawyers and academics and the protean transfers between these categories. The construct is found, in a summary way, to be structured around certain antinomies, some of which are:

Integration	National Sovereignty
European Community	Nation-State
Peace	War
Cosmopolitanism	Nationalism
Progress	Decay
Law	Politics

And, as Bergeron has shown so vividly, with the jurisprudence of the European Court, the Community and its law are formed and exalted as epitomes of progress and the universal in their intrinsic opposition to the atavistic and reactionary realms of nation (Bergeron, in press). But, as Bergeron also shows, the grander claims of integral Community do strain credibility in confrontation with a drab and diffuse actuality.

The most resolute proponents of the Community as essentially and distinctly supranational can hardly avoid an obvious incompleteness in the very law on which it is founded, an incompleteness in both the law's range and its efficacy, and in its continuing dependence on nation for much of its effect. This deficit is readily resolved in the mythology of Europeanism where such shortcomings become both an obstacle and a spur to a progress which is overcoming them. Much of the diversity or plurality of law within the Community can be accommodated within a unitary frame by seeing it as something that is being countered in this progress.

The way in which all this is being done is spectacularly unoriginal. The Community proceeds by replicating and mimicking the character of the very nation it is intrinsically set against. The Community's more indulgent observers would dissent. In the words of one of them, 'the institutional, juridical, and spatial complexes associated with the Community ... constitute nothing less than the emergence of the first truly postmodern international political form', and hence we need a new 'epistemological posture' to deal with it (Ruggie, 1993, pp 140, 169). On the contrary, Bergeron would argue, 'the Court of Justice, in a consistent development of case law supported by a plethora of Community legal scholars, has colonised the structures of modernity which characterise national law' (Bergeron, in press). And a wearyingly familiar epistemology is sufficient to accommodate that.

It is not necessary to deal extensively here with the parallel between the formation of European nations and the development of the Community. It would be tempting to see it in Marx's terms as tragedy the first time around and farce the second if the elements of tragedy and farce were not so well-mixed for both. All that need be done here is to look very briefly at the development of the Community – its trajectory, its overall configuration – and simply evoke the parallels with nation, remembering always that nation is the locus of the 'new' cultural fundamentalism.

Like nation, then, the European Community is elevated in transcendent terms – terms of universal consummation which are secured against the dissipated and decadent arena of the particular and local. That arena – a limitless domain of hybridity and contestation – constantly challenges its diminishment in quasi-national terms and Schepel has vividly revealed as much for legal pluralism 'in' the European Community (Schepel, 1995). The Community and its legality do not, of course, merely seek to suppress such things. And complete suppression would in any case deny the Community its dynamic of identity and coherence in opposition to these things. The Community treats with its others, accommodates and incorporates dimensions of them. It does this, however, not in a postmodernist responsiveness to and regard for these things in themselves, but in a monadic orientation of them in terms of its own work, its own project. European Community is, after all, a community of the classic imperial, occidental kind.

Again, as with nation, the terrain for outflanking, for encompassing the arena of the particular and the local, is created in an ultimate alliance between the Community as a totality in the form of a state and the subjects and citizens of that state. This is not an alliance forged from the perfect pre-existence of contracting parties. It is more a matter of, as d'Azeglio put it in another setting, 'we have made Italy, now we have to make Italians' (see Hobsbawm, 1992a, p 44). The means adopted have usually been as calculating and tawdry as those used by national elites – the cultural creation of traditions, rituals, public symbols and ancestor figures (see Shore, 1993; Shore and Black, 1994). The question of their efficacy so far is another matter.

One need go little further than the immense legal literature on European integration, and the utterly central part of law and the European Court in this, to find correspondences to the prime part law plays in the formation and sustaining of nation. Most obviously, yet in another way most remarkably, the European Community is now enshrined in a singular, modernist legal system of the universally encompassing variety. It is not, in its pervasive scale and in its tentacular reach, confined to the multiple residues of other systems, to keeping them together or holding the ring. It increasingly subsists in a direct relation to its distinct, individual, legal subjects now recognisable as its own citizens in terms of Article 8 of the EC Treaty. Nor is the Community confined ultimately in terms of the subject-matter of its constituent treaties. To quote Bergeron, quoting in part someone else: 'Created in negation of the chaos of European national rivalry and competition, the Community law evokes "a unity capable of transcending its diverse and contradictory elements, thus making coherent legal order possible"' (Bergeron, in press).

In a summary kind of way, it could be said that all this is not so much a matter of the Community outflanking the nation as one of nation outflanking the Community. Most immediately, there has long been a persistent and plausible line of analysis which would not only affirm the exuberant survival of member nations and their law, but would also see the Community itself as an extraversion of nation which retains its predominant force. The impact of nation here is not confined to sovereign territorial terms. It is far more, even infinitely, expansive. 'Nationalism and cosmopolitanism', says Derrida, ' have always gotten along well together, as paradoxical as this may seem' (Derrida, 1992, p 48). So, in pursuing what Derrida also calls nation's 'capital paradox of universality', we need not necessarily or even usually expect to find the so-called international claims of the Community being incompatible with those of nation (Ibid, p 71).

Nationalism in the nineteenth century served to mark off a collectivity of certain nations as exemplary of the universal and as the impetus of all that is becoming universal. That elevation was and still is effected in racist terms. The excluded are now also invited as nations to come within the realm of the universal and the exemplary. To accommodate the ambivalent identity that results from the call to be the same and the exclusion of the different, nations and cultures are stretched between various polarities, the developed and the undeveloped, the normal and the backward – the usual list. The excluded serve to organise and classify the world along a spectrum ranging from the most 'advanced' liberal democracies to barely coherent nations always about to slip into the abyss of ultimate alterity (see generally Fitzpatrick).

As similar and, in ways, mutually integral as they may be, there are still two contesting nationalisms here – that of the member states and the nationalism of a looser but still effective Community state. The challenge of the Community as a nation writ somewhat large to the member state consists not only in the explicit and trumpeted conflict between them (the little Englander always obliges with instances). Rather, the Community's challenge to the member state comes just as much from the similarities as from the differences between them. The Community, as the universality of nation, increasingly enters into the particularity of the member states in ways that would absorb them into equivalence. As with nationalism's claim to a comity of elect nations, the Community increasingly calls on member nations to become the same as each other, not, or not just, through adhering to the uniform external prescriptions of the Community, but by shaping the commonality, or potential for it, that supposedly exists within each of them. The European Court stands, as ever, ready to hasten the process with, for example, its location of Community-wide fundamental rights supposedly extracted from national locations, or with its imposition of general requirements for the interpretation of national law.

CONCLUSION

This difference in similarity between the Community and the member state – the fact that they are competing nationalisms but nationalisms nonetheless – indicates both opportunities for change through law and the limits of those opportunities. Community law has had large and positive effects in areas such as gender equality and environmental protection. The potential effects of the legal provisions already in place are even greater. In both its actual and potential dimensions, Community law encompasses and transcends the confined particularity of member states and their legal systems. It embodies the universal transforming thrust of Enlightenment – one which would brook no barriers of territory or ascribed status. This self-justifying sweep resonates happily with the foundation of the Community in the market, in a 'common market'.

The benign and seemingly inevitable consequence can be illustrated in Article 119 of the main Treaty insisting on 'the principle that men and women should receive equal pay for equal work'. As the European Court has it:

> Article 119 pursues a double aim. First, in the light of the different states of the development of social legislation in the various member-States, the aim of Article 119 is to avoid a situation in which undertakings established in States which have actually implemented the principle of equal pay suffer a competitive disadvantage in intra-Community competition as compared with undertakings established in States which have not yet eliminated discrimination against women workers as regards pay. Secondly, this provision forms part of the social objectives of the Community, which is not merely an economic union, but is at the same time intended by common action, to ensure social progress and seek the constant improvement of the living and working conditions of their peoples.[2]

There is a muted dissonance here. In terms of the first aim, all 'women workers' are universally the object of its dispensation. But the second 'social' objective relates ambiguously to 'peoples' of the member states.

The ambiguity comes closer to a resolution in other provisions of the Treaty set against discrimination. Article 48 can be taken as an instance:

1. Freedom of movement for workers shall be secured within the Community ...
2. Such freedom of movement shall entail the abolition of any discrimination based on nationality between workers of the Member States as regards employment, remuneration and other conditions of work and employment.

This is one of the foundational 'freedoms' which, in terms of the Treaty, are necessary for the effective operation or even for the existence of the market. Confining protection to 'workers of the Member States' – still ambiguous, admittedly, but meaning nationals of those states – is every bit as antithetical to the market as discrimination on the ground of gender would be. Even in the narrower terms of ensuring parity of conditions between member states, the market is just as distorted or just as much undermined by disparity in pay on national or racial grounds and by disparity in measures countering this as it would be by the discrimination on grounds of gender countered by Article 119.

Nationalism then, together with its integral racism and cultural fundamentalism, remains prime. The very ability, in terms of Article 8 of the Treaty, to take on a putatively supranational citizenship of the Community depends on, and depends solely on, being a national of a member state. Nationalism, as we saw, was inherently capable of assuming this supposed supranational dimension. The national foundation of the Community and its law thence imports a limit on change through legal action. But this very national foundation in its universalist claims also makes it possible politically to contest that limit.[3]

NOTES

1. Following on from this Treaty, the term 'European Community' will be used here. Its other dictated usage, 'European Union', will not.
2. *Defrenne* v. *Sabena (No. 2)* [1976] 2 CMLR 98 at 122.
3. For example, the (European) Parliament has resolved to call 'on the Commission to work for the application of the principle of equal treatment and freedom of movement to all citizens, including those from third countries, in the Community' (see Pollard and Ross, 1994, p 97).

7
Defining the Refugee by Race: The European Response to 'New' Asylum-seekers

Patricia Tuitt

Notwithstanding the apparent focus of this chapter on 'race', 'new asylum-seekers' and the place of refugees within contemporary Western Europe, I propose also to explore the history of definitions of the 'refugee' in Western Europe. For it is within that history of seemingly racially neutral, legal constructions of refugees that we can trace the conditions under which the present explicitly racial category of refugee emerged. The main argument in what follows is that international legal definitions of refugee, being 'fundamentally a product of European legal culture' (Hathaway, 1990, p 181), assume 'refugees' to carry the racial characteristics of the dominant 'white' majority in Europe. As such, dimensions of race are endemic in refugee discourse. This chapter challenges the view that the dimension of race is new to refugee discourse.

ABOUT DEFINITIONS

By way of setting the scene, I will begin with what I hope are some uncontroversial observations: that to define is predominantly to exclude; that to make sense of the process of defining, the excluded category must necessarily be greater than the included category, for to embrace all variables within a definition would be to render the process obsolete. Further, that the motive driving any given definition is usually either to confer a benefit on or to remove it from the excluded or included class. Finally (and obviously), that by reason of the definition, the excluded category is left qualitatively better or worse off. It follows from this that 'defining' is a process or activity which is uniquely open to interrogation and inquiry. Or to put it another way, defined categories are prima facie suspect, not merely because the rational basis of the category of the 'included' requires scrutiny, but because so too does that of the 'excluded'.

ANALYSIS OF REFUGEE DEFINITIONS

Whether scholars of the phenomenon have ever evaluated definitions of the idea of the refugee – which emerged in the first half of the twentieth century – from this logical, and quite justifiable, point of suspicion is to be doubted. It was, and still is, largely contended by such scholars that the motive driving early definitions of the refugee and the motive prima facie suggested by accompanying legal instruments, were one and the same: to confer a positive benefit on certain defined categories of 'refugee'. The alleged benefit was what one might loosely describe as a right 'to seek and enjoy asylum from persecution'.[1] On this analysis, refugee definitions were a necessary prerequisite to the establishment of a regime of protection in respect of designated people. Thus it has been said that: 'the purpose of any definition or description of the class of refugee is to facilitate and to justify aid and protection' (Goodwin-Gill, 1983, p 2). This account of the moving forces behind early refugee accords is necessarily premissed on the view that the process of defining the refugee was focused on the category intended to be *included* within the definition – and that the aim was to effect a positive enhancement of the status of the included class.

There are many proponents of this proposition and of the claim implicit in it that it is supported by the drafting history of refugee accords. I am not here going to undertake the lengthy and arduous task of challenging the historical record, not least because this has been undertaken very effectively elsewhere (see Hathaway, 1991, ch 1). For the purpose of this argument, I will concede there was at least a marginal humanitarian focus to early refugee accords. But humanitarianism can only be advanced as a sufficient explanation behind early refugee accords if it is accepted that the defining lens was focused on the class included within the particular category of 'refugee', who, ostensibly, gained a benefit from the refugee definitions. It is argued here, however, that definitions of refugee were principally focused upon the *excluded* category and that the primary motivation was to remove a 'right' or 'benefit' which had previously been enjoyed by the excluded class – although not necessarily to an extent equal to the included refugee category. This argument necessarily involves three propositions:

1. That, contrary to the established record, no significant enhancement of status was conferred upon the included category of 'refugee' by the legal definitions from which she was constructed.
2. That, by reason of the definition of 'refugee', the excluded category lost a valuable *theoretical* right of free movement between states.
3. That the excluded category constituted broadly those who potentially might challenge the assumed racial category of 'refugee'.

Since propositions 1 and 2 are merely two sides of the same coin, I will deal with them together, briefly, in the next section. Proposition 3, the central argument of this chapter, is explored in the remaining sections.

THE BENEFITS AND DETRIMENTS OF REFUGEE DEFINITIONS

The supposed positive benefit or enhancement of status derived from refugee definitions in relation to the included class is often articulated as a 'right' of territorial asylum, or a 'right' to be protected against 'refoulement'. Asylum and non-refoulement are not the same: there is greater content to the former concept. However, for present purposes the distinction is not important. We can locate the common denominator between both these concepts and explain it in everyday language as a right to migrate to an alien territory and to remain within that territory until the need for protection is eliminated. In other words, the benefit ostensibly gained by the included category was a right broadly akin to that of free movement to a state, provided this 'right' was exercised against a background of 'persecution' or other form of injurious activity directed against the person seeking to exercise the 'right'.

To sustain this 'benefit analysis', it must be assumed that, prior to the drafting of refugee definitions, migrants, of the voluntary and involuntary kind, were confronted by closed state borders which were miraculously opened to *involuntary* migrants by states who were signatories to the various refugee accords and conventions. Such was manifestly not the case. Indeed, Krenz argues that the notion that states in their sovereignty were at all preoccupied with the exclusion of aliens is one which goes hand in hand with the 'rise of nationalism' (Krenz, 1966, p 95). Hathaway also locates the rise of refugee definitions with the withdrawal rather than the conferment of the benefit of 'free movement'. In Hathaway's opinion, transborder movement was, until the twentieth century, a 'function of the particularized needs or ambitions of would-be migrants':

> Prior to this century, there was little concern about the precise definition of refugee, since most of those who chose not to remove to the 'new world' were readily received by rulers in Europe and elsewhere. (Hathaway, 1991, p 1)

It seems, then, that if the term 'benefit' denotes a positive and significant enhancement of status, no benefit had been conferred on the 'included' category of 'refugee'. At best they were beneficiaries merely in comparison to their excluded counterparts – they had escaped being accorded less. They were not empowered to move more freely than they had been in the days before the introduction of refugee status. What is clear, however, is that the position of the excluded category had become qualitatively worse. Their movement, far from being theoretically free and unfettered, was to be 'closely controlled to the maximum advantage of sovereign nations' (Hathaway, 1991, p 1).

THE EXCLUDED CATEGORY: IDENTITY AND HISTORICAL CONDITIONS

The creation of refugee definitions, at the behest of Western European states,[2] was causally linked to the fundamental changes in relations between states caused by the two world wars. Without that crisis states were content with the 'unwritten law' governing asylum-seekers which had accommodated 'refugees' for many centuries (Grahl-Madsen, 1966, p 9). The first formal resolution on refugees was drafted by the Council of the League of Nations in 1921, following the flight of large groups of Russian nationals between 1917 and 1922. (For an account, see Goodwin-Gill, 1983, p 2; Grahl-Madsen, 1966, p 92; and Hathaway, 1991, p 2.) However, it was the estimated 11 million non-German nationals displaced after the Second World War which brought the potential of significant movements of people 'into glaring focus' (Carlin, 1982, p 3) and prompted more formal definitions of refugee.

Whilst this timely response to the plight of the 11 million might suggest a humanitarian focus to refugee law, it cannot be overlooked that the aftermath of the Second World War brought not just a problem of a definable number of displaced persons in need of instant protection, but also the need for states significantly to reassess their previous perceptions of a relatively stable world. The Second World War 'refugees' were as much a symbol of the future as of the immediate past. States thus had a vision, admittedly imperfect, of future refugee movements. From this ill-defined group of future refugees was constructed a class of legally defined refugees who could continue to seek protection in the territory of an alien state. The fate of the remainder was left unspecified.

THE DEFINITION OF REFUGEE UNDER THE GENEVA CONVENTION

The particular category of refugee which guides international protection can be found within Article 1A(2) of the Geneva Convention Relating to the Status of Refugees 1951.[3] In its unamended form, Article 1A(2) defines a refugee as one who:

> As a result of events occurring before 1st January 1951 and owing to a well-founded fear of being persecuted for reasons of race, religion, nationality, membership of a social group or political opinion, is outside the country of his nationality and is unable, or

owing to such fear is unwilling to avail himself of the protection of that country; or who, not having a nationality and being outside the country of his former habitual residence as a result of such events, is unable, or owing to such fear, is unwilling to return to it.

Article 1(b) of the Geneva Convention inserted an important qualification to the protection of even the included class, which although since removed clearly demonstrates the assumed European racial category of refugee. That article provided that 'For the purposes of this convention, the words, "events occurring before 1st January 1951" ... shall be understood to mean either

a) events occurring in Europe before 1st January 1951; or
b) events occurring in Europe or elsewhere before 1st January 1951' (see Mbuyi, 1994, for text).

Both Article 1(b) and the words emphasised (above) in Article 1A(2) were amended in 1967 by the New York Protocol to the Convention Relating to the Status of Refugees, which removed the temporal and geographical limitation on the extension of state protection to refugees. Whilst there was no longer an explicit preference for territorial protection of the European (predominantly white) refugee, it has been argued that the substantive definition of refugee was equally 'Euro-centrically partisan', because of its emphasis on the protection of civil and political rights as opposed to socioeconomic rights, the latter category of excluded rights revealing an area of 'Western vulnerability' (Hathaway, 1991, p 8).

I would support Hathaway's conclusion as regards the ideological slant of the Geneva Convention's definition of the refugee. The refugee definition under the convention, as it stands and as it has been widely interpreted, is closely guided by a particular European conceptualisa-tion of fault, linked to Western European tortious principles, which work to exclude the majority of de facto refugees. In particular, its sustaining link with the tortious concept of 'reasonableness' in establishing a well-founded fear of persecution, allows for the imposition of localised concepts of reasonability which are clearly culturally determined (Tuitt, 1995, ch 5). The particular conception of fault, implicit in the definition and supported by the jurisprudence, places emphasis on deliberate, culpable actions by those in authority within a state, or those for whom the authority is vicariously liable (see, for example, UNHCR, 1979, para 65). In the context of Western jurisdictions, such actions can usually be counted upon to attract legal responsibility, whereas natural events or accidents which may lead to the same degree of harm, are less widely acknowledged as justifying legal responsibility. This Western view of 'fault' and 'responsibility' is sustained by an emphasis on persecution and an interpretation of that word which again stresses deliberative actions ('to pursue with malignancy or to oppress ...' *(R* v. *Secretary of State for the Home Department ex p Jonah* (1985)).

This substantive conception of the type and extent of harm which the 'refugee' must be exposed to, and the methodology which must be adopted to 'prove' harm, is one which is peculiarly geared to the European refugee, who is after all a part of the 'legal culture' from which the concepts governing the definition are articulated, understood and practised. It derives from a society in which harms are generally thought to emanate from culpable acts, in their broadest sense, rather than one sensitive to harms of less discriminating origin. The refugee definition under the Geneva Convention was not intended to embrace human suffering caused by accident or natural disaster – famine, drought or disease – harms which, of course, beset a large number of the excluded category, about whom, it is argued, European definitions of refugee were primarily directed.

From this brief exploration, it can hopefully be seen that until the late 1960s and the amendment of Article 1A(2) by the 1967 Protocol, 'refugee' was explicitly of 'European origin' and refugee movement was seen to be a European phenomenon (Frogaman, 1970, p 47). This explicit understanding has been implicitly maintained by giving the notion of refugee a substantive content which expresses European notions of right, harm and the particularities of proving injurious conduct. At this level, 'race' was always an aspect of refugee protection in the sense that it worked to silence any but the assumed racial category in relation to whom any disadvantages associated with refugee definitions were carefully averted.

THE CHALLENGE TO THE ASSUMED RACIAL CATEGORY OF REFUGEE

The assumed racial category of refugee was first explicitly challenged by the Organisation of African Unity Convention Governing the Specific Aspects of Refugee Problems in Africa in 1969. Whilst that convention adopted the Geneva Convention definition of 'refugee', it also extended protection to:

> every person who, owing to external aggression, occupation or foreign domination or events seriously disrupting public order in either part or whole of his or her country of origin or nationality, is compelled to leave his or her place of habitual residence in order to seek refuge in another place outside his or her country of origin or nationality. (Art 1(2))

This definition introduced a category of refugee which, at its lowest, expressed a sharing of the racial characteristics of both the 'European' and the 'African' refugee. The OAU Convention adopted the European 'model' refugee, but rejected that 'model' as being an all-embracing definition of 'refugee'. The definition, in de-emphasising 'individualised persecution' and in acknowledging generalised violence as a cause of refugee suffering, specifies the predominant forms of refugee-producing phenomena in the African continent. Other regional definitions followed, notably the Organisation of American States (Cartagena Declaration 1984) to which many Latin American states adhere. Moreover, the Organisation of African Unity definition of refugee has been adopted by most states in Africa.

The category of refugee created within these regional instruments thus extended across the spectrum of racial, ethnic and cultural identities. These instruments seemed, partially at least, to restore to a more broadly defined group of refugees the historical 'right' to seek asylum from persecution which had been suddenly removed by Western European refugee definitions. I emphasise that the 'right' was only *partially* restored because whilst African states were seemingly prepared to construct a definition of refugee from the point of a broad racial consensus, there was no corresponding sharing by Western European states. Thus the original 'excluded' category from the dominant concept of 'refugee' were still excluded from the European conception of refugee and thus from European shores.[4]

This ensured that during the late 1960s and early 1970s the challenge to the assumed racial category of refugee had a limited impact on the number of non-Western refugees present in Western states. Western states were never in danger of entering into any reciprocal arrangement with states in the developing world to adopt those states' refugee definitions in any more than a marginal form, despite the wholesale export of a European concept of refugee to states in the developing world and beyond (see note 3). Moreover, despite the rather loose employment of the notion of a 'right' to seek asylum within this chapter, any such 'right' was necessarily constrained by technological factors which ensured that intercontinental, as opposed to inter-regional, refugee movements were largely unheard of. In essence, the assumed racial character of 'refugee' had been challenged in the global arena, but, significantly, had not been challenged within the territories of Western states. This challenge was soon to confront Western states, and that challenge, has, perhaps not surprisingly, been portrayed as creating a racial dimension to refugee protection which had hitherto not existed.

INTERCONTINENTAL REFUGEE MOVEMENTS

The explicit racial category of refugee, by which I mean the focus in refugee discourse on the racial origins of asylum-seekers as much as their reasons for seeking asylum, has its immediate roots in the 'technological revolution'. This 'revolution' allowed refugees from developing countries in Africa and Asia to travel to Western European states to seek asylum, bringing with them a challenge to the assumed racial category of refugee, this time *within* the territories of Western states. The claim of the 'new' refugee (who was in reality 'new' only to Western states) to be included in a category of 'refugee' – and to obtain benefits from which they had been expressly and deliberately excluded – revealed, as many commentators have observed, 'new tensions and hostilities in Western receiving states' (see, for example, Feller, 1989, p 49; Hocke, 1990, p 38). Western states have continued to perceive the majority of these refugees according to their excluded status.

Exclusion has continued along ideological lines, promoting a single European conception of refugee and relying upon geographical and technological factors to ensure that refugees without that identity remain within their country of nationality or domicile. What has altered in recent years – since the 'technological revolution' – is the extent to which Western states are forced to expressly confront technology in order to stem the pressure it creates for a genuine system of intercontinental refugee protection. This has been achieved largely by an increasing reliance on visa restrictions and carrier sanctions, targeted toward refugee-producing states.

The United Kingdom Immigration (Carriers' Liability) Act 1987, as amended by section 12 of the Asylum and Immigration Appeals Act 1993, has received widespread criticism as being a deliberate measure intended to discourage asylum-seekers from travelling to UK ports. Similar measures have been introduced in most countries of the European Union. The compatibility of such legislation with obligations undertaken by state signatories to the Geneva Convention has been questioned. Erica Feller argues that carrier sanctions are 'broadly inconsistent with Article 31 of the Geneva Convention' (1989, p 58). Article 31 prohibits the imposition of penalties on refugees in respect of their illegal or irregular entry. While it is to be doubted whether such measures are unlawful, since the Geneva Convention only operates once a person is outside her country of nationality and the primary purpose of carrier sanctions is to keep refugees within their home states, the measures clearly prevent access of refugees to state determination procedures. However, given that notwithstanding these measures some advances have been made by non-European refugees toward the territories of European and other Western states, exclusion must also exist in the physical as well as the ideological and metaphorical sense – both to expel refugees from the territories of Western receiving states as well as to exclude or isolate 'new' refugees temporarily or permanently within host states. This factual or physical exclusion has taken many forms. For example, the scope within the refugee definition under the Geneva Convention for utilising specific Western jurisprudential ideology based upon a particularised conception of fault has been increasingly utilised in asylum determination processes to 'baffle' the asylum-seeker, and thus to present her as either 'bogus' or simply not credible. In particular, in assessing her 'well-founded fear of persecution', Westernised conceptions of reasonability are used, often inappropriately and non-contextually, to impugn the reasonableness of the refugee claimant's fear of persecution. A particular example relates to refugees who, often prompted by the very fear of authority which compels their flight from their country of nationality, fail to bring their asylum claim promptly to the authorities of the receiving state. This failure is often perceived by the receiving state as a cynical attempt to circumvent the normal asylum processes, rather than the expression of a fear of authority which has a rational psychological basis (Anker, 1987). There are many examples of an asylum-seeker's claim being adversely affected by such a finding (see, for example, *R* v. *Secretary of State for the Home Department ex p Alupo* (1991). In the United Kingdom, paragraph 340 of the Statement of Changes in the Immigration Rules (1993) provides that a delay in bringing a claim to the authorities, which is deemed to have been occasioned 'without reasonable excuse', can alone lead to an application being refused. There is a large margin afforded to states in determining what constitutes a reasonable excuse. These 'technocratic' devices (the term is Hathaway's) are complemented by the emerging idea that Western states can reliably locate 'safe' non-refugee-producing countries, thereby relegating a refugee's personal claim to fear persecution to the margins.[5]

As far as non-European refugees temporarily or permanently settled within the host state are concerned, Western states have seemingly created a '... breeding ground for social tension and unrest' (Hocke, 1990, p 38) by constantly emphasising the fact that many asylum-seekers are from the developing world, exciting racial tension and generating serious forms of racial violence (see, for example, Fekete, 1994 generally and pp 154–6 in particular). Whilst the 'ancient cultural and ethnic affinities' between 'old' refugees and Western states created the possibilities for their integration into host states, (Hocke, 1990, p 38) this has been made impossible by these measures and others designed to keep 'new' refugees not only at the margin of legal protection, but also at the margins of society.[6] They face not only de facto exclusion from the territories of Western receiving states, but 'even if they do succeed in obtaining entry are commonly physically removed from the mainstream of society and placed in cramped and overcrowded refugee camps and settlements' (Ibid, p 37).

CONCLUSION

For many years, the racial dimension to the notion of refugee was thought to be of recent origin. Indeed, this assumption dominates much scholarly writing on refugees, which is geared, quite justly, to the condemnation of a refugee regime now quite explicitly governed by issues of race. I hope this chapter has gone some way to showing that there has always been a strong, but unspoken dimension of race within ideas of refugee protection. Had there been no challenge to the assumption that refugee protection was fundamentally geared to European refugees, this silence would have remained. Once challenged, the question as to how protection should be distributed between refugees has, sadly, but I fear inevitably, been superseded by the less humane question of how much racial diversity Western states are prepared to permit.

NOTES

1. The wording is taken from Article 14 of the Universal Declaration of Human Rights.
2. For an examination of the historical development of refugee accords, see: Hathaway (1991, ch 1); Grahl-Madsen (1966, vol 1); Goodwin-Gill (1983, ch 1).
3. It is widely accepted that Article 1A(2) of the Geneva Convention Relating to the Status of Refugees 1951 carries the principal legal definition of refugee. The convention is said to be binding upon states in the international community, firstly because it is the most widely acceded to accord governing refugees (there are approximately 110 state signatories). Secondly, it has been argued that the main obligation under the convention is not to 'return (refouler) a refugee to the frontiers of a territory in which his life or freedom may be threatened on grounds of race, religion, nationality, membership of a social group or political opinion'. Article 33 has evolved into a rule of customary law, binding even non-state signatories (see, for a discussion, Goodwin-Gill (1982, p 302)).
4. The Organisation of African Unity category of refugee has not been formally acknowledged and implemented by Western states. However, some recognition is afforded to refugees fleeing 'generalised violence' in the form of 'de facto' or 'B' refugee status. Such status is conferred largely at the discretion of Western states and the juridical content of the status differs within states (see Spijkerboer, 1993, pp 16–17). It is clearly a second tier of humanitarian assistance, moreover, there is some evidence that the incidence of the grant of de facto status is being rapidly reduced in some Western jurisdictions. The form of de facto status granted in the United Kingdom is known as 'exceptional leave status'. The number of grants of exceptional leave fell by half in 1993 (see Immigration and Nationality Law and Practice 1994, p 18).

5. On 1 December 1992, the EC Ministers of State adopted a number of resolutions and conclusions governing the provision of asylum on a regional basis in Europe. I am concerned here with the conclusions on Countries in Which There is No Serious Risk of Persecution. The 'Conclusions' are not presently binding on member states of the European Union, but can be used as 'guides' to assist states to individually determine whether or not a refugee has made out a 'well-founded' fear of persecution in relation to a given state (see for discussion, Guild (1993); Tuitt (1995), ch 5).

6. Other measures include the compulsory fingerprinting of all asylum-seekers under Section 3 of the Asylum and Immigration Appeals Act 1993, and the increasing use of the power to detain asylum-seekers. These two measures inevitably lead to a blurring of the boundaries between the immigration and criminal law, and consequently adversely impacts on the ability of refugees to integrate into the society acting as 'host'.

8
Race and Criminal Justice
Makbool Javaid

The unemployed and the lumpen never have been a revolutionary force. If the unemployed get lower benefits, they will be quicker to start looking for work, and they won't turn to political trouble-making. As for the lumpen, coloured people and Irish ... the only way to hold them in check is to have enough well-armed police. (Sir Alfred Sherman, ex-head of the Centre for Policy Studies, quoted in the Guardian, *6 February 1992)*

Sixteen years have passed since Lord Scarman's enquiry (Scarman, 1981) into the Brixton disturbances and its acknowledgement that the ethnic imbalance in the prison population was in part due to the relationship between the black community and criminal justice agencies. The recommendations that flowed were largely well received, as were the attempts to implement them, particularly as regards selection, training and organisational procedures. Nevertheless, we have seen of late an ominous resurgence of the view that the criminal justice system is not 'colour-blind' and that the growing disparity between the incarceration rates of black people and their proportion in the population is due to their disproportionate criminality. A public expression of this reading of the data is rare other than from maverick conservative politicians and the tabloid press. Unlike the US, academic criminologists in this country so far have resisted such theories on the whole.

Indeed, one can only surmise that the recent Royal Commission actually subscribed to this notion since the incidence of racial discrimination and its consequences was largely ignored in its much awaited report. Public disquiet was the catalyst in the equation of miscarriages of justice (many of which involved victims from racial minorities) that led to the Commission's establishment. In spite of this and the fact that while the Commission deliberated, further examples of blatant injustice came to light (for example, the Tottenham three and the Cardiff three), the Commission could do no more than call for further research and ethnic monitoring.[1] Instead of acknowledging with its authoritative voice the existence of racial discrimination, another brick was added to the wall of silence on the issue. The effectiveness of any criminal administration system has to be judged not only by the likelihood of the guilty being convicted and the innocent acquitted, but also by measuring the treatment that is afforded to the vulnerable, oppressed and poor. As the Institute of Race Relations put it in its submission to the Commission, 'the prism of race offers a unique perspective through which to expose and evaluate the underlying failings of the criminal justice system as a whole'. By that yardstick, we have a system that is not only in a state of crisis but which appears actively to accommodate and facilitate racial prejudice. There will always be those who remain reticent and defiant in the face of the overwhelming evidence which confirms this. Indeed, in the circle of academic criminologists the issue is not if, but the extent to which, racism flourishes within the criminal justice system. The wealth of research which reiterates the prevalence of direct and indirect discrimination on the part of every agency and at every stage of the criminal process is made up of the following findings:

- At the outset, black people (irrespective of their age, or socio-economic status) are more likely to be stopped and searched by the police (Smith, 1983).
- Afro-Caribbeans, in particular, are much less likely to be cautioned or otherwise diverted from the courts, and more likely to be arrested (Skogan, 1990; Jones et al., 1986).
- Afro-Caribbeans are more likely to face more serious charges for the same substantive offence (Blom-Cooper and Drabble, 1982).
- Black people are more likely to be subjected to 'proactive policing' leading to more cases of the police looking for evidence to implicate black suspects and less involving independent witnesses. In addition Afro-Caribbeans are also more likely to be charged with 'victimless' crimes (such as motoring offences, drunkenness and possession of drugs) (Walker, 1990; Cain and Saddigh, 1982).
- Black people are more likely than whites to be remanded in custody. Their over-representation in the remand population is even greater than convicted prisoners. A much higher proportion of cases go to the Crown Court as a result of committal by magistrates than from choice by the defendant. Magistrates closely following CPS recommendations are more likely to make such committals in the case of Afro-Caribbeans (Jefferson and Walker, 1992).
- Afro-Caribbeans (and Asians between the age of 21 and 25) are more likely to be tried in a Crown Court.
- Black people are far less likely to have social enquiry reports ordered (Hood, 1992a).
- Black people are more likely to receive custodial sentences (Roger Hood in his study of a number of Crown Courts in the West

Midlands was of the view that the greater probability stood at around 16 per cent (Hood, 1992a)) and for longer periods.
• Black people are less likely to receive probation orders (Home Office, 1989; Moxon, 1988).

Whilst the above pattern is drawn from a number of diverse studies with varying methodological bases, and thus not capable of perhaps providing conclusive evidence of discrimination, the inference is nevertheless patently obvious. A separate study on the issue carried out for the Royal Commission of Criminal Justice found indirect discrimination was 'pervasive and significant' and a 'discriminatory chain reaction operating against black people' (Fitzgerald, 1993).

The judiciary, as Roger Hood has shown, is the final link in the discriminatory process that is more likely to lead the black defendant inexorably into custody. The prison statistics alone must cause alarm. The proportion of black prisoners has been steadily increasing from 12.6 per cent in 1985 to 16 per cent in 1992 compared to the 5.5 per cent representation in the general population. Among male prisoners, 15 per cent are from racial minorities; among women, the figure is 26 per cent (Hood, 1992b). The over-representation of black women in prison, even when foreign resident black women are excluded, stands at 13 per cent. This is still grossly disproportionate when compared with their representation in the population at large (Hood, 1992b).

It is hard to follow the logic of the Royal Commission's recommendation in the light of the extensive research that is currently available and the fact that s 95 of the Criminal Justice Act 1991 already obliges the Home Secretary to provide ethnic monitoring information. It is interesting to note that the Secretary of State appears to be in breach of his duties under the Criminal Justice Act since the s 95 obligation appears not to have been complied with in the last two years. For the black community it is yet another example of the lack of will to challenge racial prejudice. The disproportionate number of black men on death row in the United States paints a harrowing picture of a nightmare scenario which draws ever nearer as the capital punishment lobby gains momentum.

The black communities remain impoverished with the highest unemployment rates, poorest housing, worst education and health – all factors that lead them to become the prime targets for increased proactive policing. The importance of socioeconomic factors in criminalisation is vividly illustrated by the Afro-Caribbean and Asian stereotype, which has changed over the years. Recent studies show that Pakistanis and Bangladeshis are consistently bottom of the pile when indices of progress are analysed. We are now seeing the image of militant youth in East London and elsewhere and Asian youth are now being constructed as being more combative, less deferential and more 'crime-prone'. It is therefore not surprising that stories of Asian gangs have begun to circulate and we can expect to see a corresponding change in the police statistics. If we are to rid ourselves of the disease of racial prejudice and to eradicate discrimination, a well thought out and concerted strategy has to be devised. Such a strategy can include the following measures:

- tighter controls on police stop-and-search powers;
- better access to legal advice and a right to black lawyers if so desired;[2]
- a review of cautioning policy to eradicate over-reliance on discriminatory social criteria;
- a review of substantial discounts for guilty pleas because of the potential adverse impact on black defendants;[3]
- establishment of an independent skilled interpreter service for use particularly by suspects at police stations;
- abolition of judicial discretion under section 3(1) Criminal Justice Act 1991 not to order pre-sentence reports;
- review of bail criteria to eliminate disadvantage to black defendants;
- tighter control of judicial discretion in sentencing (clearer guidelines to eliminate racial discrimination);
- ethnic monitoring of criminal courts and police stations;
- introduction of multiracial juries as proposed by the Commission for Racial Equality;
- greater commitment to increasing representation of racial minorities in all criminal justice agencies.

Whilst the Royal Commission's failure to make recommendations along the lines of the above proposal can be explained on the basis that its terms of reference were extremely restricted, some have argued that this was a deliberate ploy. The position of the government, however, is not so easily excused since much of the research has been produced by the Home Office. What is even more perplexing is that government policy now seems hell-bent on pandering to the 'law and order' lobby within its ranks. The legislative programme is aimed at taking away the minimum protection that currently exists safeguarding the rights of the individual against the state in the criminal process. The abolition of the right to silence is only one of many provisions in the Criminal Justice and Public Order Act which will exacerbate racial discrimination.

It is as well to remember that black people are also disproportionately victims of crime and there has been a shocking escalation in the number of racial attacks in the past two years.[4] The call for legislative measures to provide better remedies to victims has been ignored in spite of the fact that the inadequacy of the law and the hostility of the enforcement agencies has been conclusively established. There are an increasing number of black people who have now totally lost faith in the legal system as a whole. An observational analysis of campaigns and demonstrations will show that, unlike in the past, very few black people participate in such initiatives, principally because they have failed to bear fruit. The sense of frustration is turning more and more to anger, since unlike the academic criminologists who ponder over statistics, the figures represent to the black community real men and women whose lives are blighted through injustice and violence. The numbers in prison and who are murdered as a result of the increase in racial intolerance cannot be allowed to continue.

If the present trends persist and remain only the subject of further research by criminologists then the legitimacy that is essential to the survival of the criminal justice system will not be found in the black community ever again. When that happens, and I sincerely hope that we never reach that stage, we shall have to do more than ask for Lord Scarman to come out of retirement and rummage through the rubble that will be the remains of our inner cities.

NOTES

1. Royal Commission on Criminal Justice (1993), *Report*, Cm.2263 (London: HMSO), Recommendations 2 and 3.
2. Recent Law Society research indicates that ethnic minority communities are not getting the kind of service they are entitled to from solicitors.
3. In spite of the extensive research on this topic, the Royal Commission supported discounts for guilty pleas (Recommendation no. 156).
4. Estimated at 140,000 by the CRE and others.

Part Three

Gender

9
Arguing Equality: Recognising the Traps
Gillian More

The aim of this chapter is to pinpoint the ways in which the liberal conception of equality poses significant barriers to the advancement of the claims of equality-seeking groups. In particular, it seeks to explore the conceptual difficulties in advancing the cause of women's equality.

The early arguments made for women's rights were premissed in the philosophy of liberal individualism. They were based on the idea that women were as capable as men of acting as rational, self-determining beings. Mary Wollstonecraft argued that women had been deprived of the ability to reason – reason being a prerequisite for a person being able to bear rights – because of the restricted nature of their education:

> Women have been allowed to remain in ignorance and slavish dependence many, very many years ... Let an enlightened nation then try what effect reason would have to bring them back to nature and their duty; and allowing them to share the advantages of education and government with man ... (Wollstonecraft, 1792, pp 184–5).

Over fifty years later, John Stuart Mill wrote in the same vein, arguing that women's exclusion from education and from government had created a false inequality of the sexes:

> That the principle which regulates the existing social relations between the two sexes – the legal subordination of one sex to the other – is wrong in itself, and now one of the chief hindrances to human improvement; and that it ought to be replaced by a principle of perfect equality, admitting no power or privilege on the one side, nor disability on the other. (Mill, 1869, p 219)

The liberal arguments for women's suffrage were founded on the belief that women are essentially similar to men: women have the same capacity as men to reason and, therefore, should be accorded equal rights.

115

Equality was conceptualised as predicated on similarity. Indeed, the liberal conception of equality merely followed the centuries-old Aristotelian conception of equality: '... things that are alike should be treated alike, while things that are unalike should be treated unalike in proportion to their unalikeness' (Aristotle, trans. 1925, pp 1131a–1131b). If one is alike, one may be treated in the same way; if one is unalike, one is to be treated differently. Moreover, treating like persons differently is to treat them unequally.

However, modern thinking has highlighted a number of flaws in the Aristotelian conception of equality. Its fundamental defect is perceived to be its failure to define a referent point for similarity. Westen, for example, describes the concept as 'empty' and 'tautological'. He observes, '[the concept] tells us to treat like people alike; but when we ask who "like people" are, we are told they are "people who should be treated alike"' (1982, p 547). This lack of referent allows courts and policy-makers to adjudicate equality by substituting their own sense of the dominant standard: in the case of racial equality, the referent is invariably the white norm (Crenshaw, 1991, pp 1372–81); in the case of sexual equality, the referent is usually the male norm (MacKinnon, 1989, p 220). The use of this dominant standard leads, then, to a second vital problem: in order for the equality-seeking group to claim the right to equal treatment, it must thus demonstrate similarity to the standard. Yet, in many cases of inequality, the equality-seeker is differently situated and cannot demonstrate similarity to the dominant norm. Considering, in particular, the case of women, this is a striking conceptual obstacle to the pursuit of equality: first, women are biologically different from men; and second, women are generally socially constructed to perform a different role. It is frequently difficult for women to demonstrate any kind of similarity to men. It is in this sense that the concept of equality is often criticised for its failure to accommodate difference (Wolgast, 1980).

Liberal theory contributes, moreover, to the construction of woman's 'difference' from man. Looking back at the work of the early liberal feminists, it is evident that woman's different social role was accepted rather than challenged. This has led contemporary theorists to criticise the early feminists for conceiving the issues of women's inequality too narrowly. Zillah Eisenstein, for example, notes that although both Mill's and Wollstonecraft's visions of sexual equality were indebted to liberal individualist philosophy, they were at the same time restricted by their acceptance of liberal 'separate sphere' ideology (Eisenstein, 1984, p 104). Although Mill broached the issue of whether what were considered natural differences between men and women were in fact socially constructed differences,[1] he did not in the end sufficiently challenge the assumption that a woman's role was primarily that of mother and homemaker and that men were rightfully occupied with 'public' activities, such as commerce and government. Tulloch describes this as

> ... an inherent tension ... between advocacy of sexual equality in the realm of civic rights for women and a simultaneously held implicit acceptance of traditional sex roles, together with an expectation that most women will in fact choose marriage as their career and should restrict themselves to home duties during their child-rearing years. (Tulloch, 1989, pp 9–11)

This 'tension' in liberal thought reveals the subtle interrelationship between 'separate sphere' ideology and the liberal similarity-based conception of equality. Primarily, the ideology of private and public spheres sustains the belief that woman's role is different from man's (Thornton, 1991, p 452). For example, housework and care of both children and the elderly are conducted predominantly by women within the invisible private sphere of the home. The location of this type of work in the private sphere has two effects: first, housework and caring work cannot lay claim to equal value and equal recompense with labour in the public sphere of the 'workplace'; secondly, domestic and caring work carried out in the 'workplace' is traditionally undervalued as unskilled work (that is, it comes 'naturally' to women). The 'polarised spheres of liberalism' (Thornton, 1991, p 452) therefore perpetuate the construction of sexual differences – differences which in turn preclude women from being able to demonstrate similarity to men.

The liberal conception of equality dominates equality legislation in the United Kingdom. For example, section 1(1) of the British Sex Discrimination Act 1975 requires a woman to compare herself to a comparably situated man in order to prove discrimination;[2] Section 1(4) of the British Equal Pay Act 1970 requires a woman to find a comparator man with whom to compare her work in order to establish that it is of equal value. Moreover, current debates over the merits of positive action suggest that public perception has been shaped to consider positive action as unfair on the grounds that it treats similar persons differently. The following sections of this chapter will briefly consider each of these three interrelated issues – discrimination, equal pay and positive action – in more detail.

SAMENESS, DIFFERENCE AND PREGNANCY DISCRIMINATION

The limitations of the liberal conception of equality have been most clearly exposed in the context of pregnancy discrimination. Women lawyers' outrage at legal decisions which had found pregnancy discrimination *not* to be sex discrimination sparked off what came to be known as the 'sameness–difference' debate in the early 1980s (Law, 1984; Littleton, 1981; Williams, 1982; Wolgast, 1980). The debaters sought to challenge the reasoning of the courts which had held that, since pregnancy was a condition unique to women, it was not discrimination to treat pregnant women differently from men.[3] Writers differed on the issue of how pregnancy should be treated in the workplace: should it, in keeping with the Aristotelian model of equality, be conceived of as analogous to some kind of physical disability suffered by men (Williams, 1984); or, alternatively, should women argue that pregnancy be treated as a unique characteristic (certainly not as an illness) and, hence, be accorded special rights (Law, 1984; Wolgast, 1980)?

This debate around pregnancy was itself criticised as having been ensnared by the liberal trap (MacKinnon, 1989). The sameness–difference debaters merely replicated both sides of the Aristotelian paradigm: whilst one side argued that women were the same as men in order that they could receive identical treatment; the other side argued that women were different in order to justify differential or special protective treatment. Whether one argued for women to be treated similarly or differently, the referent point was still the same: man was the measure for both sides (MacKinnon, 1989, pp 220–6).

The debate around pregnancy proved useful in that it helped to reveal how sex discrimination law is conceived of from the 'male point of view' (MacKinnon, 1989, p 231). Moreover, in certain jurisdictions, courts attempted to move away from the similarity/comparative approach in cases of pregnancy discrimination and instead inquired whether women had been treated in a disadvantageous way on grounds of their pregnancy.[4]

In the United Kingdom, however, the conceptualisation of pregnancy discrimination is still teetering in the middle ground, using either the special protection (difference) rule or the comparative approach, depending on the action brought. As a result of EC Law, UK courts have been forced to recognise that pregnant women enjoy special protection against dismissal and other special rights during their maternity leave period. In these circumstances, no hypothetical male comparator is necessary (despite the wording of s 5(3) Sex Discrimination Act 1975).[5] This development was initially hailed as positive. However, in 1996 the Court of Appeal used this 'no comparison possible' approach as a shield to justify the denial of a benefit to a pregnant woman where a sick man would have received such a benefit.[6] The court in effect employed the Aristotelian reasoning that because pregnant women are differently situated, it cannot be discriminatory to treat them differently.

In other cases, meanwhile, courts have continued to permit a comparison between pregnant women and sick men.[7] There is no doubt, therefore, that UK equality law is caught within the 'sameness–difference' trap. The area of pregnancy discrimination has become a notorious quagmire: at the time of writing, no less than five preliminary references were pending before the ECJ on the topic; moreover, certain lawyers are advocating the view that reliance on the anti-discrimination provisions of the Sex Discrimination Act is ill-founded and that legislative codification/clarification of maternity rights is the best route forward.

EQUAL PAY FOR WORK OF EQUAL VALUE

The campaign to achieve equal pay for men and women took a great stride forward when it was recognised that, not only should women have the right to claim equal pay when their work is identical to that of a man, but that this should also be the case where they can demonstrate that their work is of equal value to work done by a man.[8] This move neatly bypassed some of the problems caused by the liberal conception of equality: namely, since the workforce is sexually segregated, with men and women often performing quite different types of work (and 'women's work' being consistently paid less), it was not possible for women to make a direct comparison with men doing the same (or similar) work in order to claim the same level of pay.

The idea behind a claim of equal pay for work of equal value is to enable women to challenge current rationales for determining the pay of existing hierarchies of jobs. In other words, it presents the opportunity for the undervaluation of women's work to be challenged. To a certain extent, then, it could allow for the myth of public/private spheres to be exploded. The procedure is such that a woman must find a male comparator with whom to compare her job, and request a job evaluation to assess the skills, knowledge and responsibilities involved in both jobs. Yet, the procedure is notoriously complex and, moreover, there are many barriers (both hidden and unhidden) to attaining equal pay. First, there is the problem that a woman must find a suitable male comparator with whom to compare her job. In the United Kingdom, in particular, comparison is restricted to men employed in the same establishment or group of establishments.[9] If a woman is employed in an industry where pay is traditionally low (as many women are), then the male comparator chosen is likely also to be low-paid relative to other industries. Moreover, under the UK Equal Pay Act, the employer is given the chance to defend the pay differential, if it can be shown that there is 'a material factor' which differentiates the two jobs.[10] This defence clearly allows for many gender-based perceptions to infiltrate the claim, and yet again, notions of difference are used to counter claims for equality. A market forces defence is acceptable under both UK and EC law, yet the labour market functions on the basis of gender segmentation and, in this way, discrimination is simply perpetuated in the defence.[11]

Furthermore, job evaluations, originally conceived of as management tools for classifying hierarchies of workers, are problematic. It is often assumed that there can be a gender-neutral evaluation of the characteristics of a job, yet perceptions of skill are gender-biased: work which produces goods is generally valued more highly than human service work (Armstrong and Armstrong, 1991, p 112); an evaluation of responsibility is strongly influenced by the status of the job (hence, since women's work has less status, it is attributed less responsibility (McColgan, 1993b, p 45)).

The final defect in the equal pay for work of equal value procedure, in the United Kingdom at least, is that the claim is individualised.[12] One woman winning a claim does not mean that all other women in her job class are automatically entitled to the same adjustments. They too must institute claims (Central Statistical Office, 1993). This, it is argued, is but a product of a highly individualised, adversarial legal process, which does not serve the needs of many disadvantaged groups (Smart, 1989, p 145).

The impact of the Equal Pay Act in the United Kingdom has been limited. In 1995, women in the United Kingdom earned 71 per cent of men's wages (EOC, 1995). Moreover, the Act has seen very few successful claims and delays in the outcome of cases are notorious (currently, four cases still have to be determined almost ten years after the claim was first lodged: EOR, 1994). The strategy for the future must be, therefore, to push for a radical reform of the legislation: to force proactive steps by government and employers; to allow group actions; and to carefully scrutinise both defences and job evaluations for hidden bias. Looking at how pay equity legislation functions in other countries is one constructive way to design a more effective system (McColgan, 1993b). Moreover, campaigning for improved legislation at the level of the European Union may be one option to realise change within the United Kingdom.

MAKING A CASE FOR POSITIVE ACTION

Positive or affirmative action to help promote the interests of disadvantaged groups is a well-known, although sometimes controversial concept in the United States and Canada. Positive action works on the basis of a substantive conception of equality: it seeks to achieve an equality of results and rejects the futility of formal, identical treatment for everyone. Positive action recognises that not everyone is identically placed: it strives to remedy the situation of society's disadvantaged groups (Greenawalt, 1983, p 117).

Positive action normally takes the form of setting goals or quotas for recruiting/promoting employees, or for admitting students to educational institutions.[13] In the United Kingdom, positive action is permitted only in the context of education and vocational training programmes.[14] In the context of employment, positive action is considered as prohibited discrimination and as unfair preferential treatment of undeserving individuals. This was recently illustrated in the decision of the Industrial Tribunal which condemned as discriminatory the Labour Party's (now-abandoned) policy of giving preference to the selection of women parliamentary candidates.[15] Similarly, the Disability Discrimination Act 1995, considered by many as a progressive piece of anti-discrimination legislation, removed provisions of the Disabled Persons (Employment) Act 1944, which previously had required employers engaging more than twenty employees to fill at least 3 per cent of jobs with registered disabled people.

This general resistance to positive action as a proactive way of promoting equal opportunities is, in this author's opinion, curious. It appears to stem from the liberal notions that positive action interferes with free choice and, moreover, that it permits people to be recruited or promoted without merit. This view can itself be countered by the observation that there are already numerous preferential systems in operation in today's employment market: for example, many people are recruited on the basis of which school or university they attended or on the basis of family links. These systems of recruitment are precisely those which systemically discriminate against society's disadvantaged groups.

In Aristotelian/liberal terms, positive action can be justified: it can be explained as compensation for past discrimination (namely, different treatment for those who have been differently situated) (Rosenfeld, 1991, p 64). However, perhaps it is this (narrow) conceptualisation of positive action which leads to positive action being viewed as objectionable: it focuses on, and hence entrenches, difference; moreover, since the concepts of sameness and difference are hierarchically constructed, positive action may result in the stigmatisation of those groups intended to benefit from positive action.

What is necessary, therefore, is a new conceptualisation of the basis of positive action. Rosenfeld, for example, presents an optimistic vision of a new social consensus whereby positive action is seen as a way of affirming the identities of social groups (Rosenfeld, 1991, pp 239–336). This is arguably already happening in certain Canadian provinces where broad-ranging 'equity plans' are both promoting the employment, and encouraging the mobilisation, of previously marginalised social groups.[16]

In the case of women in the UK, it is possible that EC Law could provide a new impetus for the reconceptualisation of positive action as a non-discriminatory form of treatment. Despite the controversial judgment of the European Court of Justice in *Eckhard Kalancke* v. *Hansestadt Bremen*, the general consensus is that positive action to recruit/promote women in employment is still permissible in EC equality law: indeed, the EC Commission is proposing amendments to the 1976 Equal Treatment Directive to make this explicit. Even without such an amendment, it appears that the exception in the UK Sex Discrimination Act 1975 for positive action is considerably narrower than what is permitted under EC Law. Women in the UK are not therefore entitled to the full potential of their rights of equal opportunity granted under EC Law. Creative litigators should bear this in mind!

It is suggested therefore that a reconsideration of the role of positive action is necessary in UK equality law. Glass ceilings do exist and rather than waiting for the ad hoc nature of litigation to challenge discriminatory barriers, a proactive approach to removing such barriers is an eminently more sensible and efficacious route to eliminating systemic discrimination.

CONCLUSION

The aim of this contribution towards critical lawyering has been to raise an awareness of the hidden pitfalls and defects in the use of the concept of equality in relation to women's rights. In particular, it has sought to demonstrate how prevailing approaches to equality are locked into the Aristotelian model of equality, which conceives of equality in terms of sameness and difference. This approach is a fundamental barrier to many of women's equality claims since women are unable to demonstrate similarity to the comparator class – men. Indeed, it is apparent that man is the measure of equality and that woman's 'difference' from this standard is the measure of her inferiority. The public/private divide, it has been argued, is one principal way of constructing such 'difference'.

If women are to use discrimination law, then we must strive to change the mode of reasoning used by the courts. Sex discrimination should come to mean being disadvantaged on the ground of gender alone, with no comparison nor special protection rule being necessary. Equal pay law, it has been argued, must also be subject to a radical overhaul in order that a non-biased evaluation of women's work can start to realise the goal of equal pay.

Finally, it has been argued that we must look further than litigation as a way of realising equality. It has been suggested that proactive policies, in particular, the use of positive action programmes, may be one way to promote the role of women in modern society. As with many of the issues in this book, what this requires, however, is both a rethinking of society's priorities and a commitment to public re-education.

NOTES

1. There is speculation that it was Harriet Taylor's hand that did this, not Mill's.
2. Section 5(3) underlines this aspect of the comparison: 'A comparison of the cases of persons of different sex or marital status under section 1(1) or 3(1) must be such that the relevant circumstances in the one case are *the same, or not materially different*, in the other' (emphasis added).
3. *Geduldig* v. *Aiello* (1974); *Bliss* v. *AG Canada* (1978); *Turley* v. *Allders Department Store* (1980).
4. *California Federal Savings & Loan Association* v. *Guerra* (1987); *Brookes* v. *Canada Safeway* (1989) at 1243; Case C-177/88 *Dekker* v. *Stichting Vormingscentrum voor Jonge Volwassen (VJV-Centrum) Plus* (1990). For a general move away from the comparative formula, see the decision of the Supreme Court of Canada in *Andrews* v. *The Law Society of British Columbia* (1989).
5. *Webb* v. *EMO Cargo (No.2)* (1995).
6. *Clark* v. *Secretary of State for Employment* (1996).
7. *Brown* v. *Rentokil* (1995) (reference pending before the ECJ).
8. First recognised by ILO Convention 10 of 1951.
9. See, however, the decision of the EAT, broadly interpreting s 1(6) EqPA in *Scullard* v. *Knowles* (1996).
10. s 1(3).
11. Case C-127/92 *Enderby* v. *Frenchay Health Authority* (1993) (for a critique of this decision, see Fredman, 1994).
12. Compare with, for example, certain Canadian pay equity acts (Fudge and McDermott, 1991; McColgan, 1993b).
13. See, for example, *Regents of University of California* v. *Bakke* (1978).
14. See ss 47–48 Sex Discrimination Act; ss 37–38 Race Relations Act. However, the Fair Employment (Northern Ireland) Act 1989 does allow for limited positive action in providing contract compliance and monitoring procedures as ways of improving the representation of Catholics in workplaces in Northern Ireland.
15. *Jepson & Dyas-Elliott* v. *The Labour Party* (1996).
16. See, for example, the Ontario Employment Equity Act 1993.

10
Feminist Perspectives on the Law of Tort

Joanne Conaghan

The engagement of feminism with such a well established field of common law as tort may, at first glance, seem strange if not even inappropriate. After all, a perusal of the hallowed texts which make up the corpus of traditional torts scholarship would suggest that feminism and tort law have little (if anything) to say to one another. Tort law in general and negligence in particular define standards of behaviour which bind everyone, male and female. Moreover, the victims of torts do not find their rights and remedies formally contingent upon their sex or gender. What, then, can feminists possibly have to say about tort law?

One starting-point might be to highlight a strange but rarely perceived contradiction not addressed by traditional analyses on the subject. It is this: while women are frequently victims of torts (being battered, assaulted, raped, harassed, molested and sometimes even killed), they are poorly represented in the case-law, whether as plaintiffs or as defendants. If one looks at the 'leading' cases comprising the traditional torts concerned with protecting the individual from deliberate assaults on his/her bodily integrity – assault, battery, false imprisonment – they consist, typically, of situations involving either male-on-male aggression (*Tuberville* v. *Savage* (1669)) or confrontations between the individual and authority (*Fagan v Metropolitan Police Commissioner* (1968)). Violent confrontations between men and women, particularly possessing a sexual dimension, are rarely if ever to be found in the casebooks or in the courtrooms. Yet we all know that these confrontations occur and that they are tortious.

Women's relative absence from that realm of tort law where, perhaps, one might most expect to find them is indicative of their general scarcity throughout. It is true that they do crop up now and then in the context of negligence, usually as distraught mothers who have witnessed serious injury to their children (*Hambrook* v. *Stokes* (1925); *McLoughlin* v. *O'Brian* (1982)) or, perhaps, as widows suing on the estates of their deceased husbands (*Videan* v. *British Transport Commission* (1963); *Roles* v. *Nathan* (1963)). Occasionally too they will appear as

124

defendants, although usually in a set of fairly circumscribed roles: as an overworked schoolteacher (*Carmarthen CC* v. *Lewis* (1955)), a harassed manageress of a tearoom (*Glasgow Corporation* v. *Muir* (1943)), or the inevitable woman driver (*Nettleship* v. *Weston* (1971)). However, on the whole they keep a surprisingly low profile in negligence (at least in so far as it takes the form of appellate cases), while in more robust and solidly 'economic' contexts such as industrial disputes or business transactions, they are virtually invisible.

What, then, are we to make of this relative absence of women from the stories and dramas which occupy and comprise tort law? Might it suggest that those areas of everyday life which tort law typically penetrates are more populated by men than by women or that those wrongs which tort law traditionally recognises are more likely to occur to men? Correspondingly, is it possible that the realms which women habitually occupy and the harms which they most frequently sustain are least likely to be caught and remedied by the tort system? Is women's limited presence in the tort system evidence of a gendered content in the distribution of social benefits and burdens, a dimension which traditional analysis does not reveal?

Such suggestions require verification and, indeed, that is one of the primary tasks which currently occupy feminist tort theorists (Forell, 1992; Bender with Lawrence, 1993; Conaghan, 1996). Thus feminist scholarship has added a new twist to an old question. The enquiry is no longer simply: what are the interests which tort law protects, but additionally: are those interests male? Such enquiries have strategic implications also: if tort law does, by and large, express and protect male interests, the question arises as to whether it can be reformed and redeployed to remedy particular female harms such as sexual harassment or the injurious effects of pornography (Conaghan, 1996; MacKinnon, 1979, pp 164–74 and 1994, pp 29–47).

However, the rehabilitation of tort law is more than just a strategic question. It requires close feminist scrutiny of the fundamental principles upon which tort law is based. To what extent are *they* compatible with the ideological and strategic goals of feminists? Are the doctrines which underpin tort law also tainted by gender bias (or at least gendered assumptions)?

THE 'REASONABLE MAN'

An obvious starting-point here is the traditional test of the 'reasonable man' representing the standard of care in negligence. While this ubiquitous character has long claimed to be an objective expression of all that is prudent and sensible in human nature, doubts have frequently been expressed both by judges and academic commentators as to the veracity of this claim (Cane, 1987, pp 35–9). At issue is the lurking suspicion that the 'reasonable man', despite his impressive pedigree in terms of case-law and legal reasoning, is little more than a fictitious representation of a particular judge's point of view. As Lord MacMillan forthrightly observed, 'It is still left to the judge to decide what in the circumstances of the particular case the reasonable man would have had in contemplation ... here there is room for a diversity of view' (*Glasgow Corporation* v. *Muir* (1943)).

The extent to which the 'objectivity' of the 'reasonable man' test is compromised by the interjection of a particular judicial viewpoint begs the question as to what exactly that viewpoint is and how it is arrived at. In this context, factors such as a judge's class, race, experience and indeed gender are often acknowledged to influence the outcome. Thus it has frequently been asserted that the practice of recruiting the judiciary from an extremely narrow slice of human experience – namely the English public school and Oxbridge – has produced an orthodoxy in terms of judicial opinion which belies its partial and subjective content (Griffith, 1985).

Into the fray of existing conflict enter feminists anxious to explore the gender dimension of the debate about judicial partiality. Is tort's 'reasonable man' in law also a man in fact? Does he express a standard which accords with male rather than female conceptions of what constitutes reasonableness? Indeed, do men and women reason differently? There is certainly a common perception that they do, one which is humorously captured by Sir Alan Herbert's depiction of women in his classic parody of the common law:

> There exists a class of beings illogical, impulsive, careless, irresponsible, extravagant, prejudiced and vain, free for the most part from those worthy and repellant excellences which distinguish the Reasonable Man ... (Herbert, 1936, p 648).

Herbert's picture presents women as emotional and frivolous beings not capable of rational consideration of the weighty matters which more appropriately preoccupy men. While widely acknowledged as a caricature, in the sense of greatly exaggerating perceived differences between men and women, Herbert's portrayal retains its humour (and therefore its power) because it continues to draw, at least to some extent, on popular perceptions of gender difference in respect of rationality. These may take the form of traditional disparaging characterisations of women as 'emotional' and therefore incapable of the kind of abstract conceptual analysis which 'reason' requires, or they may manifest themselves in more positive (and often self-consciously feminist) assertions which challenge conventional perceptions of what constitutes reason and highlight the virtues of alternative modes of analysis and forms of decision-making, typically involving the rejection of abstract thinking in favour of the 'contextualisation' of issues in association with 'relational thinking' (see, for example, Gilligan, 1982; Ruddick, 1989). Regardless of what form they take (including whether they are biologically or socially based), such assertions of gender difference evidence a strong perception pervading both conventional and feminist legal thought which acknowledges that the conception of reason traditionally deployed in legal analysis is male.

Such a contention is most dramatically highlighted in recent debate about the alleged gender bias inherent in the criminal defence of provocation. But such gendered perceptions are arguably (although perhaps less obviously) evident in tort law also. Most striking perhaps is the frequent difference in perception between men and women as to what constitutes wrongful behaviour in the context of sexual harassment (Lester, 1993, pp 227–9). The reasonable man and the reasonable woman might well differ as to what is and what is not offensive for these purposes. Even in the context of negligence it has been argued that judges, when evaluating the conduct of a woman, may well apply to her a standard which relies upon a male assessment of the situation and the appropriate response. (See, for example, Robin Martin's entertaining discussion of the plight of a woman locked in a public toilet who injured herself in an attempt to climb out attracting a judicial pronouncement of contributory negligence in *Sayers* v. *Harlow UDC* (1958) (Martin, 1994, pp 348–9)).

THE 'REASONABLE PERSON'

The feminist critique of negligence's 'reasonable man' raises issues of form as well as substance. In other words, it is not just the *content* of the standard being applied which is under scrutiny, it is also the application of a single and allegedly objective, universal standard to human behaviour at all. What feminist legal theory reveals (in the company of critical legal theory in general) is that law is neither politically nor morally neutral but is value-laden: it is an expression of particular values and assumptions about the distribution of resources in society (and individual access to them) which has blatantly political consequences (Conaghan and Mansell, 1993). Thus judges when assessing reasonable behaviour, whether they are articulating their own subjective opinions or whether they are engaged in a genuine attempt to give expression to what they believe are prevailing social standards of proper behaviour, are making, in effect, policy-based decisions, that is, decisions which appeal to particular values and moral preferences governing individual relationships with each other and with the state (Martin, 1994, pp 342–51). These are values about which reasonable people may well disagree.

Thus the conventional understanding of the reasonable man as an objective measure of human behaviour (*Vaughan* v. *Menlove* (1837)) is a legal fiction: he is in fact merely a particular expression of appropriate human behaviour inevitably reflecting the values and assumptions, experience and understanding of those responsible for his birth and subsequent upbringing. For this reason it is not enough to simply replace the 'reasonable man' standard with an appeal to the 'reasonable person' as is the practice in some of the more 'politically correct' textbooks (for example, Hepple and Matthews, 1991). The reasonable person is no more objective than the reasonable man. Indeed the claim to objectivity is itself contentiously male: objectivity, it is alleged, is the method by which men's point of view is privileged and women's silenced. As MacKinnon observes:

> Male dominance is perhaps the most pervasive and tenacious sytem of power in history ... it is metaphysically nearly perfect. Its point of view is the standard for point-of-viewlessness, its particularity the meaning of universality. (MacKinnon, 1983, pp 638–9)

Thus, not only does the standard of reasonableness express a particular point of view masquerading as the *only* point of view but it is also a point of view with which feminists, among others, take issue. For example Leslie Bender, a leading feminist writer in the field of tort scholarship, calls for the rejection of the 'language of economics' in the application of the reasonableness standard (Bender, 1990a, p 760). In her view, the prevailing cost–benefit approach to measuring carelessness, which weighs the costs of the accident against the costs of taking precautions (see the classic judgment of Learned Hand J. in *US* v. *Carrol Towing Co* (1947)) is dehumanising in reducing human life to questions of economic cost. Moreover, such an approach is implicitly male, both in its preoccupation with the economic consequences of particular actions and in its tendency to abstract specific features from a particular context for the purposes of engaging in economic calculations. Bender argues for an alternative standard of human behaviour which focuses on 'the promotion of human safety and well-being' instead of 'algebraic formulations' (1988, p 32), an understanding of legal responsibility in terms of 'taking care of' (1990a, pp 767–73), a shift in the dominant ideology from 'individualist to interconnected' (1990b, p 907) and the adoption of a new duty to exercise 'the conscious care and concern of a responsible neighbour or social acquaintance' (1988, p 31).

Thus Bender, accepting that moral preferences inform and define the legal standard of the reasonable man, rejects that standard by attacking the moral preferences underlying it. Instead, she argues for an alternative standard, equally informed by moral preferences but expressing an ethics which she believes to be more just, more compassionate and therefore more desirable. So, although she is subscribing to the adoption of a single standard it is not an 'objective' standard, but rather one which, on its merits, is preferable to the one currently prevailing.

THE 'REASONABLE WOMAN'

Bender's approach takes us a step forward in a number of ways. Not only does she demonstrate the partiality of the traditional standard of care but, by carefully unpacking its underlying values, she reveals its gendered content. Moreover, by highlighting the moral dimension in the 'reasonable man' standard she shifts the focus away from spurious assertions of its objectivity to a proper discussion of its ethical merits and demerits. However, it might still be argued that Bender's position is problematic because she continues to subscribe to the idea of a single standard of care by which to evaluate human behaviour. The recurring problem with the application of a single legal standard to diverse situations and human actors is that it continues to express a particular point of view about social behaviour, a view which inevitably operates in a way which reinforces the perspectives of some, while excluding the point of view of others. Thus, for example, while Bender's standard of care might fit well with the moral point of view and social circumstances of liberal middle-class American feminists, it might seem less attractive when applied to the circumstances of those less well situated to embrace Bender's generous conception of responsibility.

Furthermore, there are those who express scepticism about the 'ethics of care' which Bender's view represents on the grounds that it is not a *genuine* female attribute but rather a feature ascribed to women by a system of male domination. For example, Catharine MacKinnon observes that 'women value care because men have valued us according to the care we give them' (MacKinnon, 1986, p 39). Thus she regards the alleged gender differences which the work of Gilligan and Bender (implicitly) celebrate with wary circumspection: 'For women to affirm difference, when difference means dominance, as it does with gender, means to affirm the qualities and characteristics of powerlessness' (p 39).

In gentler fashion, Lucinda Finley has warned against the dangers of deploying female stereotypes, however positive, in the search for a standard of care which recognises women's perspectives (Finley, 1989, pp 63–5). Thus, for example, the implicit assumptions that women are more caring, more nurturing and less self-motivated, which hover unspoken in Bender's articulation of an alternative ethical standard, have arguably served to oppress rather than to distinguish women in the past. Moreover, where women have chosen to depart from these standards they have been subject to harsh judgement and social stigma not accorded to men.

For this reason Finley is ambivalent about the recent development in American courts of the standard of the 'reasonable woman'. This is a concept which has emerged to address situations where there is an alleged difference in perception between men and women as to how particular behaviour should be judged. The most obvious example is litigation involving sexual harassment where, not surprisingly, the 'reasonable woman' has had a considerable airing. Thus in *Rabidue* v. *Osceola Refining* (1986) while the majority of the court held that the 'reasonable person' would not have been offended by the work environment which was the subject of the complaint (a woman in a predominantly male workplace adorned with posters of nude and scantily clad women – her complaints were met with reprimands, sexual taunts, obscenities and, on occasion, 'fatherly advice'), Keith J., in a powerful dissenting judgment, evoked the standard of the 'reasonable victim' to challenge the majority's assessment of Ms Rabidue's predicament. His judgment became the benchmark against which later cases considered and in some instances applied a 'reasonable woman' test to determine whether particular conduct was offensive for purposes of establishing sexual harassment (see for example *Ellison* v. *Brady* (1991); *Robinson* v. *Jacksonville Shipyards Inc* (1991)); the Supreme Court in *Harris* v. *Forklift Systems Inc* (1992) has recently declined the opportunity to explicitly endorse or outrightly reject the 'reasonable woman' test.

Despite Finley's wariness, the 'reasonable woman' test has met with considerable favour among many feminists who applaud its application at least in circumstances where the harm in question has an evident gender dimension, such as sexual harassment or rape (Forell, 1992; Lester, 1993). But there remain some who continue to be uncomfortably aware of the dilemma which a gender-based standard of reasonableness evokes: does it in fact advance women's interests or does it inevitably 'stereotype and disempower' (Cahn, 1992, p 1398)? Moreover, does it rely on an 'essential' conception of woman, that is one which attributes to women (and to men) a series of fixed characteristics and features and which is blind to the considerable range and diversity of experiences and attributes which go to make up and define individual identity? It may be that the answer to this dilemma may ultimately lie not in a principled adoption or rejection of the 'reasonable woman' standard but in the careful and pragmatic consideration of its desirability and application in particular contexts. Such a pragmatic and strategically focused approach to its deployment may help to avoid the essentialism inherent in its rigid application and at the same time give recognition to those instances where the dominant feature of identity is gender. At the same time such a focus avoids the 'all-or-nothing' approach of conventional rationality by recognising that the utility of the 'reasonable woman' approach may depend less on abstract principle and more on concrete application.

CONCLUSION

The feminist critique of the 'reasonable man' standard has taken critical debate a good deal further than simply trashing his claim to objectivity: feminists have queried the notion of objectivity itself. In the context of tort law this has allowed debate to shift away from relatively sterile assertions of judicial partiality towards a fuller, freer, debate about the moral values underlying tort law and their desirability. Thus scholars such as Bender have helped to redefine the agenda in terms of ethical preferences. However, this still leaves unresolved a number of issues which feminist writers in tort law need to address. The first is the question of the desirability of universally applied standards. In the context of negligence this issue becomes: is the standard of care best defined in terms of a single principle (or set of principles) as Bender appears to contend, or should it be subject to a variety of contextually situated standards, as advocated by Robin Martin? Moreover, how should these standards be set – by the courts or the legislature? Martin contends that the legislature is better placed to determine standards than the courts and there is strength to this argument. After all, once it is acknowledged that the determination of standards is essentially a political question (or at any rate a question about which there are legitimate differences in opinion), the legislative process does appear to be a more appropriate forum than the courts.

A second issue present, particularly in Bender's writing on tort law, is an understanding of gender in terms of a set of fairly fixed and rigid set of attributes which define 'male' and 'female'. To what extent is the characterisation of particular positions in gender terms either accurate or helpful? Is there not a serious danger here of relying on an essentialist understanding of gender difference which reinforces rather than undermines gender stereotypes? After all, however attractive Bender's articulation of a feminist ethics, it certainly does not speak for women as a whole. Does that matter?

It may be that to identify a discourse in terms of gender (masculine/feminine) does not necessarily imply a fixedness either in terms of biology or social identity, particularly where gender is understood in terms of social construction and social construction is understood in terms of multiplicity of identity. The confusion lies in a tendency for issues of biology and ideology to coalesce both in popular understanding and in feminist writing. It follows that there is no necessary essentialism in Bender's writing, *properly understood*, but therein lies the problem. Thus, it is important for feminists engaged in law to recognise the fluidity of gender both conceptually and socially. Such recognition avoids the dangers of rigid and oppressive demarcations of identity along gender lines and at the same time allows for the possibility of organisation and political activity on the basis of commonality.

Finally, it is worth observing that the agenda of feminist engagement with tort law is different from that traditionally set by radical legal theory which has focused attention on tort law as a mechanism of compensation rather than as an expression of ethical standards to guide human behaviour. It may be that the left's preoccupation with compensation in the context of a now depleted welfare state has led to neglect of those ethical issues which tortious principles and feminist legal theory now address, and for this reason the shift in focus is welcome. But at the same time it must be recognised that feminist writing in tort appears to be guilty of making the same unnecessary assumption which has informed traditional perspectives on the subject over the years, namely the assumption that responsibility should determine compensation. There is no inherent reason why the right to compensation should depend on any ascription of responsibility: the connection is entirely ideological, based on an assumption of individual responsibility and a correspondingly limited concern for the misfortunes of others. But surely a conception of limited responsibility is precisely what Bender seeks to challenge? It is arguable that so long as feminist theory remains wedded to the most fundamental assumption underlying tort law – the assumption that our duty to *care* derives from some *individual* failure on our part to act or act properly (however evaluated) – it will not succeed in toppling the enduring edifice which continues to constitute tort law.

11
Women, Law and Medical Power
Sally Sheldon

A starting-point for this analysis is recognition of what has been described as the 'medicalisation' of daily life (Zola, 1977; Illich, 1975). Within this movement, increasingly large areas of human experience are defined as falling under the authority of the medical profession: it is doctors who are authorised to define when life begins, when death takes place and to classify who is healthy and who is sick. In this sense, doctors have become the new 'therapeutic clergy', taking on much of the power and moral authority which had previously been attributed to priests (Foucault, 1989). Medical expertise becomes generalised beyond the bounds of a mere technical competence. Furthermore, as Ian Kennedy has cogently argued, a great many decisions which are made not exclusively or even primarily with reference to medical criteria fall to be decided by doctors (Kennedy, 1985, p 22). As such, the limits to be placed upon the exercise of medical power and the role to be played by law in such an enterprise become a vital area of research for any critical legal project.

In this chapter, I wish to examine how far the need to ensure that the power of the doctor is not abused can be seen to have informed the legal regulations which govern encounters between doctors and women. This will lead me to provide a brief sketch of how medical power is reproduced in statute and case-law or, rather, how both carve out a space to be left to medical discretion and to focus, far more specifically, on how this has operated in a particular area of importance to women: the regulation of abortion. This will lead me to attempt some more general conclusions. Before doing this, however, I would like to provide some explanation of why I feel it particularly necessary to focus on the medical treatment of women.

WOMEN AND MEDICAL POWER

If the expansion of medical power would appear to concern us all, I would argue that it is of even greater significance for women (see generally Foster, 1995). First, women use health services more frequently than men and are more subject to a routine, daily medical control

(Roberts, 1985; Davis, 1988; Kane, 1991). Secondly, medical discourse has constituted women as particularly *psychologically* and *socially* vulnerable and therefore in need of close medical surveillance, advice and guidance (Turner, 1987, p 102; Showalter, 1987). Thirdly, women have often been depicted within medical discourse as *biologically* natural patients, at the mercy of our bodies or hormones. Female biology has been constructed as more problematic than male, hence more in need of medical attention (Turner, 1987, p 109; Ussher, 1989). In particular, as will emerge more clearly below, the female reproductive process has been well staked out as especially in need of medical supervision and control.

The existence of such medical surveillance and the use of such medical power in the policing of female behaviour with the restraint of potentially 'dangerous' feminine traits has a long and dubious history. Medical texts have attributed to women irrationality, sexual passivity, and a desire for maternity (Martin, 1987; Easlea, 1981) and various historical studies have demonstrated how doctors have acted to ensure female compliance with these constructions through such draconian measures as ovariectomies (Scully, 1980), lobotomies (Showalter, 1987) or committal to psychiatric institutions (Smart, 1992, p 38). This latter was practised well into this century under the Mental Defectives Act 1913 for unmarried mothers on the grounds of moral imbecility or feeble-mindedness. Further, in the late nineteenth century, the deployment of medical knowledge was integral to the attempts made to keep women in the home, through claims that studying outside it would damage their reproductive capacities (Ehrenreich and English, 1978; Thomson, 1995).

Although the claims and methods of the medical science of more recent years seem (by and large) far less dramatic,[1] evidence of the same pattern of medical enforcement of appropriate female behaviour is still visible. Barrett and Roberts, in their (1978) study of GPs and female patients, found that GPs and hospital specialists would often relate to women in terms of non-medical, social criteria in order to reinforce women's traditional social role and that frequently doctors would use the authority of their medicomoral language to offer not neutral, clinical advice but a set of prescriptions based on the conventional wisdom of their own social milieu (see also Roberts, 1985; Davis, 1988 Thomas, 1985; Foster, 1995).

It would seem, therefore, that women are doubly susceptible to medical power and that female patients are consequently doubly in need of empowerment vis-a-vis the medical profession.

LAW AND THE REPRODUCTION OF MEDICAL POWER

How far has the law attempted to bolster the position of the patient in the face of medical power? The law displays a clear preference for self-regulation by the medical profession, with intervention justified only in exceptional cases. Jonathan Montgomery has expressed this well:

> Medical practice is, in effect – although not technically in law – a professional monopoly, its ethical standards are set and policed by medics, and malpractice suits are almost exclusively based on negligence which turns out to make liability depend on the expert opinions of doctors. While judges have suggested that they might intervene to establish standards, actual activity of this sort has been conspicuous by its absence. (Montgomery, 1989, p 319)

Montgomery thus argues that the law in England and Wales has been dominated by an acceptance of the claims of medical professionalism. This is supported by a process of 'mystification' whereby medical control can be justified by reference to the existence of a field of highly specialised medical knowledge which is accessible only to the trained practitioner. Claims that only doctors can understand what doctors do have provided a compelling justification for a high degree of self-regulation, with much left to internal disciplinary procedures. The judiciary are cautious and reluctant when requested to police those areas which have been constructed as involving medical discretion. The path-breaking case of *Bolam* v. *Friern Hospital Management Committee* (1957) established the principle that a doctor's conduct must be measured against the standards of his or her peers: a doctor will not be guilty of negligence if he or she 'has acted in accordance with a practice accepted as proper by a responsible body of medical men skilled in that particular art'. Thus it is doctors themselves who establish the standard of care which will be required by law. Montgomery locates this case as part of a 'general and consistent refusal by the judges to set substantive standards for the medical profession' (1989, p 322).

Bolam has had far-reaching effects in medical case law. It has also served to ground a judicial refusal to recognise any place for a doctrine of 'informed consent' in English law, whereby patients would have a right to know exactly what risks a treatment involves before consenting to it. Rather, the courts assert that the amount of information which a patient should be given is to be determined by the doctor. In so far as a doctor would be acting 'in accordance with a practice accepted as proper by a responsible body of medical men skilled in that particular art' in withholding certain information, she/he will not be liable to the patient in damages. The justification provided for this is the doctor's superior knowledge of what lies in the patient's best interests: how much it is (medically) advisable for the patient to be told (*Sidaway* v. *Board of Governors of the Bethlehem Royal and the Maudsley Hospital* (1985); *Gold* v. *Haringey Health Authority* (1987)). Moreover, the Court of Appeal has affirmed that the doctor has no duty to reveal particular risks even when the patient enquires specifically about their existence (*Blyth* v. *Bloomsbury AHA* (1987)).

Judicial intervention has thus carved out a broad area which will be left to medical discretion, and within which standards will be developed and policed largely by the medical profession itself. The courts have likewise repeatedly refused to intervene in decisions regarding the allocation of health care resources, most recently in the Court of Appeal decision in the well publicised case of the ten-year-old leukaemia victim, B (*Times Law Reports*, 15 March 1995). A similar pattern emerges in statute law, which leaves broad areas of discretion to medical judgment.

WOMEN, LAW AND MEDICAL POWER: THE REGULATION OF ABORTION

As was noted above, a prime locus for the deployment of medical power over women has been the control of reproduction – contraception, pregnancy and birth, abortion and, more recently, assisted conception. The growth of medical knowledge regarding the reproductive process, in particular the development of the foetus, has served to firmly establish reproduction as a domain which should fall under medical control. This 'staking out' of reproduction as a matter for medical control has been mirrored in legal rules. Here I would like to make some brief remarks regarding the regulation of abortion as one area where feminists have criticised the extent of medical control and highlighted the problems which it poses for female autonomy.

Abortion has increasingly come to be seen as a narrow, technical, medical matter (Sheldon, 1995) and the regulation of abortion has been very clearly marked out as an area for medical discretion and control (Keown, 1988). Unlike many other European countries, Britain accords the woman no right to an abortion in early pregnancy. Rather, a woman seeking an abortion must always obtain the signatures of two doctors: she is never legally entitled to authorise the termination of her pregnancy herself. Two amendments which sought to relax medical control over abortion in early pregnancy were rejected in 1990 when MPs were again given the possibility to vote on the regulations governing abortion. I have argued elsewhere that the fact that such access to abortion is to be controlled by doctors, rather than the pregnant woman herself, rests on assumptions of women's irresponsibility, irrationality and immaturity: women are not seen as sufficiently capable or competent to make such decisions for ourselves (Sheldon, 1993).

Lord Silkin, introducing his (1966) Bill to the House of Lords, gives a clear flavour of the assumptions made by reformers regarding the sort of woman who would be the beneficiary of improved access to legal abortion:

[t]here] are women who suffer from illnesses, which ... will ... make them less able to bear the burdens of motherhood ... There is the case of the woman who is in prison, serving a long term commencing between the beginning of the pregnancy and the time at which she will give birth. Obviously that woman is inadequate to be a mother of a child. There is the persistent offender, or the shop-lifter, and there is the mother who has in the past been found guilty of neglecting or ill-treatment of her existing children. These are some of the cases I have in mind. There is the drug taker or the alcoholic. I am sure the right reverend Prelate (the Bishop of Exeter) would not suggest that such a mother is a fit person to be in charge of children. There is the woman who already has a large family, perhaps six or seven children ... There is the question of the woman who loses her husband during pregnancy and has to go out to work, and obviously cannot bear the strain of doing a full day's work, and looking after a child. There is the woman whose husband is a drunkard or a ne'er-do-well, or is in prison serving a long term, and she has to go to work. These are the cases I have in mind.[2]

Given the construction of the woman seeking abortion as a desperate, downtrodden or deviant individual, it is small wonder that Kevin McNamara feels it appropriate to ask 'Who is the mother to make the judgment?'[3] Rather, it is believed safer to leave this decision in the hands of the calm, responsible medical professional.

The fact that this decision rests with the doctor has posed considerable problems in terms of women's access to abortion. Firstly, it means that we have to go cap in hand to request termination of pregnancy, and if we are granted such access, this may only be after intrusive questions and a normative, moralising lecture as to acceptable sexual behaviour. This process has been frequently reported as extremely upsetting and often demeaning, as the following examples, taken from interviews, indicate:

The GP was very rude. He basically said: 'my wife had her first child at 19, so what's the problem?' I was living with a junkie at the time, in a squat in Bath. (The *Guardian*, 9 May 1994)

The worst part was going to my doctor, who was very insensitive and cruel. My doctor refused flatly to grant a termination but offered a second opinion by another doctor. The second was a lady who still did her best to make me feel like a monster for wanting an abortion. (Davies, 1991, pp 69–70)

Such accounts remain anecdotal but are sufficiently common to demand serious attention (see also Winn, 1988; Neustatter and Newson, 1986; and Davies, 1991 for comparable examples).

A further problem arises with regard to funding. If a woman chooses to go to a non-NHS clinic she will normally have to pay for her own abortion. The law has left control over which terminations shall be performed in the hands of the senior doctors who have controlled NHS facilities – in this case the senior hospital gynaecologists and obstetricians. This results in the anomalous situation whereby in 1992, 93 per cent of women in North Tyneside had their pregnancies terminated within the NHS, as compared to just 1 per cent of women in Coventry and Dudley district health authorities (where the hospitals are controlled by anti-choice doctors).[4]

Thus the medicalisation of abortion – its construction as a technical, medical issue – has restricted women's access to safe, legal abortion, particularly in the sense of leaving both the abortion decision and control over what operations are to be performed in NHS facilities in the hands of doctors. However, it seems to me to be equally clear that the medicalisation of abortion has also *facilitated* women's access to abortion services. This can be seen in the decriminalisation of abortion itself – had David Steel's Medical Termination of Pregnancy Bill (later to become the 1967 Abortion Act) not commanded the support of the medical profession it is highly unlikely that it could ever have passed onto the statute books. The possibility of redefining abortion as a matter for medicine obscured the political significance of decriminalisation and defused, or at least diluted, opposition to such reform.

Further, the effects of medicalisation are still clearly visible in the British legislation today. In comparison with other Western abortion statutes, the Abortion Act is notable not merely for its 'illiberal' failure to accord the woman more autonomy in the early weeks of pregnancy, but also for its relatively high, 'liberal' upper time limit of 24 weeks. This seeming paradox becomes less confusing when located as part of the codification of abortion as a medical event. As has been seen, medicalisation serves to ground an abdication of legal control and the granting of a large area of discretion to doctors. The Act allows terminations late into the course of a pregnancy, provided they are performed and authorised under strict medical control. Moreover, the limit of 24 weeks was itself chosen for its coincidence with the medical event of viability (capacity to sustain independent life) and was supported by all of the major groups which represent doctors' interests (Sheldon, 1995, pp 115–16). The adoption of viability as the appropriate 'landmark' is indicative of the increased focus of the abortion debate on the issue of foetal development (as medically defined). In practice, this has meant that women can get access to abortion even comparatively late in pregnancy.

Finally, the perception that abortion is a matter for medical discretion has made it particularly difficult for a woman's partner to challenge her decision to terminate a pregnancy. In *Paton* v. *British Pregnancy Advisory Service* (1978), a man tried to challenge his wife's decision to terminate her pregnancy. Refusing his request for an injunction, the court held that:

> [not] only would it be a bold and brave judge who would seek to interfere with the discretion of doctors acting under the [Abortion] Act, but I think he would really be a foolish judge who would attempt to do any such thing, unless possibly, there is clear bad faith and an obvious attempt to perpetrate a criminal offence. Even then, of course, the question is whether that is a matter which should be left to the Director of Public Prosecutions and the Attorney General. (at p 992)

The protection of medical discretion here serves to shield women from the opposing claims of their sexual partners. It seems here that the protection of medical discretion in law has served simultaneously to carve out some limited space for increased female autonomy. It has meant that (some) women get improved access to (some) services.

FEMINIST POLITICS AND MEDICAL AUTONOMY: A POTENTIAL ALLIANCE OF INTERESTS?

Law's abdication of a large degree of control to doctors who act as gatekeepers to abortion services is illustrative of the more general tendency to carve out broad areas which will be left to medical discretion, as outlined above. This reluctance to police medical activity, I have argued, has particularly important implications for *female* autonomy for, as was seen above, women are more subject to medical power than are men. However, I have also aimed to demonstrate that at least in one instance the adoption of medical knowledges and constructions in law and the judicial protection of a realm of medical discretion has equally (paradoxically) resulted in *greater* freedom for women.

Although I do not have the space here to expand this argument, I suspect that other examples might also be supplied to make the same point: for example, access to infertility treatment services. Unlike French law, which takes an extremely prescriptive stance as to who should (not) be allowed access to such services, the Human Fertilisation and Embryology Act 1990 leaves massive discretion to doctors. This means that many women who would not be able to receive such treatment in France are not debarred from receiving it here. Yet women who have tried to challenge the exercise of medical discretion in this area, and in particular the decision to refuse them treatment, have met with little success in the courts for precisely the reason that access to such treatments has been constructed as a matter for medical judgment (*R* v. *Ethical Committee of St Mary's Hospital (Manchester) ex p Harriott* (1988); Millns (1995)). Again the British tendency to privilege medical discretion is revealed as a mixed blessing for women.

Such discussion undoubtedly poses more questions than it resolves. I would, however, like to draw two general conclusions from it: first in terms of the relationship between law and medicine; and secondly the implications of the medicalisation of abortion for a feminist politics.

First, then, what should have become clear is that to view law and medicine as non-contradictory components of a homogeneous, monolithic male power is clearly impossible and the way that some feminists have theorised instances of medical power is equally untenable. To continue the example of abortion, and to cite the way which its decriminalisation has been described by one feminist writer from across the Atlantic:

> the availability of abortion frames, and is framed by, the extent to which men, worked out among themselves, find it convenient to allow abortion – a reproductive consequence of intercourse – to occur. Abortion will then, to that extent, be available. (MacKinnon, 1983a, p 28)

I would contend that what is clear from the above analysis is that whilst law and medicine may be imbued with gendered male values, it is impossible to assume any continuity of interests between them. Although more often it does not, law *may* offer empowerment in the face of medical power: the protection of medical discretion in law may offer women some space for autonomous action, shielded from the claims of male partners.

Secondly, I would like to return to my contention that the depoliticisation effected by the medicalisation of the abortion debate is a double-edged sword. Above, I sought to highlight the negative effects of medicalisation in terms of its role in creating and entrenching certain concrete problems for women who seek abortion. I also feel that medicalisation has been harmful in a more pervasive, though perhaps less tangible, way. For a long time abortion was the focal point for broader debate both inside and outside the women's movement and could scarcely be talked about outside the context of broader issues of sex education, contraception, maternal health, control in sexual relations, childraising responsibilities and so on. Now it seems the only factors which need to be discussed are those which relate to foetal status and development (as medically defined) (Sheldon, 1995). As Peggy Foster has written:

> Whilst women's problems are thus individualized and medicalized, the medical profession and the health care industry more generally can be regarded as playing at least some part, if not a major role, in disabling women as a group and distracting them from the fight for political, social and economic solutions to their collective problems. (Foster, 1995, p 180)

Today it is more usual to talk about women's plurality and difference than it is to assert collective problems. However, feminists should be careful lest the medicalisation of abortion allows the broad, structural problems which contribute to unwanted pregnancy to slip off the agenda. Is it really true that it is no longer relevant to ask why women experience unwanted pregnancy? What can the incidence of abortion tell us about the effectiveness and availability of contraception and sex education, and women's potential to resist unwanted penetrative (hetero)sex? Why is a given pregnancy unwanted? Would it be equally undesirable if the overwhelming financial and emotional burdens of raising children did not fall on individual women as opposed to couples or other family groups, or indeed such family groups as opposed to the state? Today, the increasing acceptance of a consensual medicalised framework which focuses on the development of the foetus provides scope for compromise precisely because it makes it easy to avoid ever thinking about such issues.

NOTES

1. However, Hudson (1987) relates the case of a woman who developed obsessive behaviour as a result of living with a sadistic husband. The recommended medical 'cure' was to operate on her. Roberts (1985, p 33) gives the example of another woman who, following an illness which consisted of a refusal to do any housework, was given a course of six ECT treatments and subsequently discharged as 'well' again.
2. Lord Silkin, introducing his (1966) Bill to the House of Lords, in Hindell and Simms (1971, p 150). See Sheldon (1993) for many more comparable examples.
3. McNamara, HC Deb., Vol. 730, Col. 1129, 1966 (22 June).
4. OPCS statistics, published by the Birth Control Trust.

12
The Campaign to Free Kiranjit Ahluwalia
Pragna Patel

This is the essence of my culture, society and religion, where a woman is a toy, a plaything. She can be stuck together at will, broken at will ... It is the culture into which I was born and where I grew up, which sees the woman as the honour of the house. In order to uphold this false 'honour' and 'glory' she is taught to endure many kinds of oppression and pain in silence. In addition, religion also teaches her that her husband is her god and fulfilling his every desire is her religious duty. A woman who does not follow this path in our society has no respect or place in it. She suffers from all kinds of slanders against her character; and she has to face much hurt entirely alone. She is responsible not only for her husband's family but also his entire family's happiness ... For ten years I lived a life of beatings and degradation and no one noticed. Now the law has decreed that I should serve a sentence for life? No one asked me why all this has happened ... Today I have come out of my husband's jail and entered the jail of the law ...

These powerful words launched the campaign to free Kiranjit Ahluwalia. Her cry against injustice, expressed so clearly in the words 'No one asked me why' is a severe indictment of a criminal justice system which fails to acknowledge violence against women, yet condemns without understanding the actions of those women who seek to defend themselves and survive. By the time Kiranjit walked out of the Old Bailey as a free woman in September 1992 her case had come to symbolise women's resistance against domestic violence. From the beginning, what drove us at Southall Black Sisters (SBS) was the recognition, born out of the day-to-day experience of the women who come to our centre, that Kiranjit and women like her had been wrongfully imprisoned, and that the issue of domestic violence had to be placed high on the agenda. Most of all, we needed to extend the definition of 'miscarriage of justice' to include the cases of battered women in prison.

KIRANJIT'S STORY

Crawley Women's Centre alerted us to Kiranjit's plight around October 1989. Her story had exploded in the local papers, in which lurid and sensational headlines proclaimed her a 'killer mum'. A line or two, buried deep within the text, mentioned that she had suffered violence at her husband's hands. The need to place Kiranjit's experience in this context was crucial. SBS offered to provide her lawyers with a report outlining the constraints and pressures on Asian women who attempt to escape the stifling and violent confines of marital life. Without insight into the cultural context in which she experienced domestic violence, the court's understanding of her circumstances would be partial at best. Our offer was dismissed outright by Kiranjit's lawyers who, worse still, stated that they would turn to her family for an account of the cultural expectations and customs should the need arise!

For ten years Kiranjit experienced violence and abuse from her husband on an almost daily basis. The final straw came when she discovered that while he was beating her and neglecting his duties to their children, he was having an affair with another woman upon whom he was lavishing gifts and attention. She felt humiliated but trapped. She had made numerous attempts to end the relationship, often appealing to her family and his for help and assistance. She had sought court injuctions to restrain him from further violence but fell under pressure to reconcile for the sake of maintaining family *izzat* (honour). She attempted suicide on two occasions. Despair drove her to concede to his every whim at the expense of her own self and identity.

On the fatal day itself, Kiranjit was assaulted by her husband with a hot iron and threatened with further violence. She made one last attempt to talk to him about their marriage. His indifference triggered off a rage in her that had been building up for some time. She threw petrol and then a lighted taper at him whilst he slept. Then, dressing her son, she ran into the garden and hid behind a shed. Her husband died about ten days later from severe burns. She was charged with his murder.

The entire criminal justice system failed Kiranjit. The courts were not concerned with the violence she faced, nor why a woman would destroy the very things which society teaches her to covet. Throughout her interviews with the police, Kiranjit was made to focus only on the immediate events surrounding the killing, despite her pitiful attempts to explain the history of her actions. Her story was suppressed at every stage of the criminal process. Unable to control or even recognise her own story, Kiranjit allowed herself to be silenced, thereby sealing her own fate as a long-term prisoner. We knew that there could have been another outcome had the courts understood how countless women live their lives in violent circumstances. The challenge had to take place at two levels. We had to find legal grounds to re-open her case and, at the same time, mount a campaign to educate and inform the public about the injustice of her case.

The first hurdle was to find new lawyers who would examine the case for grounds of appeal. We turned to Rohit Sanghvi who, together with barrister Andrew Nicol, showed genuine respect for our views and a willingness to cooperate with the wider campaign. For at least 18 months they scanned the trial proceedings. Their efforts were all the more remarkable given the absence of legal aid. The search for grounds for appeal became a learning process for all concerned, a process which showed us both the possibilities and the constraints of the law as an arena of resistance.

THE NEED FOR A CAMPAIGN

When Kiranjit was convicted of murder, we knew that it was going to be an uphill battle to force the Court of Appeal to overturn her conviction. We were sure that unless a major public campaign was also mounted to coincide with the legal action, she would not succeed. For us, the issue was not simply about an individual case of injustice but about the rights of an entire group of battered women. Initially, we were anxious about how the barristers in the case would receive our involvement. We envisaged the campaign and the legal team working closely together. When we look back, we can honestly say that the process of collaboration was as vital as the outcome itself. We have never been able to recapture that spirit of cooperation with lawyers with whom we have worked on criminal cases since. It was one of those rare occasions where we felt involved, rather than patronised or marginalised as a campaigning mob whose job was to 'help' the lawyers win the case by making a noise outside the courts!

We had always envisaged the campaign raising political demands beyond narrow legal confines, important at a formal level as the legal arguments were. It took the lawyers some time to understand this aspect of the campaign. This sometimes led to tensions between the lawyers and ourselves. Often their prejudices about feminism and feminist demands would guide their views of the campaign, betraying their ignorance of its objectives and also the diversity of opinion which existed amongst us as feminists. They had a tendency to perceive us as a homogeneous group of radical women obsessed with direct action, unable to appreciate the subtleties or the constraints of the law. There is an urgent need for those in the legal profession who are committed to challenging human rights abuses to see themselves as participants in wider social struggles. The alliance is vital if we are to push the boundaries of the permissible, within and outside the courts, and if we are to close the ever-widening gap between legal and other political forms of resistance.

THE LEGAL ISSUES: GENDERING 'JUSTICE'?

The lawyers were to develop three substantive grounds of appeal over the course of the two-year campaign. Rohit Sanghvi's painstaking examination of the trial judge's summing up revealed the error which gave us our first foothold in the Court of Appeal. In directing the jury on the objective limb of the provocation test, the trial judge drew their attention to the 'relevant' characteristics to be taken into account. These he said to be Kiranjit's age, marital status, ethnicity and education. But nowhere in the closed checklist that he presented did he refer to her as a battered woman. This omission had major implications for the way Kiranjit's trial had been conducted.

We submitted reports to show that Kiranjit suffered from 'battered woman syndrome', a concept borrowed from the US which describes the inability of some women to leave an abusive relationship due to cycles of depression, despair and hopelessness. Counsel, Geoffrey Robertson QC tried to avoid truly medicalising the debate by arguing that, in Kiranjit's case, the jury could have applied their common sense understanding of domestic violence without the need for expert medical evidence. However, the court was only willing to entertain the notion of battering as a sufficiently permanent characteristic if supported by medical opinion in the form of psychiatric reports. Although the necessary medical evidence was lacking, the Court of Appeal was clearly willing in principle to recognise battered woman syndrome in the context of provocation.

But many of us in SBS were troubled by the implications of our arguments. The problem with the concept of battered woman syndrome is that it undermines the meaning of women's anger. It reinforces an image of women as passive victims rather than as survivors whose actions are rooted in the harsh realities of their everyday lives. What is more, contradictions within the concept abound. It cannot explain why it is that when a battered women kills, her action is ultimately one of survival. Battered woman syndrome sits uncomfortably within a defence which requires evidence not of depression or anxiety, but anger. Its interpretation as a permanent characteristic is equally problematic. Those of us who work with battered women are aware that once the violence disappears, more often than not, their personalities and characters change. Clearly, the battered woman is a social construct and not a medical one. Many of us feel that battered woman syndrome is yet another route by which the criminal justice system seeks to 'privatise' the phenomenon of domestic violence and so render women's actions and anger palatable to society. But, despite our discomfort, the need to free a wrongly jailed woman had to take precedence.

The second ground of appeal was the challenge to the subjective limb of the definition of provocation, specifically the requirement that the defendant experiences a sudden and temporary loss of self-control. Such a challenge had been mounted unsuccessfully exactly one year earlier by Anthony Gifford QC on behalf of Sara Thornton. The injustice of denying the defence on this ground is self-evident once the context in which the fatal actions take place is made clear. Many battered women cannot respond immediately, due to their size and strength, but above all, their fear of retaliation. What is more, the law of provocation is constructed on the basis of male experiences of conflict. In the course of our campaign we tried to show that anger can express itself in a variety of ways and that many battered women are likely to 'store up' their anger as the provocation in the form of abuse and violence escalates. Often that anger erupts when the assailant is asleep, inebriated or otherwise incapacitated.

For the first time, in Sara Thornton's case the concept of a 'slow-burn' reaction to acts and/or words of provocation entered legal debate. The Court of Appeal, however, concluded that Sara Thornton was a cold and calculating murderer. Her curious behaviour and appearance of outward calm following the killing of her husband did not fit the court's perception of a provoked woman. Sara did not fit the stereotype of a battered woman. She was outspoken, articulate and daring. Her protests, ranging from her hunger strike in 1992, through to her open defiance and contempt of authority, have all played a part in her continued incarceration.

The court in Kiranjit's case rejected this second ground of appeal. In the process, however, it made a significant concession to the feminist critique. Lord Taylor accepted the notion of a 'slow-burn' anger and declared that the time lapse between the act of provocation and the act of killing need not be construed as a cooling-off period as a matter of law. Instead, the matter should be left to the jury. This shift in judicial interpretation has rightly been hailed as a major change which defenders of battered women are encouraged to explore in future cases.

The third ground of appeal involved the use of medical evidence which pointed to the state of Kiranjit's mind at the time of the killing. Evidence of endogenous depression, indicating diminished responsibility, though available, had not been adduced at the trial. Fresh medical reports to show that she was depressed at the time of the killing were presented to the Court of Appeal. Unsurprisingly, it was this ground, which neither questioned previous decisions nor male power and authority, which secured Kiranjit's re-trial at the Old Bailey in September 1992. Mr Justice Hobhouse made it clear that he had only accepted her plea of manslaughter on the grounds of diminished responsibility and not provocation. She was sentenced to three years and four months' imprisonment, exactly the time she had already served. She was not required to undergo any form of medical treatment. She walked out of court a free woman.

RACING JUSTICE?

Although race was not a component of our legal challenge, in my view, the original trial judge made an error in relation to Kiranjit's background. In his summing up he said, 'the only characteristics which you specifically know that might be relevant are that she is an Asian woman, married incidentally to an Asian man ... You may think she is an educated woman. She has a University degree.' It is not too difficult to see that, in the judge's mind, her education and her Asian background stood as two polarised and mutually exclusive opposites. In this context, being Asian became synonymous with ignorance, passivity, compliance and submission. Whilst not forming a plank of her appeal, this compelled us to explain, in the form of a specialist report, the specific cultural context in which women like Kiranjit experience and negotiate their lives. We attempted to explain how culture does have a bearing in terms of the strategies available for Asian women to escape violence. But we had to tread a very narrow tightrope. Whilst not wanting to construct Asian culture as some monolithic and static phenomenon, problematic or pathological, we needed to spell out exactly how Asian women can be constrained by their families and communities.

Race and gender are entwined in such complicated ways, producing multicultural assumptions and notions which operate to the detriment of black and minority women, often strengthening both patriarchal and racial forms of domination. We cannot therefore afford to talk in terms of stereotypes. This last point is vital if we are to rethink legal concepts so that they reflect more accurately the reality of people's lives. Indeed, Kiranjit's powerful critique of her own specific circumstances, her culture, religion and her experiences of domestic violence gave the lie to the implicit assumptions about her 'Asian-ness' expressed by the original trial judge. The need to guard against race and gender stereotypes whilst working within the framework of the legal system proved to be our major preoccupation as case and campaign progressed.

Whilst the overriding priority has to be to do what is in the best interest of the individual client, a critical analysis of the content and direction of change is crucial if the law is to be divested of its patriarchal, race and class power. We have always been at pains to avoid stereotypes, but in Kiranjit's case, we did not wholly succeed. Perhaps inadvertently, we have reinforced stereotypes on both race and gender questions. The success of the campaign rested on the presentation of Kiranjit as a long-suffering battered Asian wife held back by the traditions and value system of her community. The powerful codes of honour and shame which bind and oppress women played no small part in the public image we were to construct. Also, Kiranjit's story drew on notions of a good wife and mother, a woman with no previous convictions, a construction which again rendered her less threatening to society.

CAMPAIGNING AND EMPOWERMENT

The campaign to release Kiranjit Ahluwalia had to lay bare the gendered assumptions of homicide laws and the legal structures through which women's powerlessness has been entrenched. But we realised that to focus solely on the legal issues would not be enough. The case could only succeed if we could create a climate in which social and political consciousness around the issues of domestic violence were sufficiently raised to enable the legal challenge to take place. Raising consciousness meant politicising the issue of battered women who kill. Our slogans, therefore, included the need for women to defend themselves against violence and oppression. 'Women's tradition, struggle not submission' and 'Domestic violence is a crime, self-defence is no offence' have since become the rallying cries of all feminists against domestic violence.

The failure of Sara Thornton's appeal forced us to recognise that the task of overturning Kiranjit's conviction would be even more difficult. And so we began the long journey, involving endless meetings with lawyers, students, women's groups, teachers, law centres, anti-racist groups, community activists, MPs and anyone who would hear us. The issue became one which was supported by politicians across the political spectrum. We formulated petitions, organised seminars, conferences, public meetings and benefits and supported others who wanted to do so on our behalf. With the help of women's sections up and down the country, we forced through resolutions committing the Labour Party to law reform. In the first six months, we organised regular pickets outside the Home Office denouncing the government's intransigence on the issue. We sang songs and shouted, whistled, banged drums and played musical instruments. We were noisy, loud and had fun.

Our main allies were radical feminists, in particular Justice for Women, countless Asian and other women's groups, including the Women's Institute. The alliance we forged had two main aims: to free battered women and to demand legal change. There were many divisions between us. Should we agitate for reform to existing law, campaign for entirely new laws, laws which were gender-specific, laws which take into account aggravated circumstances such as racial violence? At SBS we had to fight injustices faced by black communities as a whole at the same time as challenging gender, class and caste oppression from within. The experience has left us in no doubt that to elevate any one struggle at the expense of others is to lend tacit support to a variety of systems of oppression.

The campaign had a huge impact and for a while seemed to become a permanent feature in the media. To our surprise, even the tabloids featured articles that were both sensitive and supportive of battered women in jail. The *Daily Mirror* carried one of best articles on the issue that we have ever seen. It managed to convey difficult legal concepts in a language that was intelligent, sensitive and accessible. Yet the relationship of the Kiranjit campaign to the media was not always without its tensions and frustrations. The inherent racism of the media often betrayed itself. It was 'easier' to get a quote from Sara Thornton than from an Asian woman. Outside the courts, it was more acceptable to elicit a response from a white woman rather than from one of the many Asian women from refuges and centres.

Desperate for media coverage, we began to think like journalists, constantly preoccupied with how to utilise opportunities that arose, how to attract journalists with photo-opportunities and how to obtain more serious coverage of the issues in the papers. Although we wanted to ensure that the press did not simply portray the case as an 'Asian' one, out of desperation for pre-appeal coverage, we found ourselves having to focus increasingly on the Asian aspect of the case. But this meant that we lost an opportunity to address the Asian community and to document the changes and attitudes to women and to domestic violence within the Asian community.

White and black, young and old, activists and non-activists, we were involved in one of the most empowering mobilisations of women against domestic violence ever mounted. The women who use our centre and refuge wept and laughed with joy at Kiranjit's release. We came out of the Court of Appeal jubilant and victorious. Multicoloured bright balloons floated over the towers of the mighty institution and we felt as if we were floating with them. We felt powerful. Yet in the midst of our victory a journalist said, 'Surely the judgment represents a defeat for you?' I turned to the journalist and said, 'Look at the women and the public around you, look at their power, does this represent defeat to you?' The campaign enabled us to feel our own collective power. Our challenge was vital not only because of its outcome but also because the very act of struggle is transformatory in itself. In this campaign we redefined women's relationship to the criminal justice system, and, with it, the very notion of justice itself. Our struggles built upon past feminist struggles and will, we hope, affect all future struggles against male violence.

13
Feminist Perspectives on Law
Katherine de Gama

This chapter has two objectives: first, to provide a critical introduction to feminist perspectives on law; second, to flag and put into context key issues raised by other contributions in this section, specifically, sameness, difference and epistemological oppression (Gillian More), the denial of women's experience in criminal law (Pragna Patel), the relationship between legal and medical control of women's bodies (Sally Sheldon) and feminist issues in tort law (Joanne Conaghan). Central to all our pieces is the problematic nature of equality and rights discourses for feminist legal practice.

The law has always been an important focus for feminism, whether seen as a source of oppression or a strategy for reform. However, recently we have begun to liberate ourselves from ultimately fruitless discussions about the usefulness of law and instead are seeking to dismantle the dichotomy between theory and practice by exploring the way in which law constructs and reproduces sexual divisions (Smart, 1989). The dialectic between theory and practice will be the focus of the earlier contributions. Our chapters examine, instrumentally, the consequences of legal decisions and, symbolically, the strength of law as ideology, as a discourse which imposes a particular definition of reality on events, and which in doing so silences and disempowers. First, however, it is important to outline what is specific about feminism's perspective on and engagement with law.

THE CAMPAIGN FOR LEGAL EQUALITY

Early feminism was committed to legal reform. Law was accorded a high profile on the political agenda because it erected crude barriers to what women argued to be fundamental rights (Atkins and Hoggett, 1984; Banks, 1981; Strachey, 1978; Tong, 1992). Law defined and delineated separate and unequal roles, placing a woman under her husband's tutelage, like a child or a chattel. Under the doctrine of couverture, marriage united a woman and a man in the social body of the man, such that a woman's being and social identity were entirely subsumed within that of her husband. At common law a married women forfeited the right to hold property. She had no right to the custody of her children. Her husband, however, had far-reaching rights over the lives and bodies not only of his children but also his wife. He had the right to restrain and chastise her. If she left him, she could be forced to return to *his* house. Although women were able to sue for divorce from 1857, a husband's right to imprison a wife was not even questioned until 1891 (*R* v. *Jackson* (1891)). It was assumed that a husband had the right to punish a wife physically, as long as he used a stick no thicker than his thumb (Stetson, 1982).

Feminism attacked the oppressions enshrined in family law and also the discriminatory rules and practices which barred women from access to education, employment and the 'male' sphere of the market. In a series of cases brought before the courts between the 1860s and the 1930s, women went to law to claim equal treatment with men (see *Chorlton* v. *Ling* (1868); *R* v. *Harrald* (1872); *Jex Blake* v. *Senatus* (1873)). The issues were constructed in such a way that the question the courts had to ponder was not whether these women were equal to their male counterparts in terms of personal and educational qualification, but whether they were 'persons' in the eyes of the law (Sachs and Hoff Wilson, 1978; see also Mossman, 1986). The outcome of the 'persons cases', as they became known, was the legal construction of appropriate gender roles. The decisions, cursory and undisciplined, clearly expose two very powerful myths: first, the myth of judicial neutrality; second, the myth of male protectiveness. Blackstone, writing in 1765, claimed, 'the disabilities a woman lies under are for the most part intended for her protection and benefit, so great a favourite is the female sex in the laws of England' (Blackstone, 1765, p 445). But an analysis of the persons cases clearly suggests otherwise.

One of the least convincing declarations of chivalry is provided by Lord Neaves's judgment in *Jex Blake* v. *Senatus*. In the 1860s the University of Edinburgh achieved a dubious accolade. It was the first university to admit women students to its medical school and the first university to require them to withdraw. In 1869, seven women were admitted and, for reasons of decency and propriety, taught anatomy in separate classes. But still, their admission provoked uproar and civil disorder on such a scale that the university was persuaded to renege on its decision. First, it offered the women the opportunity to sit examinations only if they bound themselves to not demand their degrees. When they refused, the university terminated their classes. The women sought redress in the courts. The basic question, addressed by the Court of Session in Scotland, was whether women should be barred from public function by reason of their sex alone. The women argued that, if suitably qualified, they could not be excluded from public or professional life unless Parliament imposed disabilities on them in the clearest possible language. Male academics, professionals and administrators argued that women were inherently incapacitated and could only be relieved of their disabilities by the explicit command of Parliament.

The court, therefore, had to decide if women were equal or inferior, and whether they could properly be included within the term 'persons'. The judges chose to depict women alongside the insane and the insolvent, as too delicate to undertake public functions. But they insisted they were granting a privilege, not imposing a disability. It was in women's best interests to be excluded. In the words of Lord Neaves, 'there is little doubt that ... the want of feminine arts and attractions in a woman would be ill supplied by such branches of knowledge that a university could supply' (cited in Sachs and Hoff Wilson, 1978, p 18). Before the close of the century, in a different context, the House of Lords in *Allen* v. *Flood* (1898) stated discrimination to be lawful at common law, 'for the most mistaken, capricious, malicious or morally reprehensible motives'.

Today freedom of contract is mediated and to some extent fettered by notions of freedom from discrimination. In family law massive victories have been won on divorce, custody, property and violence. The crude obstacles to women's emancipation have been removed. It is, therefore, no longer self-evident why contemporary feminism should continue to engage with law. Yet, feminism in the twentieth century remains trapped in a potentially very dangerous liaison with law and liberalism.

THE MALE AGENDA

In the 1960s and 1970s feminism allied itself with liberalism (Tong, 1992, ch 1). Its focus was on assimilation or the elimination of difference. Its successes, instrumental and symbolic, were the Sex Discrimination Act 1975 and the Equal Pay Act 1970. The political aim was the opening up of the public sphere. But then came a rigorous and systematic critique of liberalism's assertion of a social distinction between public and private which has its counterpart in the sexual division of labour (see Gillian More in this collection). It was this discourse, which defined only the public sphere as appropriate for legal regulation, which informed and underpinned the legal subordination of women. Feminist theory identified the 'public/private divide' not as analytically discrete spheres capable of being sustained at the level of theory, but as itself a creature of the public. Public and private were understood not as separate but as interdependent and mutually reinforcing (Benn and Gaus, 1983; Elshtain, 1981; Thornton, 1991). In this context, law was identified as being of critical importance as a boundary definer. By its presence or absence it constitutes both public and private (O'Donovan, 1985). The achievement of 1970s feminism was to debunk and demystify the private. Ideas of privacy, constructed by legal decisions, preclude intervention in the family. Feminism, however, talked about the operation of power within the hitherto unquestioned paradigm of the family. Its slogan and rallying cry was 'the personal is political'. If this is true, then the private is public.

That the personal is the political is clear in the hearings surrounding the recent Minneapolis anti-pornography ordinance drafted by Andrea Dworkin and Catharine MacKinnon (Lacey, 1993). The ordinance defined pornography as the 'graphic, sexually explicit subordination of women through pictures and/or words' which either depict women as dehumanised objects, enjoying rape, incest or sexual assault or in postures of sexual submission or servility. Dworkin and MacKinnon sought to place a feminist perspective on pornography at the very centre of the legislation. Pornography was skilfully defined as sex discrimination because, first, it exploits, and second, it differentially damages women. In drafting the ordinance, necessarily and inevitably they placed one constitutional right, the right to free expression, against another, that of equal protection. The US Court of Appeals was therefore forced to come out and state publicly that what it acknowledged as a very problematic example of free expression was more important than women's rights to equal protection. But although instrumentally a 'failure', the hearings were of crucial importance in that they gave voice to women whose stories had been silenced. As such, the hearings constituted an official forum which, by claiming the personal to be political, thoroughly undermined the claimed dichotomy of public and private.

Feminism, from the mid 1970s, recognised that women's oppression is located in the private. Feminism celebrated sexual difference and claimed femininity as a source of value and strength. Its focus was on mothering, sexuality, women's experience, combined with a powerful critique of masculinity. The problem, however, with the 'woman-centred approach' is that, like liberalism, it assumes and celebrates the public/private divide. In the early 1980s Carol Gilligan published *In a Different Voice*, a thesis which went further in that it informed the notion that law is *male* (Gilligan, 1982). It inspired the beginnings of a new feminist jurisprudence, informed and underpinned by an ethic of care. Gilligan argues that women and men have different experiences of mothering which have implications for moral development. Women are expected to assume responsibility for the care of others, while men are encouraged to be autonomous individuals. Women subscribe to a caring conception of morality, while men subscribe to a rights-based conception of morality which defines fairness in terms of equality and objectivity.

The model of formal legal equality – rational, objective and procedurally correct – describes a male model of justice. As Catharine

MacKinnon argues, 'the state is male in the feminist sense. The law sees and treats women the way men see and treat women.' She continues, 'when the state is most ruthlessly neutral, it will be most male; when it is most sex blind, it will be most blind to the sex of the standard being applied' (MacKinnon, 1983, pp 644, 658). Feminism, however, seeks to distinguish the parochial from the universal. Equality, under this model, is not fairness. The liberal state is not autonomous of gender. The premiss of equality, that everyone should be treated the same, is blind to the public/private divide, constraining gendered stereotypes and the unequal distribution of power.

Defining equality as problematic, the 'sameness/difference debate' raged throughout the 1980s (see Gillian More, in this collection). Should feminism demand equal or special rights? (Bacchi, 1990; Williams, 1991). The key focus of the debate was pregnancy. The problem of seeking to accommodate women's reproductive capacities within the paradigms of equality or difference are seen in two cases. In *Turley* v. *Allders Department Store* (1980) the Employment Appeal Tribunal denied a pregnant woman's claim of sex discrimination because, under legislation based on individual comparisons, she could not, of course, find a pregnant man to compare herself with. However, on similar facts, in *Hayes* v. *Malleable Working Men's Club* (1984) the Employment Appeal Tribunal stated that pregnancy was a temporary ailment and that a pregnant woman could compare herself with a sick man. So, in order to establish that difference is sameness, the courts in the UK either deny women a remedy or resurrect anachronistic, damaging stereotypes. More recently, the same reasoning was applied by the Court of Appeal in *Webb* v. *EMO Cargo* (1992). However, on appeal to the European Court of Justice, dismissal for pregnancy was held to be sex discrimination without drawing on arguments of sameness and difference. Long before this tentative retreat, feminism recognised the debate as fruitless and circular. It was assumed, first, that either sameness or difference should be the chosen strategy and, second, that the two strategies remain mutually exclusive.

Both arguments fail to question the Aristotelian paradigm of equality, which maintains that, 'things that are alike should be treated as alike, while things that are unalike should be treated as unalike in proportion to their unalikeness' (Aristotle, 1925, pp 1131). Therefore, if similarly situated people are treated differently they are discriminated against. But both the sameness and difference strategies measure women against a male referent or comparator. 'Sameness' offers remedies to women whose biographies approximate to male biographies. The difference argument gives resonance to stereotypes of women as weak and in need of protection. But politically the pitfalls are more immediately dangerous in issues not of pregnancy but custody. The 'men's movement' seeks to use the principle of equality to deny women's claim to children by asserting that women are 'having it both ways', demanding equal rights in the public sphere and special, preferential rights in the private. But this is merely an artefact of the narrow constraints within which the debate has been constructed. It is male agendas which have determined the parameters of the debate. But given that joint custody, the focus of the fathers' rights lobby, offers no guarantee of parental care and responsibility, a gender-neutral approach, premissed on the assumption that equality is possible through assimilation to a male standard, is clearly inappropriate. This is because it ignores the massive advantages which accrue to men from the current sexual division of labour.

The way out of the impasse of liberalism was suggested by MacKinnon, who argued that feminist issues should not be framed in terms of sameness and difference and 'equal rights'. Feminist issues are more appropriately framed in terms of hierarchy and power (MacKinnon, 1987, ch 2; 1989, ch 12). Equality, therefore, was problematised. What is important about MacKinnon's work is that it offers a praxis – a theory, based on women's experience, from which action flows (MacKinnon, 1983a, 1987, 1989). However, her work has been subjected to a vigorous race, class and lesbian critique (Cain, 1991; Crenshaw, 1991; Williams, 1991). Feminism today speaks of epistemological oppression. It is crucial to ensure that white, middle-class, heterosexual feminism does not silence in the same way as orthodox legal discourse.

EQUALITY, NEUTRALITY AND UNIVERSALISM?

When speaking of epistemological oppression, feminism questions law's claim to 'truth', in the sense of an ungendered, objective pursuit of it. It challenges law's shiny ideological claims to equality, neutrality and universalism. Law's emphasis on rules, rights and their enforcement fosters and privileges a historically and culturally specific form of ordering the world. Rights discourse, law's legitimating ideology, speaks of an individualising and competitive system of values in which connectedness and community are systematically effaced. Law imposes a detached, mechanistic view of the world. Law is of crucial importance to feminism because it is an instrument to silence and disempower. By denying the experience of the subject it denies – even degrades and distorts – women's experience.

Examples abound, but the most vivid are from criminal law. The most interesting are found in the areas of provocation, diminished responsibility and rape. In provocation, law embraces male charac-terisations of appropriate male and female responses. The defence is based on the curious notion of the reasonable *man*. Under the Homicide Act 1957, s 3 provocation operates as a partial defence, reducing murder to manslaughter and thereby opening up discretion in sentencing. The classic direction is from *R* v. *Duffy* (1949). Here, Lord Devlin defines provocation as

> some act or series of acts, done by the dead man to the accused, which would cause any reasonable man, and actually causes in the accused a sudden and temporary loss of self-control, rendering the accused so subject to passion as to make him or her for the moment not master of his mind.

R v. *Camplin* ([1978] AC 705) decided that s 3, which includes words as well as acts, abolished all common law rules. Lord Diplock held that the reasonable man was no longer a legal abstraction found in *R* v. *Lesbini* (1914) or *R* v. *Bedder* (1954). Instead, he is endowed with the power of self-control to be expected of someone with the relevant physical, social and psychological characteristics of the accused, excluding, following *R* v. *Newell* (1980), drunkenness and excitability.

R v. *Imbrams* ((1981) 74 Cr App R 154) and, more recently, *R* v. *Thornton* (1992), reaffirmed *Duffy*'s requirement that there should be a sudden and temporary loss of self-control. The jury, now, must take into consideration the nature of the provocation, the defendant's sensitivity and the time lapse between the provocation and the response. However, as yet there are no cases on whether a reasonable woman is to be construed to be the same person as a reasonable man. But, in *R* v. *Ahluwalia* (1992), the Court of Appeal accepted, *obiter*, the concept of 'battered woman syndrome', a psychiatric construct premised on the assumption that women who experience domestic violence become victims, paralysed by depression and despair. Provocation and diminished responsibility are conflated, and therein, the authenticity of their actions as women who kill denied (O'Donovan, 1993).

What is more, as a legal category provocation is arbitrary and open-ended. Outcomes are determined by assumptions and expectations which are gendered. There is an incongruity between women's experience and the legal version of reality. Typically, women who kill are victims of physical and sexual abuse who act in order to protect themselves. But domestic violence is rarely explored in the courtroom in such a way as to convince a jury of the practical and emotional problems of leaving a violent relationship (O'Donovan, 1991; see Pragna Patel in this collection). Instead, the actions of women who kill are constructed as cold-blooded and calculated. Women's and men's experiences are unevenly represented in law. Moreover, as words alone may constitute provocation subjective evaluations of appropriate response have extraordinary power. For example, men have successfully pleaded provocation having killed nagging and unfaithful wives (Rajinder Bisla, 1992; Asher, 1981; Wright, 1975). From Blackstone it has always been a far greater offence for a woman to kill a man than a man to kill a woman. To kill a wife in the act of adultery is 'the lowest degree of manslaughter ... there could not be a greater provocation' (Blackstone, 1765).

Women who kill may seek to avoid the stigma of conviction for murder and a mandatory life sentence by pleading either provocation or diminished responsibility. However, it is likely that discretion in sentencing will be differentially exercised. Provocation claims a greater 'legitimacy' than diminished responsibility in that, although the outcome remains punitive, implicit in the structure of the defence is the assumption that the actions of the accused have meaning and authenticity. Yet the courts are happy to accept an image of us as mad, bad and pre-menstrual (Edwards, 1988). Sandie Craddock (who later re-offended in the name of Smith), Christine English and, more recently, Ann Reynolds committed horrifying acts, yet successfully claimed diminished responsibility and, in the language of the tabloids, 'walked free' from the courtroom because of pre-menstrual syndrome (PMS) (*The Times*, 4–26 November 1981; *New Law Journal*, July 1988, p 456). There is no consensus in the medical profession as to whether PMS, as a condition capable of generating violence of the kind perpetrated in these cases, actually exists (Dalton, 1991). Yet it is accepted uncritically by the courts. As a medical construct it is an assertion of age-old myths about the pathology of female biology, the notion that women are at the mercy of raging hormones. This biological reductionism reinforces a notion of us as physically, intellectually and emotionally inferior to men.

Rape, however, is an example of the way law treats women as victims. The myths which inform the substantive and procedural norms of the courtroom are premised on the assumption that women bear the responsibility for the actions of men. By implication, they reinforce the notion of the pathology of the 'real' rapist, diverting attention from the relationship between rape and culturally approved forms of behaviour (Box, 1983). Brownmiller, however, rejects any notion of 'uncontrollable passions', denying that rape is a sexual act which can be attributed to the lustful excesses of individual men and thereby depoliticised. Instead, she ascribes to rape a universal social function. It is 'nothing more than a conscious process of intimidation by which all men keep all women in a state of fear' (Brownmiller, 1975, p 15). Her thesis is supported by legal doctrine. Although statutory provisions have emerged for the protection of the victim, procedural rules, informed by dichotomised notions of sexuality, have been instituted to protect the defendant. Legal principle and juridical practice have assimilated prevailing constructs of heterosexuality premised on the activity of men and the passivity of women. Certainly, the sexual typifications which inform the assumptions and practices of the courtroom reflect polarised images of women as good/bad, chaste/ unchaste, virgin/whore. Law denies and distorts women's voices (Smart, 1989, pp 26–50). The test for recklessness in rape is subjective: *R* v. *Caldwell* (1982) is spuriously distinguished by the claim that recklessness in rape relates not to consequences but to circumstances. Not surprisingly, the acquittal rate is higher than for any other offence.

FEMINISM AND LAW TODAY

It is difficult to speak about where feminism is today because of the rich plurality of its vision. However, tentatively, the focus now appears to have shifted to rights. Rights discourse is the common sense of liberal legalism. The questions we are now asking are about whether we should pursue rights or whether rights merely silence and disempower (Herman, 1993; Hunt, 1990; Kingdom, 1991; Smart, 1989; Schneider, 1991). The limits of rights discourse are self-evident. But, as the common sense of liberal legalism, rights do at least provide us with a forum for resistance. As objective or as rhetoric, rights offer us an opportunity to debate and engage with many agendas. But as Eisenstein points out, we need also to subvert these agendas. The goal for women, she argues,

> should by no means be to learn to act like, think like, and adopt the values of men and the male-dominant culture. [Instead] concepts such as autonomy, power, authenticity, self-determination – all these should be re-examined and redefined by women. (Eisenstein, 1984, pp 66–8)

What is foremost on *our* agenda, as academics, practitioners and campaigners, is the need to create a feminist jurisprudence which gives voice not to ungendered, abstract rights but to real lived experience.

Part Four

Environment

14
An Idiomatic Discussion of Environmental Legislation
David Wilkinson

Are you acquainted with environmental law can't fail to be impressed by its dramatic expansion in the twentieth century. It is now upon us at every turn. Open any textbook on the subject and it is immediately apparent that what is commonly thought of as a "niche" activity compares a vast body of legislation.

Another, the more interesting issue, which an overview of this area of statutory regulation might attempt to address, are, first, the reasons why environmental law has expanded so rapidly in the twentieth century and, secondly, its possible implications. However, that will be done. The overriding objective of critical legal study is to get back to reveal of orthodoxy, unmasking the analysis of the deeper continuities and tensions of areas of law otherwise taken for granted, as Gordon puts it, to deliver "thickly described accounts of how law has been embodied in and has worked to structure the most routine practices of life (Gordon, 1984, p. 125).

There is not one canonical approach to critical legal theory. In this chapter, I will address these questions within two idioms – an idiom being neither as complete nor as constraining as a "theory", but rather a way of talking about, hence understanding, a thing or a process (Wale, 1992, p. 36) – the rational choice idiom, which I will represent here by interest group theory, and the structuralist idiom, which will be represented by Marxist theory.

THE RATIONAL CHOICE IDIOM

THE RATIONAL CHOICE IDIOM

The distinguishing feature of the rational choice idiom is that societal decisions are viewed as the outcome of rational choices made by individuals. More specifically, legislation is said to be a product of pressure brought to bear by self-interested individuals on self-interested politicians. Public attention focuses from time to time on environmental events, an intensification which often coincides with extensive media coverage (Chloe 1993, p. 27). Public attention magnifies environmental events in the public perception, attracting further media attention, and

161

14
An Idiomatic Discussion of Environmental Legislation
David Wilkinson

No one acquainted with environmental law can fail to be impressed by its dramatic expansion in the twentieth century. It is now upon us at every turn. Open any textbook on the subject and it is immediately apparent that what is commonly thought of as a 'niche' actually comprises a vast body of legislation.

Amongst the more interesting issues which an overview of this area of statutory regulation might attempt to address are, first, the reasons why environmental law has expanded so rapidly in the twentieth century and, secondly, its possible 'hidden' functions. How should this be done? The overriding objective of critical legal study is to 'peel back' the veneer of orthodoxy, enabling fresh analysis of the deeper constructs and functions of areas of law otherwise taken for granted: as Gordon puts it, 'to deliver ... thickly described accounts of how law has been imbricated in and has helped to structure the most routine practices of life' (Gordon, 1984, p 125).

As there is no one canonical approach to critical legal theory, in this chapter I will address these questions within two idioms – an idiom being neither as complete nor as constrained as a 'theory' but, rather, a way of talking about, hence understanding, a thing or a process (Weale, 1992, p 38) – the rational choice idiom, which will be represented here by interest group theory, and the structural idiom, which will be represented by Marxist theory.

THE RATIONAL CHOICE IDIOM

The distinguishing feature of the rational choice idiom is that societal decisions are viewed as the outcome of rational choices made by individuals. More specifically, legislation is said to be a product of pressure brought to bear by self-interested individuals on self-interested politicians. Public attention focuses from time to time on environmental events, an intensification which often coincides with extensive media coverage (Enloe, 1975, p 271). Public attention magnifies environmental events in the public perception, attracting further media attention, and transforming them into environmental issues (Ibid, pp 11–46). Politicians then come under significant pressure to legislate because, whatever other interests they may have, they are undoubtedly motivated by the desire for re-election. As Downs observed: 'Parties formulate policies in order win elections rather than win elections in order to formulate policies' (Downs, 1957, p 28). This seems to have occurred. The Clean Air Act 1956, for example, followed directly from the 'Killer Smog' of 1952 and the Deposit of Poisonous Wastes Act 1972 followed extended media coverage of the hazards to young children of playing on land where dangerous waste had been tipped in the Midlands.

The difficulty with the rational choice idiom at this level of generality is that it provides insufficient detail concerning the actual mechanism by which legislators are influenced. This deficit is remedied, in part, by interest group theory. According to interest group theory the lobbying of organised groups is the major source of pressure on politicians. In the context of environmental legislation the two key lobbying groups are environmentalists and industrialists.

Environmentalists
Environmentalists have always strongly promoted their own interests in democratic political systems. Yet accounting for environmental legislation as a response to pressure from environmentalists creates some apparent theoretical difficulties, especially if we accept the assumption of interest group theory that only *collective* action is likely to have a strong effect on legislative activity. The problem lies in Mancur Olson's observation that rational individuals will not, of their own accord, work towards the collective good. According to Olson, collective action is unlikely to occur unless the group can offer 'selective' incentives – incentives which apply exclusively to group members (Olson, 1971, p 34). According to Farber, a group that offers benefits to non-members provides rational individuals with no incentive to join: the well known 'free-rider' problem. Farber concludes:

> [t]he Olson paradigm appears to have a straightforward implication for environmental legislation: there should not be any. For example, air pollution legislation benefits millions of people by providing them with clean air; it also imposes heavy costs on concentrated groups of firms. The theory predicts that the firms will organize much more effectively than the individuals, and will thereby block the legislation. (Farber, 1992, p 60)

The rest of this section takes issue with Farber's analysis on the ground that it overlooks a number of factors. The first problem with the Olson paradigm is that, as Olson himself admitted, it works poorly for philanthropic groups (Berry, 1984, p 72). Altruistic environmentalists are unlikely to be thwarted by free-rider problems since they are unlikely to object to others obtaining a benefit from their activities. Indeed empirical research shows that many members of environmental interest groups (EIGs) join precisely because the activities of the group contribute towards making the world a better place for the current and future generations (Lowe and Goyder, 1983, p 39). Free-riding is, ironically, one of the main benefits (not drawbacks) for the altruistic environmentalist. For the non-altruistic environmentalist, EIG membership provides many selective benefits: information which facilitates individual lobbying opportunities; 'a source of meaning and identity' (Eyerman and Jamison, 1989, p 102); a rosy 'saving the world' glow; and more tangible goods such as newsletters, reports and purchasing opportunities.

Not only are individual environmentalists likely to organise collectively into EIGs, but EIGs are, in turn, likely to organise collectively into 'super-EIGs'. Individual EIGs suffer from the disadvantage of representing relatively narrow interests and run the risk of pulling in opposite political directions. Super-EIGs present a common face on potentially divisive issues, thereby multiplying member EIGs' political credibility. Super-EIGs which have been effective at the UK and EC level in influencing legislative outcomes include the Central (later British) Correlating Committee, the Council for Preservation (later Protection) of Rural England, the Council for Nature, the Council for Environmental Conservation or CoEnCo, Wildlife Link and the European Environment Bureau (EEB) (Evans, 1992; Lowe and Goyder, 1983, pp 163–76). The EEB has been particularly important in providing a pan-European grouping for hundreds of affiliated EIGs to lobby EC institutions (Kramer, 1991, p 130; Mazey and Richardson, 1992, p 95).

A substantial literature testifies to the influence of EIGs and super-EIGs in promoting environmental law at all levels (see for example Evans, 1992; Bramble and Porter, 1992; Prince and Finger, 1994; Stair and Taylor, 1992). The legitimate interest of EIGs in the policy arena is now widely recognised: the Bruntland Report, for instance, recommended that governments establish official consultation with EIGs to share information, strategies and resources and participate in all aspects of environmental matters (World Commission on Environment and Development, 1987, p 213); a recommendation now enshrined in Principle 10 of the Rio Declaration on Environment and Development.[1] Interest group theory reminds us that, whatever other factors may be at play, it is important not to underestimate the influence of EIGs in determining legislative outcomes.

Industrialists

The industrial lobby is clearly a powerful determinant of government policy. According to Farber, environmental statutes impose heavy costs on industry and should, therefore, be universally and successfully resisted; a conclusion which he uses as the *reductio ad absurdum* of interest group theory. I suggest, on the contrary, that interest group theory can help to explain industrial acquiescence in environmental law if modified to take account of the fact that industry will not always (i) be able to or (ii) desire to block proposed environmental legislation.

Industry's ability *to resist legislation*
There are a number of reasons to believe that industry will often be less than fully able to resist environmental law. In any industrial organisation there is likely to be an incomplete match between employees' personal interests and the interests of the employing organisation. Environmental legislation that runs counter to the interests of an organisation as a whole may further the status of employees within departments responsible for such matters. It may also satisfy the personal preferences of a substantial number of employees, including managers, for high levels of environmental quality. Employees, even those in influential management positions, may therefore lack the necessary reactive motivation.

'Bounded rationality theory' (Simon, 1975, pp 79–83) also predicts significant limitations in the ability of industrial organisations to respond to proposed environmental legislation. The impossibility of obtaining full information about the likely costs of proposed statutes; the cost and time required for assessing corporate response strategy; and the problems of mobilising reaction – each of these factors reduces the effectiveness of even genuinely concerned companies. This factor is exacerbated by the 'anarchy of capital': industrial sectors are fragmented and competitive (Alford and Friedland, 1985, p 283) and thus may be either unable to respond with the degree of coherence attained by comparatively cooperative EIGs or unwilling to do so in view of potential market advantages to be obtained by legislation which impacts differentially.

Industry's will *to resist legislation*
In some cases industry may actually welcome proposed environmental legislation. In his seminal theory of regulation, Stigler proposed that much regulation arises in response to demand (not resistance) from industry for government-supplied benefits (Stigler, 1971). These benefits are said to include financial subsidies and control over the entry of rival competitors to the market. The Stiglerian view would be that, in these respects, environmental law is no different from other regulation.

Consistent with the Stiglerian hypothesis we find that much conservation legislation revolves around subsidies. A case in point is the regime providing for Sites of Special Scientific Interest (SSSI), contained in the Wildlife and Countryside Act 1981. Payments may be made to landowners under the 1983 Financial Guidelines for Management Agreements (made under s 50 of the 1981 Act) on the basis of 'profit foregone'. The availability of these payments encourages some site owners to make bogus claims that they intend to carry out damaging operations (House of Commons Committee of Public Accounts, 1994, pp 6–8). Some SSSI are bought and sold on the strength of management agreement payments (Pearce, 1993, p 36).

Most environmental laws provide indirect 'subsidies' from the creation of markets for new goods and services: after all, one firm's costs are another firm's profits:

> this regulatory thicket translates into both more investment in environmental technologies and more jobs and profit for the environment industry ... The challenge no longer lies in finding a lucrative seam to exploit but in ensuring that British companies win significant shares of the spoils on offer. (Wilkes, 1995, p 9)

Pollution controls, especially those concerned with the production of waste, stimulate markets by providing incentives for manufacturers to find economic uses for by-products. For example when North British Distilleries were prevented from continuing discharges to their local river they discovered that, dried, it could be sold as cattle-feed. Similarly, British Steel was able to recover a considerable proportion of the £25 million spent on compliance costs at their various works by sale of the resulting iron oxide dust (Clapp, 1994, pp 219–37).

The thesis that environmental legislation is partially explicable in terms of economic benefits for industry extends to EC Directives. Once an industry is subject to national environmental controls which impose *true costs* it will be motivated to press for harmonisation of controls across the Community to achieve the benefit of a level playing-field. The EC Commission is generally in favour of harmonising cost burdens on competitors and, indeed, has argued before the European Court of Justice that harmonisation is the 'principal objective' of much EC environmental legislation.[2] Once the Community has legislated in an area, exclusive competence in external agreements relating to the same subject-matter passes to the Community, and member states' competence to promulgate domestic controls is limited to certain measures that are more restrictive than the Directive or Regulation in question.[3] This has the effect of constantly shifting power to Community institutions.

Consistent with Stigler's theory, there are also examples of environmental legislation which control market entry. This is true, for instance, for regulations which require the application of specific anti-pollution technology. Tucker, for instance, alleges that the American Environmental Protection Agency's decision in the 1970s to specify catalytic converters as the solution to vehicle exhaust pollution had as much to do with 'locking out' Japanese competition from the 'stratified-charge' engine as it had to do with environmental protection (Tucker, 1980, p 149). Market entry barriers are created by most pollution legislation since these usually require substantial investment by new operators. The regime of integrated pollution control that applies under the Environmental Protection Act 1990 illustrates the point well. Her Majesty's Inspectorate of Pollution (HMIP) have interpreted the legislative term 'Best Available Techniques Not Entailing Excessive Cost (BATNEEC)' in a way that penalises new businesses. According to HMIP, improvements to existing plants may be made gradually, and in line with the profitability of the individual plant, considerations that will not be taken into account when considering whether new planned operations meet the BATNEEC standard. Similarly, the need for new waste management operators to provide financial securities (Environmental Protection Act 1990, s 74) provides a market obstacle to smaller operators. Legislation imposing expensive 'best technology' solutions on market entrants will, therefore, tend to be supported by the larger, more vocal (hence politically effective) industrial organisations. As we have seen, the benefits that flow from the supply of goods and services lead to the conclusion that *net* costs of environmental legislation are never as bad as they seem: 'According to the calculations of the American Council of Environmental Quality at least a million dollars is pocketed in the course of the elimination of three million dollars worth of damage to the environment' (Enzenberger, 1974).

Industrialists may not be strongly motivated to resist environmental legislation where they think that there is an opportunity to pass these costs on to consumers. The advantages of 'cost pass-through' have long been evident to manufacturers. Over a hundred years ago, the manufacturing chemist James Napier actively proposed banning all discharges of manufacturing waste into rivers on the grounds that:

> If the Prohibition were made general and imperative, manufacturers would find other ways to prevent it, the cost of so doing being put upon the manufactured article and the public (the parties benefited eventually) would have to pay. (Royal Commission on Pollution of Rivers, 1872, p 153)

Howarth, for instance, suggests that criminal fines imposed on corporate water polluters have no real impact since they are simply passed on to customers through infinitesimally small price increases (Howarth, 1994, p 32). The state may assist by engineering the regulatory framework such that the public have no choice but to pay. For instance, the capital investment required for the improvement of sewerage treatment works to meet EC environmental quality standards is passed on to water consumers directly as a component of water charges levied under the Water Resources Act 1991.

The remaining real costs of environmental legislation can be softened by the use of framework legislation which allows public demand for action on environmental issues to be satisfied quickly whilst leaving the precise course of action open to later manipulation. Legislating for a general framework only, leaves detailed matters to be added at a later stage by statutory instruments, agency standards or, worse still, non-statutory unchallengeable codes of practice (McAuslan, 1980, p 42), a strategy described by Farber as 'strike while the iron is cold' (Farber, 1992, p 68). Costs can be further reduced by phasing in legislative changes gradually through the extensive use of Commencement Orders. The much criticised implementation of the Control of Pollution Act 1974, for instance, was notoriously slow (Evans, 1992, p 156). Sometimes legislative measures are eventually abandoned entirely (for example, local authority registers of contaminative uses of land provided for by s 143 Environmental Protection Act 1990) giving rise to charges of 'optional legislation'.

The existence of tough-sounding legislation means little if regulators fail to set standards. The Statutory Water Quality Objectives provided for by the Water Resources Act 1991 lie virtually unused due to the (political) decision not to increase water charges more than absolutely necessary to meet EC water quality requirements. Industry is also unlikely to care much about proposed legislation if it is likely that standards will be set at such low levels that little environmental improvement (hence cost) will be involved. During a period beginning around 1977 water authorities' discharge standards were actually relaxed on a wholesale basis in order to artificially improve water authorities' compliance with the provisions of the Control of Pollution Act 1974 (Kinnersley, 1988, p 121). Similarly Jordan has doubted whether the requirement to apply BATNEEC under the Environmental Protection Act 1990 constitutes a real change from, or imposes any heavier cost burden than, the requirement to use Best Practicable means contained in previous environmental acts (Jordan, 1993, pp 416–18). Unfortunately weak discharge or emission standards merely serve to legalise, hence legitimate, continuing pollution.

Finally, industry may not wish to resist environmental legislation that is unlikely to be effectively enforced. Enforcement of environmental legislation is a notorious problem at all levels. International environmental law often suffers from the complete absence of any realistic enforcement mechanism; the EC is hamstrung by the Commission's lack of a direct policing role; and UK regulatory agencies suffer from a lack of resources (Ball and Bell, 1995, p 131) and an insidious 'conciliatory culture' in which prosecution for non-compliance is always a 'last resort' (Hawkins, 1984, pp 191–207; Scarrow, 1972). It is interesting to note that, despite much posturing as a 'tough' agency, the National Rivers Authority still prosecutes less than 1 per cent of reported pollution incidents (NRA, 1993, p 49). Even when enforcement does result in prosecution, fines have usually been an inadequate deterrent (Britain, 1984) since, except for the notable £1 million fine levied on Shell Oil for polluting the Mersey estuary, courts are still reluctant to impose fines commensurate with corporate offenders' ability to pay (Howarth, 1994, p 31).

The above discussion demonstrates that interest group theory is not, after all, in conflict with the existence of environmental legislation. Industry will not always be able or willing to block environmental legislation; indeed, it may often welcome the benefits which it brings. The supposed costs of environmental protection are usually exaggerated and are, in any case, mitigated by a variety of factors. Add to this the considerable influence of EIGs, and interest group theory begins to look much more useful in accounting for the rapid expansion of environmental legislation in recent years.

THE STRUCTURAL IDIOM

The rational choice idiom attends to individuals as the determinants of policy and legislative outcomes. At the other end of the theoretical spectrum is a body of theory which relates legislative outcomes to the underlying structure of the social system in which law is embedded. Marxist theory – the classical structural theory – considers legislation, indeed all law, to be a product of the prevailing mode of production. On this basis it is reasonable to explore the possibility that the capitalist mode of production produces environmental legislation that (i) ensures the availability of labour; (ii) protects increasingly technological modes of production; (iii) creates or encourages new markets to replace those destroyed by saturated demand; (iv) entrenches the values of nature exploitation; and (v) serves to legitimate capitalism through ideology.

Marxism and the Supply of Labour

One view is that early environmental laws, such as sanitary laws, although ostensibly designed to ameliorate the squalor of Victorian towns (Engels, 1892), were in truth a product of capital's need for a fit, healthy and peaceful working population. Environmental controls enhanced workers' productivity and lengthened their lives, thereby increasing the influence of older workers who were less prone to running in mobs and taking part in trade union activities (Ridgeway, 1971, p 25). Others have suggested that planning and development controls derived from capitalist objectives of providing a stable population of labourers, in relatively sanitary conditions, close to the factory site (Tarn, 1980) and preventing the gathering of large masses of the 'dangerous classes' (Hall, 1988, p 24).

Modern environmental law has not relinquished its function of maintaining a supply of labour. First, given increased scientific knowledge about the aetiology of disease and the damaging effects of chemicals, environmental standards are seen as necessary to protect the workforce from unacceptable risks and reduce the costs of environmental injury litigation. Secondly, the benefit of bringing employment opportunities to an economically disadvantaged area is often used to outweigh environmental considerations in planning decisions. Thus the maintenance of labour supports the accumulation of capital in the face of environmental risks.

Environmental Legislation and the Mode of Production

According to Marx, labour is the basis of profit; for profit derives from *surplus* labour. Surplus labour allows, and indeed is necessary for, the accumulation of capital. Gradually capital shifts from circulating capital (raw materials and finished products) to fixed capital (that is, machines), thereby constantly increasing the rate at which natural resources are used up and progressively concentrating capital into the hands of fewer capitalists (Marx, 1993, pp 704–15).

These three key aspects of the Marxist theory of production (mechanisation, monopolisation, and increased use of natural resources) are all, to some degree, reflected in environmental law. Pollution controls lead to further technologisation, preferably automation, and only rarely point back down the path to traditional labour-intensive patterns of operation. As already noted, the need for huge investment in new anti-pollution technologies adds to the gradual exclusion of small operators. Pollution legislation rarely restricts the input of natural materials into the manufacturing process: so long as pollution is constrained to acceptable limits, the exhaustion of the world's non-renewable natural resources continues to be characterised as a purely economic problem to be dealt with by price sensitivity to the supply/demand differential. Even international legislation that seeks to conserve renewable resources (such as fish stocks) is in many cases motivated more by the desire to obtain the 'maximum sustainable yield' and to promote 'optimum utilisation' than to achieve *environmentally* optimum resource levels.

Environmental Legislation and the Creation of Demand

Environmental legislation may be further identified as part of the mechanism to alleviate a contradiction inherent in the capitalist mode of production, namely that technological progress allows productive capacity to rise faster than consumptive capacity. Capital has two solutions to this dilemma. The first is to restrict production in order to maintain high profit levels. Andresen, for example, argues that the International Convention on the Regulation of Whaling 1946 was introduced in order to restrain the overproduction of whale oil (Andresen, 1993, p 109). The second solution is to facilitate increased consumption. This requires

> Firstly, quantitative expansion of existing consumption; secondly: creation of new needs by propagating existing ones in a wide circle; thirdly: production of new needs and discovery and creation of new use values ... a new, qualitatively different branch of production must be created, which satisfies and brings forth a new need. (Marx, 1993, pp 408–9)

Through the manipulation of the media and advertising, 'false' needs for new products and technology are stimulated (Marcuse, 1969 and 1972). Ironically, these new technologies and products, rather than the underlying mode of production, are then blamed for the bulk of the world's environmental problems (Commoner, 1989; Schumacher, 1974). When over-consumption reaches an overt stage, and is perceived as such, industry attempts to assuage public guilt by redirecting (but not reducing) purchases towards 'green products'. This whole process – stimulation, production and redirection – is made under the fragile cover of dubious claims concerning environmental *advantages* of the new products and technologies in question (Holder, 1991). Green consumerism maintains damaging economic activities.

Far from seeking to conceal the fact that environmental law is part of the machinery for sustaining economic expansion, the recently emerged ideology of 'ecological modernism' boldly posits a *necessary* relationship between environmental protection and economic growth (Weale and Williams, 1993, p 47). This relationship is evident in 'sustainable development', the fundamental tenet of environmental law.

There is little agreement about what sustainable development means or should mean. The Bruntland Report unhelpfully defined it as 'development that meets the needs of the present without compromising the ability of future generations to meet their own needs' (World Commission on Environment and Development, 1987). The UK government have not progressed much further in elaborating the definition. According to Tromans, they 'don't yet know what [they] want to say, but hope something will come to [them]' (Tromans, 1995, p 796). This ambiguity obscures fundamental disagreement about what, precisely, is to be regarded as sustainable. For the environmentalist it is the global ecosystem, or some subsystem thereof whilst, for the capitalist, it is development (that is, economic growth) itself: a system which must be maintained in the face of radical claims to alter society. Thus Pallaemerts has complained that, '"sustainable development" has become synonymous with "sustainable growth", not only in Europe, but throughout the world and, eventually, may very well end up meaning little more than sustain*ed* growth' (Pallaemerts, 1993). And, as Conaghan and Mansell note,

> Thus, so far as 'sustainable development' reflects the dominant paradigm of exploitation rather than harmony, it is arguably of little value in the struggle to save our planet. The environment in which we live should not be seen as 'capital' which we are free to dispose of or trade off as economists suggest. (Conaghan and Mansell 1993, p 126)

Legitimating Nature Exploitation and the Denial of Environmental Value

One view of environmental legislation is that it serves capital indirectly by legitimating nature exploitation. The capitalist mode of production requires 'exploration of all of nature in order to discover new, useful qualities in things; universal exchange of the products of all alien climates and lands; new (artificial) preparations of natural objects, by which they are given new use values' (Marx, 1993, p 409). This scientific mission embodies now familiar attitudes:

> [it creates] a system of general exploitation of the natural and human qualities, a system of general utility, utilising science for itself just as much as all the physical and mental qualities, while there appears nothing *higher in itself*, nothing legitimate for itself, outside this circle of production and exchange ... for the first time, nature becomes purely an object for humankind, purely a matter of utility; ceases to be recognised as a power for itself; and the theoretical discovery of its autonomous laws appears merely as a ruse so as to subjugate it under human needs, whether as an object of consumption or as a means of production. (Marx, 1993, p 410)

It is significant that this instrumental view of nature is completely antithetical to the views of many environmentalists and environmental philosophers, who suggest that nature has inherent worth (Taylor, 1986, pp 59–98). Capitalism converts natural objects into mere commodities which exist only as exchange values (Collier, 1994). Environmental law assists this process in many ways, not least by limiting environmental protection to that which is justifiable on cost–benefit analysis (CBA), by which means the environment is reduced to a non-recognisable monetary form. When cost–benefit analysis is explicitly applied to the environment – as in the Roskill Report on the proposed Third London Airport – it tends to arouse widespread indignation because it is seen as an inappropriate way of dealing with what are essentially non-quantifiable values (Kirby, 1982, p 105). Attempts to rectify the inherent bias of CBA towards monetisable values have themselves been criticised as superficial; designed more to legitimate government policy and marginalise all but moderate views (McAuslan, 1980, pp 68–9). There are forceful arguments that environmental values should be decided by open ethical debate rather than economic willingness-to-pay (Sagoff, 1988, pp 24–49). Real value is in the environment itself, not in figures on an accountant's balance sheet.

Environmental Legislation and Ideology

If law served explicitly to further the interests of capital, and that alone, it would scarcely survive a day. But, according to Marxist theory, it has a further less obtrusive function. Law is a product of democratic politics which, in turn, derive from the (contradictory) need to combine capital accumulation (hence social inequality) with political legitimacy (Habermas, 1976). This function is served by law's role as a bearer of ideology. One meaning of ideology is the 'common sense' view of the world, promulgated to preserve the existing social order from fundamental challenge (Hunt, 1991).

To act as an ideological instrument law must be elastic, not brittle; capable of absorbing demands from reformist groups within society without significantly altering the underlying (exploitative) structure of economic relations. This elasticity finds form in a tendency to give way, in limited measure; providing a vehicle for the satisfaction of subordinate interests; securing those comforting environmental benefits that contribute to the 'long-range contentment and satisfaction [necessary] to reproduce "voluntary servitude"' (Marcuse, 1972, p 22). At this point, Marxist theory meets interest group theory. Consistent with this view it has been alleged that environmentalism panders to the interests of the middle class (Tucker, 1980) or 'new class' (Inglehart, 1977) – that is, all those situated outside of the mainstream capitalist mode of production who are identified by their common concern with postmaterial values. The 1949 National Parks and Access to the Countryside Act, for instance, was founded on a compound of (middle-class) aesthetic and scientific values and (working-class) demands for wider access to the countryside (Blunden and Curry, 1989).

Challenges to the existing order may also be deflected by provisions for public participation in the environmental decision-making process. Public participation and expressions of individual environmental values appears, at first sight, to be a benign, even positive, extension of democracy. But the theory of ideology suggests that these measures are little more than palliatives – inducing an illusion of power whilst, in reality, entrenching powerlessness to change the existing social order. To use Marcuse's expression, they exist to provide 'repressive tolerance' (Marcuse, 1969). Consider, for example, public inquiries into projects, such as road schemes, which seriously damage the environment. According to McAuslan, these enquiries merely provide an opportunity for Ministers to check government policy and do not even begin to function as a mechanism by which publicly expressed values can directly influence environmental policy (1980, pp 49–74). They also deflect attention from the central debate by turning one group of environmentally concerned citizens against another; by encouraging NIMBY-ism, in which local environmental groups seek to displace environmentally damaging operations into someone else's 'backyard'. Thus we see that some environmental law disempowers the public, first by deflecting attention away from environmental policy, and second by siphoning off more radical protest which might otherwise find its expression in direct action. Perhaps it is no coincidence that increased use of direct action in environmental protest campaigns has been matched by increased frustration at the impotence of existing legal institutions in the halting of environmental destruction. Politically legitimate but non-legal direct action is, of course, precisely what those who acquiesce in new environmental law seek to avoid.

The Marxist Conclusion
The above observations indicate that environmental law could be perceived as a product of interclass conflict and as predominantly a sham; a useless tinkering with the capitalist mode of production to keep it going just a while longer; as doing nothing to alter the basic nature/worker-exploitation structure of capitalist society. Whether this will continue indefinitely depends upon the resilience of both the economic and the ecological systems. Some predict that the dawning realisation that exploitation of nature is intrinsically linked to the capitalist mode of production, coupled with the impending ecological crisis, will trigger the long awaited revolution (Enzenberger, 1974). Others seriously consider that total ecological failure, or at least serious resource failure, will reach us first if we do not change our ways (Meadows et al., 1972; Goldsmith et al., 1972).

We must, however, be careful to note that, even if correct, the Marxist critique does not establish the validity of the Marxist prescription. Marxism may offer an account of the contradictory interests which have shaped environmental law, and a useful analytical account of oppression, but its normative function is no less exposed to critical analysis than liberalism. Putting aside the question of whether any socialist state has ever been truly Marxist, there is no doubt that pollution in socialist states has generally been worse than that in Western democracies (Goldman, 1972; Komarov, 1978). Marxist prescriptions for man–environment relations have also been criticised as devaluing woman's worth.[4] Furthermore, both Marxists and non-Marxists have acknowledged that both Marxism and capitalism are informed by the (discredited?) principle of nature exploitation through scientific and technological mastery (Enloe, 1975, p 17; Grundmann, 1991; Eckersley, 1992).

CONCLUSION

The rational choice and structural idioms go some way towards constructing a critical analysis of environmental law. Literature within other idioms (institutional, ethical, policy discourse and so on) is available to fill out the picture but cannot be addressed in this chapter. It is hoped that, at minimum, critical discussion of the type engaged in here will tend to dispel the naivety that environmental law arises naturally to address environmental problems and exists solely to provide optimal protection of the environment. As we have seen, environmental legislation is, on one account, the result of rational political pressure on essentially self-interested legislators and, on another account, an epiphenomenon of the economic structure of society. Does this mean, then, that environmental legislation inevitably legitimates an essentially destructive and self-serving system? An optimistic response would be to say that law will always tend to be manipulated and suboptimal yet, nevertheless, there are many possibilities for positive change. A pessimistic response would be to doubt whether environmental law can ever be elevated from its current weak mode to serve basic human and environmental needs. On this point I remain agnostic.

Of course we must be careful not to ask too much from law as an institution. Change in environmental law may require concomitant or even prior changes in political structures. A reduction of many supposed 'goods' such as unfettered material consumption, the sovereignty of states, freedom of trade, freedom to use certain technologies, may be required if we are to achieve a high and sustainable level of environmental protection (Hartshorne, 1974; Schumacher, 1974). Some have even suggested that it may be necessary, ultimately, to impose constraints on fundamental civil liberties such as the 'freedom to breed' (Porras, 1993, pp 27–33). Certainly, we must be careful not to allow the ideology of 'ecological modernism' to lull us into thinking that real change can be achieved without sacrifice, even if the relatively superficial effects of current environmental law are less expensive than many would have us believe.

What is clear is that an evaluation of environmental law must be free from the shackles of 'progressivism': the view that things inexorably get better and better of their own accord. The very first step towards this is to recognise that just as we do not inhabit the perfect set of social and political institutions, so too we have neither inherited nor produced a perfect set of environmental laws.

NOTES

1. Rio Declaration on Environment and Development adopted 14 June 1992 at Rio de Janeiro, A/CONF.151/5/Rev.1, 31 ILM 874 (1992).
2. *Commission v. Council*, supported by European Parliament and Spain, 17 March 1993.
3. In relation to environmental directives based jointly on Articles 100 and 235, member states are only permitted to adopt stricter domestic environmental standards where this is specifically provided for in the directive. In relation to directives based on Articles 100(a)(4) and 130(t), the EC Treaty explicitly permits member states to maintain or adopt more stringent domestic standards than provided by directives adopted under those articles (subject to provisos designed to minimise negative effects on trade).
4. This attack centres around Marx's portrayal of housework and other labours typically identified with women as drudgery which is to be transcended. Simone de Beauvoir (summarised in Eckersley, ch 3) attributes the Marxist distinction between freedom and necessity to patriarchal and differential valuation of the traditional arenas of male and female work.

15
Private Rights and Environmental Protection
Donald McGillivray and John Wightman

Can private rights have any significant role to play in relation to environmental protection? Traditionally, ordinary private law (mainly land law and tort law) provided the owner of land with rights to exploit the land, and rights to prevent interference with it. But the growth of public regulation of land use during the twentieth century has seen the limitation of exploitation rights, and the activities of pollution control and planning authorities have marginalised tort claims against interference. The conventional wisdom has been that only through the attenuation of private rights by regulation in the public interest will the environment be protected.

This view of the relative roles of private rights and public regulation has increasingly been challenged by the work of economists who, fortified by theories of regulatory failure, have argued for a larger role of private rights and the market in shaping environmental outcomes. Much of the earlier work, following Coase, advocated allowing the trading of property rights in the market effectively to define environmental goals (Coase, 1960). More recent work, particularly that of Pearce, has emphasised the role of economic instruments (including tort liability) to attain politically defined goals (Pearce et al., 1989). But, in both cases, private law is seen as wedded to the market, whether it be defining bundles of rights for exchange, mimicking the market in allocating liability where no exchange is impossible, internalising externalities or transmitting incentives for pollution abatement through civil liability.

In this chapter we attempt to steer a course between these two positions. We argue that problems with traditional regulation do leave space for an important role for private law, but one that is based not on private law being a carrier of market goals or mechanisms, but on its providing a means of privately initiated (that is, unofficial) challenges to official definitions of the public interest. We begin by exploring how far private law can be used to protect public interests.

176

PRIVATE RIGHTS AND PUBLIC INTERESTS

Most private law is private in the sense that it protects the economic or bodily interests of rights-holders. Contract rights are enforceable by a party to the contract, and tort claims arise where a private interest has been infringed, typically giving rise to compensation for personal injury or damage to property. Normally, such claims benefit no one but the right-holder. In relation to the torts concerning interests in land, it is possible to identify a 'pure' form of privateness which is most closely approached in the law on what will count as an actionable interference in private nuisance. Three aspects of privateness can be distinguished. First, the nexus with land: it is interference not with any use, but the use of *land* which is actionable, and traditionally an interest in land – effectively some form of private ownership – has been required. Second, it is sufficient if a single proprietor is affected: there is no requirement of more widespread impact, and impact on others is irrelevant to whether the interference is actionable by the plaintiff. The third aspect is the requirement that there is an interference with the use and enjoyment of the plaintiff's land: this includes activities affecting amenity, but not those which merely disturb or destroy the natural world without affecting a person's use.

Even where the private right is drawn in these terms, it may be possible to use it to pursue an interest wider than the immediate concerns of the right-holder. An injunction to restrain the emission of smoke or smell will normally benefit others in the neighbourhood as well as the plaintiff. However, the 'reach' of an injunction against some polluting activity is not limited to the more obviously private interests of neighbours. There may be other classes of 'collateral beneficiaries' of a nuisance action. Thus, anglers may benefit from a riparian owner's success in obtaining an injunction to prevent pollution of a river by a sewage outfall because of the improvement in habitat for fish, while environmentalists may approve of the outcome simply because it conserves a part of the natural world, rather than on account of any amenity use they make of the river.

These examples show how law which is purely private in form may be used to pursue wider interests. More radically, it is possible for one or more of the three aspects of privateness to be relaxed as formal components of a private law action. There are clear signs of some dilution of the traditional approach to the nexus with land in private nuisance, where occupation rather than a legally recognised interest in land is now the test (*Khorasandjian* v. *Bush* (1993); *Hunter* v. *Canary Wharf* (1996)).

An important instance where a nexus with land is not essential is the protection of interests in a fishery. In the leading case *Pride of Derby Angling Association* v. *British Celanese* (1952) the plaintiff angling club obtained an injunction restraining pollution of the River Derwent. The club's standing to bring the action stemmed from its ownership of the fishing rights. In legal terms these are known as a *profit a prendre*, a legally recognised species of real property right. In origin it is similar to a right of common, protecting the right of the holder to take from an otherwise unowned source. Unlike some such rights it can exist 'in gross', that is without being attached to any neighbouring land. In origin, it was a means of preventing the unauthorised taking of fish, but is used now by angling clubs to preserve fisheries in the face of pollution of watercourses. And now that anglers normally return fish to the river, the concern is with preservation of habitat rather than the taking which was originally protected by the right. The potential to protect habitat means that fishery rights can be used not just for amenity protection, but are also of use to those who wish to conserve without using.

Public nuisance, a curious hybrid with both civil and criminal aspects, also relaxes some of the components of the pure private right. As in the case of other continuing criminal acts, it is possible for the Attorney-General in a relator action to seek an injunction at the request of affected citizens, or alternatively the local authority can bring an action under s 222 Local Government Act 1972. A person suffering special damage, that is, more than others who are affected, can claim damages. It therefore differs from private nuisance in two relevant respects: there is no nexus with land; and it is the general impact on a group, not on an individual, that matters, except in the case of a claim for special damage.

Public nuisance does not eclipse private nuisance as far as injunctions are concerned, because citizens have no right under public nuisance to seek the injunction: the decision lies in the hands of the A-G or local authority. This means that the nexus with land remains a prerequisite for a citizen to seek an injunction for any kind of nuisance. But should this particular dimension of privateness be a sticking point? The slight loosening in *Hunter* from interest in the land to occupation could go further: say noise or pollution affecting a person's place of work, or where they play sport. Of course, there will typically be an owner of land (for example, a sports club) in whose name an action under traditional principles can be brought. But the ownership by a club here is in one sense a technicality, for it simply represents the aggregate of casual users for sporting purposes, none of whom are in occupation in the sense envisaged in *Hunter*. And although the form of ownership is lacking, the same substantive reasons for protection encompass an amenity enjoyed without being in any particular place, such as bird-watching affected by deterioration in water quality or quantity essential for bird life. Here there is no citizen's remedy at present, but it is not inconceivable that private and public nuisance could move closer together and enable an injunction to be sought in these circumstances.

Although such a development to dispense with the nexus with land may seem unlikely, it is in fact precisely what is contained in the proposed EC directive on waste.[1] The proposed waste directive applies mainly to solid wastes and sludge deposited on land. It provides for strict liability for the producers and eliminators of waste, and resembles traditional private law by giving rights of action to those suffering personal injury or property damage. But it also goes beyond traditional private law in two interesting ways. First, liability attaches to any 'impairment' of the environment, including anything not in private ownership (important instances are air, and water-bearing strata). Second, the draft directive provides that common interest groups can bring actions, either to prevent impairment or for the cost of remedying damage. This proposal is striking, for not only is the nexus with land broken, giving common interest groups standing to apply for injunctions, but there is no need to show any interference with any human activity: impairment is sufficient.

In this respect the draft directive goes well beyond the provisions relating to statutory nuisance contained in Part III of the Environmental Protection Act 1990. These dispense with the nexus with land (action must be taken by local authorities, either on their own initiation or that of local residents), while persons 'aggrieved' may insist that a magistrate's court serve an abatement notice in respect of existing nuisances, allowing private initiation of actions. But statutory nuisance is, at least presently, concerned with matters 'prejudicial to health or a nuisance', where 'nuisance' is defined as either a public or private nuisance at common law (*National Coal Board* v. *Thorne* (1976)).

Of all the examples discussed, therefore, the proposed waste directive is the one furthest removed from the pure form of protecting private interests.[2] Private law can therefore be seen to encompass a spectrum of types of claim, running from the protection of orthodox individual proprietary interests to the protection of more generalised public interests in the environment, including both general amenity uses (such as bird-watching or hiking) and impact on the environment which does not affect human use. If private law were extended to recognise such claims, citizens – typically acting through common interest groups – would have a legally recognised interest as custodians, rather than as owners or even users.

Specific developments in property law suggest similar possibilities of moving away from 'pure' forms of private rights. It has been argued that there is a discernable trend towards conceiving of 'a significant "equitable property" in the quality and conservation of the natural environment' (Gray, 1994, p 188). Gray suggests the appearance of new, collective private property rights in respect of at least those parts of the natural environment considered 'ecologically imperative' (Karp, 1992–93, pp 745 et seq), making them simply non-excludable in the traditional sense. He relies heavily on examples from wilderness conservation, especially from the US where greater political and legal salience attaches to the spiritual dimension associated with exposure to wild country (see, for example, Nash, 1982). This dimension may be less important in the UK for various reasons, historical and geographical, but the basic point remains: the more that collective rights in property are recognised, the greater the law seems to be prepared to oppose the exclusory view of property which has, so clearly, gained pre-eminence with the rise of the market.[3]

PRIVATE RIGHTS AND PUBLIC REGULATION

Even if it is possible to carve out a role in theory for private rights to be used to protect public or collective interests, what happens when private law clashes with regulation? The general situation we have in mind here is where a regulatory authority has in some way licensed an activity which the plaintiff claims amounts to an actionable interference. What effect does the regulatory decision have on the private law claim? As we will see, much of the potential of private law to be used in pursuit of public interests turns on this general question, to which the courts have not yet supplied a clear answer. It is useful to explore the response by distinguishing two approaches – the single-track and twin-track.

A single-track approach seeks single 'right answers', so that both public and private law give the same response. This can arise in two ways. Either the private law claim yields to the public law permission, or (less commonly) the public law permission yields to the private right. The main instance of the former is the defence of statutory authority in nuisance, which effectively deprives neighbours of any claim in relation to anything done in the exercise of a statutory power as long as it was not done negligently (*Allen* v. *Gulf Oil Refining* (1981)). Another example is *Budden and Albery* v. *BP Oil* (1980), where a claim in negligence against two oil companies based on their use of lead in petrol was dismissed. For the Court, allowing the action would mean that valid regulations prescribing the lead content in petrol would effectively be replaced by a lower, judicially determined standard.[4]

The other kind of single-track approach, where the public law is aligned with the private right, is much more rarely found, but can be detected in remarks in *Wheeler* v. *Saunders* (1995). There, the plaintiff was successful in a private nuisance action against a neighbouring pig farmer, notwithstanding that the pig units from which the offending smell was coming had been constructed with planning permission. In the Court of Appeal, Sir John May thought that: 'If a planning authority were with notice to grant a planning permission the inevitable consequence of which would be the creation of a nuisance, then it is well arguable that grant would be subject to judicial review on the ground of irrationality' (p 713).[5] On this latter view, the content of the private law of nuisance is treated as circumscribing the powers of planning authorities in granting planning permissions.

The twin-track approach, in contrast, permits public and private law to give different answers to the lawfulness of an activity. This approach was adopted (with some ambiguity) in *Gillingham BC* v. *Medway (Chatham) Dock Co.* (1992), and (more clearly) by the majority view in *Wheeler*. In *Gillingham,* the effect of a planning permission granted to a port operator to develop the port was greatly to increase the inconvenience (especially noise) caused to local residents from the increased heavy goods traffic generated by the development. Although Buckley J rejected a direct analogy between statutory authority and planning permission, he held that the permission altered the nature of the locality, so that no actionable nuisance was found. In *Wheeler,* the Court found that the permission did not change the nature of the locality, and in *Hunter* it was held the planning permission for the Canary Wharf tower did not authorise interference with television reception in its 'shadow'.

The twin-track approach thus preserves a space for private law actions even where an interference has been licensed. So, where private law is being used (as suggested in the previous section) to pursue a public interest, there is a possibility of using it to argue for a different meaning of the public interest from that produced by the official regulatory authority. We now turn to assess how far it can be justified for the legal system to embrace conflicting understandings of the public interest.

PRIVATELY INITIATED LEGAL ACTION, PUBLIC INTERESTS AND PLURALISM

The twin-track approach in cases like *Wheeler* and *Hunter* can be explained in part as an instance of the court confining the erosion of individual property rights to cases where the legal authority is wholly explicit and affected individuals are heard. Thus in *Wheeler* the comparison was drawn by Peter Gibson LJ between the private Bill procedure before the enactment of a statutory power (which may be a defence to an action in nuisance), which gives affected parties rights of representation, and the system for determining planning applications. The latter, he noted, afforded only limited opportunities for affected parties to obtain a remedy.[6]

Thus it is precisely where the private action is being used for a purely private purpose that the case for the twin-track approach is easiest to make. But where private law is seen as a means of pursuing a notion of the public interest, not only are arguments derived from individual rights less persuasive, but there is a clear overlap with the regulatory function: both concern a conception of the public interest. The contrast between *Gillingham* and *Wheeler* illustrates this difference. In *Wheeler* there was nothing at stake beyond the conflict between the private interests of neighbouring owners whose uses conflicted. In *Gillingham* the interests of those affected by the noise nuisance were pitted against the wider benefits of the development of a port in an area of high unemployment.

So how can we begin to justify the use of private law to argue for a definition of the public interest which is at odds with that reached by a public authority? Our case for a role for private law in shaping conceptions of the public interest rests on its potential to counteract regulatory failure by providing an institutional means of opening the substance of regulatory decisions to scrutiny.

The model of environmental decision-making we envisage is pluralist in the sense that the official decision sanctioned by public law would not necessarily be the final word on the legality of an activity. Individuals and groups could privately initiate legal proceedings in which it would be possible to challenge not only the infringement of private interests, but also the regulator's view of where the public interest lay. This is not to suggest that 'private' rights should invariably prevail, only that the issue remains potentially open so that a case may be presented to a court.

In a world of perfect regulation, such institutionalised second-guessing would be indefensibly irrational. But given the various modes of regulatory failure – which apply to the identification of public as much as the treatment of private interests – an institutionalised pluralism is, we argue, desirable. Thus it is possible to regard the whole legal response to environmental issues as comprising not just the regulatory view, buttressed by its official status, but also the outrider of unofficial legal action. In this pluralist view, private law takes its place alongside other legal mechanisms, notably private prosecutions and applications for judicial review, which are unofficial since the initiation of legal proceedings is not controlled by regulatory agencies or other parts of the state.

The situation in *Gillingham* provides an example of how private law could be used in this way. By 1990, the local authority was clearly less concerned about promoting employment than it had been when, in 1982, it granted permission to redevelop the former naval dockyard. Although planning authorities can revoke permissions (if compensation is paid), in *Gillingham* the local authority was pursuing the action in public nuisance in the hope of stopping the interference from the lorries by injunction without having to pay compensation. Although this use of public nuisance was seen by the court almost as an act of bad faith, it is also possible to view it as a legitimate attempt to establish that the balance of argument had changed about whether the harm inflicted was justified on public interest grounds.[7] The private action here can be seen as a means of revising a regulatory decision, but does not second-guess the original decision at the time it was made. Rather, it provides a means of revising the balance of factors in the light of changed circumstances. This approach to the effect of the planning permission concedes that it may in some circumstances prevail over a private right. But instead of regarding it as an open-ended removal of a plaintiff's rights, it sees the planning permission only as a conditional borrowing of those rights, to be returned if the calculus of public interest changes to remove the justification for the borrowing.[8]

CONCLUSION

The argument that private law should be stretched to reflect public interests, and that it should be able to prevail over official definitions of the public interest, may seem to take us to the very edge of possible developments in private law. Even so, the emphasis on the role of unofficial legal action in shaping environmental decision-making is in tune with recent trends. Increasingly, the decisions of regulatory authorities and large utilities are questioned indirectly through unofficial legal action. In judicial review, the rules on standing have been relaxed, much of the development occurring in cases brought by environmental bodies such as Greenpeace, Friends of the Earth and the World Development Movement (see, for example, *R. v. HMIP ex p Greenpeace Ltd (No.2)* (1994); *R. v. SS for Foreign Affairs ex p World Development Movement Ltd* (1995). Also detectable is an increasing use of tort claims, especially in relation to water pollution where information is more readily available and causation less difficult to show than matters such as air pollution (see, for example, Mumma, 1992; the *Croyde Bay* (1994) case). These trends reflect not only a spreading awareness of the limitations of traditional 'command and control' regulation, but also a scepticism among environmental groups about the hubristic claims sometimes made for economic instruments.

In 1960, Coase pointed to the perverse belief in public regulation:

> When they are prevented from sleeping at night by the roar of jet planes overhead (publicly authorized and perhaps publicly operated), are unable to think (or rest) in the day because of the noise and vibration from passing trains (publicly authorized and perhaps publicly operated), find it difficult to breathe because of the odour from a local sewage farm (publicly authorized and perhaps publicly operated) ... they proceed to declaim about the disadvantages of private enterprise and the need for Government regulation. (p 26)

Ownership of planes, trains and sewage farms in the UK has changed dramatically since Coase rightly pointed to some of the problems of public regulation. Private law has a role in making regulation more responsive to the views of citizens, but it is not one that only casts it as the carrier of market goals and mechanisms.

NOTES

1. COM(89) 282 final, modified by Amended Proposal COM(91) 219 final.
2. Note that the draft directive has effectively been superseded by the Commission's Green Paper *Remedying Environmental Damage*, COM(93) 47. See also the Convention on Civil Liability for Damage Resulting from Activities Dangerous to the Environment, Lugano, 21 June 1993, 32 ILM 1230 (1993), Art 2, para 7.
3. A consequence of this for environmental protection, of course, might be that the successful use of trespass in cases such as *League Against Cruel Sports* v. *Scott* (1985) may be frustrated in the interests of a more communitarian approach to fundamental property interests.
4. Another good illustration of legislative standards effectively setting common law standards is *Cambridge Water Co.* v. *Eastern Counties Leather* (1994), where harm was defined in accordance with the terms of the 1980 EC Drinking Water Directive.
5. But see *R.* v. *Exeter City Council ex p Thomas* (1990), where it was held that a local planning authority could grant planning permission for residential development in the knowledge that, in a predominantly residential area, the development would lead, most likely, to successful nuisance actions against two existing 'bad neighbour' businesses in the area.
6. Simon Ball has suggested that one approach to a permission is to make its effect on private rights subject to procedural safeguards: '*If* there is compensation available, *if* there is a reasonable chance of a successful appeal and *if* there is less difficulty in bringing a judicial challenge, then the extinction of private rights by a public decision may be acceptable' (Ball, 1995, p 296, original emphasis).
7. If the affected householders in *Gillingham* had sued in private nuisance, then this issue could have been argued before the court. Why should the local authority bringing the action under local government legislation be in a different position? After all, it is arguable that it was acting not in its capacity as a planning authority but as a public health authority.
8. We develop arguments based on the two models of public/private interaction used here, discussing in particular the spatial variability present in nuisance actions, in McGillivray and Wightman, 'Private Rights, Regulation, Public Interests and the Environment', in O'Neill and Hayward (eds), *Justice, Property and the Environment: Social and Legal Perspectives* (Avebury, in press).

16
Your Life in Their Hands: The Case Against Patents in Genetic Engineering

Steve Emmott

Patent law used to be prescribed as a career alternative for those who found accountancy too exciting. Developments in modern biotechnology have changed all that and since the US Supreme Court ruling in 1980 on the Chakrabarty case[1] which granted the first patent on a genetically engineered micro-organism, intellectual property rights (IPR) have become a key element in the struggle for ownership of the world's genetic resources.

Trying to adapt a body of law developed in the nineteenth century for dealing with mechanical bits and pieces to meet claims for patent protection of new and modified forms of living organisms is proving problematic. As patent claims rise up the scale from modified viruses and other micro-organisms to plants, animals and even human genetic material, these problems intensify. Socioeconomic, ethical and political issues arise in a way that Henry Ford never experienced and the patent-granting institutions are proving ill equipped to respond to these concerns. This chapter will try to set out these issues and to describe the attempts by the European Patent Office (EPO) to apply the terms of its charter to genetically modified lifeforms. It will also consider the rejection by the European Parliament of the move by the European Commission (EC) in Brussels to introduce a European Union (EU) directive intended to standardise 'the legal protection of biotechnological inventions'. In what was probably the most surprising setback for the pro-biotech lobby in recent years, this directive was killed off by MEPs on 1 March 1995 after a six-year campaign by environmentalists, human rights groups, animal welfarists, women's movements, farmers, Third World development agencies and other non-governmental organisations (NGOs). It was the first time the European Parliament had exercised its new powers of co-decision-making under the Maastricht Treaty and may prove to be a turning-point in the search to apply socially acceptable and ethical criteria to the uses of genetic engineering.

THE CONCEPT OF A PATENT

A patent is said to represent a contract between the inventor and society whereby society grants monopoly rights to exploit the invention for a limited period. In exchange the inventor agrees to full publication of the details of the invention to enable others to undertake further research and development after the patent is granted. Three basic criteria are laid down for patentability. The claim must be for something new for which the necessary information was not already in the public domain. It must involve a non-obvious inventive step and it must have an industrial application or usefulness. In theory, therefore, it is clear that the mere discovery of a previously unknown object or, say, a chemical property cannot be a patentable invention since it already existed in nature and since no inventive step or useful human intervention has taken place. In biotechnology terms, this should mean that you can't patent a gene. In practice, and following the lead of the US Patent and Trademark Office (PTO), an increasing number of claims are being filed and granted for patents on genetic material which has received minimal human intervention.

THE CASE AGAINST PATENTS ON LIFE

Objections to the EC directive ranged from deeply felt opposition to the use of gene technology through to the specific impact of this particular type of IPR on sectoral interests. The following summary of these objections is taken from the literature of the 'No Patents on Life' campaign, coordinated in the UK by The Genetics Forum.[2]

Our Relationship with Nature

Our respect for life, creation and reproduction will become subverted by the reductionist and materialistic concept of life as a collection of chemical substances which happen to be able to replicate themselves, which can be manipulated and which can become private property. The very notion that someone is able to own a plant or animal intellectually, to own its whole being and purpose, is morally repugnant. The view that everything that exists can be commercialised, commodified and privately owned is deeply corrupting. Our exploitation of the planet is leading us further into an unsustainable relationship with the forces of nature. Environmental concerns and other 'value-laden' issues will be blocked out by the scientific determinism which allows of no other criteria for product approval.

Human Rights

If human beings, our parts and bodily products, physical or psychological traits and intimate genetic information can become the exclusive property of patent-holders, the fundamental concept of an individual's right to an independent existence and the right to control one's own body and lifestyle is severely weakened. The boundaries between acceptable and unacceptable intervention in our human condition will become increasingly impossible to define. Eugenics will become less unthinkable. In March 1995, the US PTO granted a sweeping patent on the basic methods of gene therapy to the National Institute of Health which immediately assigned the exclusive rights to commercial development to a private company.

Animal Welfare

Patents will stimulate the genetic engineering of animals to suffer as they serve as research vehicles, become turned into drug-producing 'pharm' animals or otherwise become high-tech food production systems. Severe stress and physical deformities will be seen as an acceptable price to pay for technological 'progress'. The 'Oncomouse', discussed in more detail below, is the first example of this phenomenon – a patented animal specifically engineered to contract breast cancer.

Farmers

Not only will farmers pay royalties on seeds, plants and livestock which they buy (and at purchase prices set to reflect the new improved 'miracle' traits) but they will become liable for charges on successive generations of crops or breeding herds when resold, since patent protection will extend to any subsequent propagation containing the patented material. In practice this could mean that small farmers will not be able to compete and since the subsequent generation rule will be difficult to police, the patent-holders may choose to do business only with large-scale industrialised farms. Both sets of pressures will force smallholders off the land, leading to a weakening of rural communities and further intensification of farming practices when agricultural and rural policy is seeking to move in the opposite direction. Increasingly broad-based claims are being made. One company, W R Grace & Co., was granted monopoly patents in the US for all forms of genetically engineered cotton crops, regardless of the gene transfer method or the trait modified, and a European equivalent on all modified soya beans. The breadth of these patents was so alarming that the US Department of Agriculture sought to overturn them and the US PTO has provisionally revoked the cotton patent, though it remains in force whilst appeals are heard. Oppositions have also been filed with the EPO.

Plant and Animal Breeders

Most of the large independent seed companies have been bought up by the industrial giants, positioning themselves to control the basic building blocks of plant life. The remaining breeders will no longer have free access to germplasm for developing new varieties of plants and animals. This freedom, which is afforded by the plant breeders' rights (PBR) regime, has already been weakened by the renegotiation in 1991 of the international UPOV treaty which governs this system. The bar on patents as an alternative (and much more restrictive) method of registering IPR was removed. There is no international equivalent animal breeders' rights system. Drawing further momentum from the pro-patent biotechnology industry lobby, the new GATT Agreement provides that there must be a patent regime for micro-organisms and that whilst plants and animals need not be patented, plant varieties must be protected either by a patent system or by an effective *sui generis* system (such as PBR) or by a combination of the two.[3]

Consumers

As consumers, we are likely to end up paying more for food, medicines and other biotechnology products with less choice. Multiple patents on different traits or parts of the production process will give rise to multiple surcharges as the price of the end-product reflects the accumulated royalties paid out. The available range of foodstuffs, for example, will be determined more by the industrial patent-holder than by the consumer's needs. Genetically engineered food characteristics will be likely to serve the needs of producers and distributors more than those of the customer. Slow-rotting tomatoes that sit on supermarket shelves for lengthy periods are examples of what has already happened in the US. They are promoted as tasting better than the real thing (whatever that means), and so 'fake-freshness' becomes a marketing tool.

Genetic Diversity

As private control over the world's genetic resources tightens with monopoly rights of exploitation, the idea of those resources as a common heritage fades away. Biotechnology R & D, aimed at providing us with seemingly attractive superstrains of high-yielding and disease-resistant crops, is in fact leading us into a monoculture mentality. Our wealth of diversity will dwindle even faster and we run severe ecological risks from unforeseen diseases and predators for which no fall-back resistant strains will remain in the wild or in our publicly-owned gene banks. Gene prospecting by multinational pharmaceutical and agrochemical companies in the Third World is now a fact of life, as are exclusive exploitation and patent contracts with hard-pressed nations. A prime example of this trend was the agreement in 1991 between Merck and the Costa Rican private biodiversity agency (InBio)[4] where the world's largest drug company paid US$1m for the right to inventory, test and commercialise plants, micro-organisms and insects from the rainforest.

Public Research

Universities and public research institutes are increasingly being funded by the private sector. In genetic engineering, the research agenda is being set by the multinationals, who demand patent and exploitation rights in return for their cash. Academic freedom to publish, the embodiment of free interchange of scientific findings, is being withdrawn in the face of the need to keep the data secret in advance of a patent application being filed. Independent experts and academics without industry affiliations needed to serve on regulatory and advisory bodies concerned with public health and environmental well-being are becoming an endangered species.

Concentration of Industrial Power

The pharmaceutical, agribusiness, chemical and food manufacturing sectors, for each of which genetic engineering promises future riches, are already dominated by multinational giants and barriers to new entrants are extremely high. Cross-sector mergers and acquisitions are helping to create 'bioagropharmachemical' giants. Patent ownership of the basic blueprints of life will exacerbate this concentration. The creation of such centres of power leaves consumers with fewer choices in our needs for food, health and a cleaner environment. It also presents government regulators with an imbalanced marketplace and leaves them facing a disproportionately powerful lobby.

The Third World

Access by Third World nations to scientific information and technology transfer will be severely diminished. Genetic resources originating in the South will become privatised by the North without compensation. Products derived from their own gene pool and indigenous cultivation will be sold back to them at royalty-inflated prices thus aggravating debt burdens, marginalising the poorest countries further. The Bio-Diversity Convention signed in Rio de Janeiro in 1992[5] sought to address this concern but the opportunity has not been taken to incorporate its compensation provisions into Euro patent law. An example of what is happening at present is the case of the neem tree, the seeds of which local people in India have traditionally and freely used for medicinal, contraceptive, insecticide and other purposes. W R Grace (again) have patented the active chemical compound, azadirachtin, derived from the tree. They admit that they were inspired by traditional knowledge but claim to have created an improved formulation of the compound. It is clear that the local farmers have acted as custodians of the tree and its products over the centuries and freely shared their knowledge. They are now being displaced by what they see as 'intellectual piracy'.

EXISTING EUROPEAN PATENT LAW

Although each of the 15 member states of the EU has its own national patent law, 14 of them (the exception is Finland) are signatories to the European Patent Convention 1973 ('EPC'), along with Switzerland. This is a multinational treaty signed by sovereign nations and is not part of the EU institutional framework. Nevertheless, it sets the terms under which it is possible to obtain a Europe-wide patent from the EPO in Munich, valid in law in each member state subject to any national idiosyncrasies. It was drafted before widespread development of the products of genetic manipulation, but it does contain some apparent restrictions on patentability in this area. The following, *inter alia*, are not patentable:

- Discoveries, scientific theories and ... presentations of information (Art 52.2)
- Methods for treatment of the human or animal body by surgery or therapy and diagnostic methods practised on the human or animal body – except products, in particular substances or compositions, for use in any of these methods (Art 52.4)
- Inventions contrary to public order or morality (Art 53A)
- Plant or animal varieties or essentially biological processes for the production of plants or animals, except for microbiological processes or the products thereof (Art 53B)

At first reading, these look like impressive defences against the patenting of animate matter, but as usual, it all depends on the interpretation. When genetic material can be isolated from its origins and replicated in the laboratory, it is held to cease to be a mere discovery. So-called 'copy genes' are thus not excluded. The ban on human or animal surgery, therapy or diagnostic methods is not an explicit bar to the patentability of humans or animals themselves, nor does it exclude engineered gene products used in the treatments. Plants or animals may evidently be patented provided the claim is not for a varietal protection. Microbiological processes are not excluded provided they can pass the inventive-step test. When bio*techno*logical processes at higher levels of life are involved, with claims of useful intervention, they cease to be essentially biological. The public morality exclusion was designed to exclude bombs not biotechnology. It requires subjective judgements not commonly found in the public servants who administer the patent system, and it has proved difficult in the past to persuade the EPO to apply this criterion. Thus the EPC, whilst providing some ostensible limitations, is not formulated with sufficient precision or in sufficient technical detail to satisfy the calls of those who wish to see clear limits to the patentability of life.

THE ONCOMOUSE PATENT AND EPO POLICY-MAKING

In 1988 the US PTO granted a patent to Harvard University for a transgenic non-human mammalian animal with an activated oncogene sequence – a mouse or other animal designed to contract breast cancer and to die in the interests of research. An application to the EPO for a European patent was initially refused on the grounds that patents could not be granted for animals as such within the terms of the EPC. This was overturned by the Board of Appeal in 1991 who went on to examine whether such an 'invention' was contrary to public order or morality under Art 53A. They found that it was necessary to weigh up the suffering inflicted on the animal against the potential benefits to humankind and held that in this case humankind's interests took priority.[6] Exercising value judgements of this kind is new territory and the EPO itself acknowledged in its 1991 Annual Report that this decision, 'added a new and largely unknown dimension to the patent system. The granting of patents no longer depends on purely technical considerations: from now on, applications will have to bear scrutiny in respect of their wider social implications'.[7]

Formal oppositions filed against the findings by animal welfarists and others mean that the case is not yet closed and further hearings were held in November 1995. The EPO report goes on to say that

> ... technological innovations invariably have to be assessed in the context of the human and natural environment ... in every area of technological innovation there will always be cases in which the patent system comes up against barriers which then have to be reassessed within the existing legal framework. In the case of the onco-mouse, this reassessment has not yet been completed ... further insights will doubtless emerge concerning the patentability of transgenic animals and plants. Hence it would seem that the granting of a patent for the Harvard onco-mouse is merely a transitional stage in a long-term process whose eventual outcome remains uncertain.[8]

Until the oncomouse application is finally determined, the EPO is operating an unofficial moratorium on animal patents.

PATENTS ON CROPS

This willingness of the EPO to listen to wider arguments is reflected in a recent response to Greenpeace's opposition to an application to patent oil-seed rape, submitted by Plant Genetic Systems of Belgium (PGS). The crop is engineered to be resistant to the herbicide Basta. This trait raises long-term concerns about damage to the environment. The EPO said these were sensitive and important issues and it needed to consider whether it was morally justified to grant a patent when this could lead to increased use of toxic herbicides, encourage the evolution of 'super-weeds' by transferring resistance traits and thus causing genetic pollution by the spread of the foreign genes to wild relatives. In the event, they rejected the argument that herbicide resistance was contrary to public morality, but struck out six of the detailed claims by the applicant, effectively granting the patent on the engineered cells but not on the seeds themselves, finding that this part of the claim would have represented a patent on a variety and thus invalid under Art 53B.[9] Whilst the EPO is prepared to listen, it is clearly handicapped by the limited number of grounds on which it can respond to arguments about the social and environmental implications of genetic engineering. If, as seems likely, it was waiting for further guidance from the patent directive, none will now be forthcoming.

HUMAN GENES

Evidence that the EPO is not always easy to convince on public morality or policy grounds is shown in the case of the Relaxin patent. Arising out of research by the Australian Howard Florey Institute, a patent was granted to Genentech, a subsidiary of Swiss drug company Hoffman-LaRoche, for the human gene coding for the hormone relaxin, isolated from the ovaries of pregnant women. The EPO rejected an official opposition from the Green group of the European Parliament that the patent was unethical and that since the gene had existed as part of the human genome for thousands of years, the claim was in fact a discovery not an invention and thus not patentable. In the light of the clear apprehension over human patents shown by MEPs in their vote to reject the patent directive, which was subsequent to the EPO's finding, the Greens are likely to appeal.

THE DRAFT EU LEGISLATION

The EC in the 1980s was pressed hard by the biotechnology industry lobby, who evidently didn't think that the EPC protected them enough. They argued that the uncertainties in European patent law were damaging R & D investment in genetic engineering and told the Commission that industry would be tempted to relocate to the US or to Japan where patent regimes were less restrictive. (Biotechnology industrialists in Japan and the US use much the same arguments with their regulatory regimes, citing Europe as an easier place to do business.) The EC decided against recommending a renegotiation of the EPC, which would have been a long process and which in any event did not sit neatly within the EU framework. In 1988 it launched its own draft directive and built the need for this law into its policy objectives as a key requirement for the promotion of biotechnology in Europe. Initially this document was presented as a simple enabling act, clarifying the scope of patentability of lifeforms. The EC's in-house bioethics advisory group concluded that there were 'no ethical grounds for opposing the patentability of inventions relating to living matter in principle ...'.[10]

The Eurocrats must have assumed that this would be a fairly speedy and straightforward process but, as described above, it provoked a storm of opposition from NGOs and fell at the final hurdle. Although the farming and animal welfare considerations were of serious concern to MEPs, the fundamental basis of their hostility was the lack of an unequivocal exclusion from patentability of human genetic material and germ-line therapies. Bio-industrialists put on a brave face and claimed that the decision was of little consequence but the failure of the directive dislodged the main plank in their campaign to get themselves written into the centre of EC policy-making. At the time of writing (early April 1995), the EC was reported to have decided to redraft the directive and to try again. MEPs were equally anxious that the initiative they had seized should not be lost and were considering ways of retaining the moral high ground they had staked out.

One of the factors troubling MEPs was the case of US citizen John Moore. Whilst receiving medical treatment in California for leukaemia, his enlarged spleen was removed and the white blood cells found to contain unusual and commercially valuable blood proteins. A cell line was created, patented and licensed to several pharmaceutical and biotechnology firms. Moore was never told of the unique properties and value of the cells, nor that his doctor had 'invented' them and profited from their commercialisation. The California Supreme Court, whilst awarding him damages for being duped, refused to allow him proprietary rights in his own tissue.[11] Whilst it may be right that Moore should not have been able to cash in on his human genetic attributes, they should surely not have been privatised either.

THE UK REGULATORS

Decision-makers within the UK government, too, have problems responding to arguments about the wider issues. When in 1994 PGS applied to market throughout Europe rapeseed oil similar to that of the patent claim discussed above, the Advisory Committee on Releases to the Environment (ACRE) and the Advisory Committee on Novel Foods and Processes (ACNFP) reporting respectively to the UK Department of the Environment and to the Ministry of Agriculture both recommended approval on the narrow scientific grounds and declined to look at other considerations. The chair of ACRE, Prof. John Beringer, in a letter to The Genetics Forum has said that

> members of ACRE are interested in the long-term implications of the use of herbicides, but it is not in our remit to advise on these, and neither should it be because we do not have the expertise to make the assessments needed.[12]

The DoE duly approved the marketing application but objections from the Danish government, responding to pressure from environmentalists and consumer groups, have triggered a reassessment by the EC, taking the consent out of UK hands. In the meantime, MAFF has approved products from the rapeseed for human and animal food use without apparent qualms about the environmental impact and is set to do the same for a herbicide-resistant soya bean intended to be imported by Monsanto.

WHERE NOW?

It is clear that until there are unambiguous statements from our legislators on the limits to patentability of lifeforms, patent applications for genetic material, products and processes at national and European levels will continue to mount and precedents will continue to be set in an ad hoc fashion. There is no space in this chapter to discuss alternative forms of intellectual property rights which will adequately protect and reward genuine inventions without granting the monopoly control that patents bestow. However, such rights are unlikely to develop until the principle that life is not patentable is entrenched in EC law.[13]

An Early Day Motion tabled in the Westminster Parliament in March 1995 with cross-party support congratulates the European Parliament on the stand it has taken on the question of patenting of life, urges the EC to rethink its biotechnology policy to ensure respect for human and animal life and the integrity of the natural environment and calls on the EPO to recognise the significance of the decision taken by the MEPs.[14] The Parliamentary Science and Technology Committee has held hearings into human genetics and reported in 1995. Meanwhile, the Inter-Parliamentary Union, with 1,500 delegates from 114 countries meeting in Madrid in April 1995, adopted a resolution calling for a ban on all human gene patents, reaffirming the inviolability of the human body. Clearly the ground is moving.

Not only is there a need for a statement of legal principle enshrining the limits to patentability, but we should be concerned to legislate for the protection of human genetic privacy to meet the commercial and social pressures that are already starting to arise from the use of genetic screening techniques. Gene therapy techniques are now in use and as the location and function of each genetic construct is mapped by the international Human Genome Project, society and individuals will face bewildering choices as to how to use that knowledge. In some cases we will have to decide whether we will choose not to use it. In the face of a list of ethical questions about the socially responsible use of gene technology which will get longer each year, we need to consider the creation of a domestic or EU standing Commission on Bio-Ethics drawing on a broad cross-section of informed opinion. International measures are also called for to regulate trade in gene products (the proposed Bio-Safety Protocol which arises from the Bio-Diversity Convention) and to consider global ethical implications (a suggested UN Bio-Ethics Charter). In the narrow world of patent lawyers, all these issues are seen as being interesting but not relevant. In the real world, patents on life are but the tip of the bio-iceberg.

NOTES

1. *Diamond* v. *Chakrabarty* (1980).
2. The Genetics Forum, 5–11 Worship St, London EC2A 2BH.
3. Section 5, Art 27.3 of Trade Related Intellectual Property Rights agreement, part of the Uruguay Round of negotiations on General Agreement on Tariffs and Trade 1994.
4. Discussed in more detail in *Seedling*, June/July 1992, pp 12–17, published by GRAIN Girona 25, pral, Barcelona B-08013.
5. The UN Convention on Biological Diversity, signed at The Earth Summit, entered into force in December 1993.
6. The Banner Report to the UK MAFF on the ethics of emerging technologies in farm animal breeding, HMSO 1995, contains a more sophisticated discussion on transgenic animals and suffering.
7. European Patent Office (1991) *Annual Report* (Munich: EPO).
8. Ibid, pp 11–16.
9. Greenpeace UK briefing note.
10. Opinion of the Group of Advisors on Ethical Aspects of Biotechnology, 30 September 1993, para 2.2.1.
11. *Moore* v. *University of California* (1990). Professor Gerald Dworkin of Kings College London discussed the legal background to property ownership of human tissue in a conference paper to the IBC, May 1993.
12. Letter to The Genetics Forum ,1 September 1994.
13. Alternatives include Plant & Animal Breeders' Rights in conjunction with protection of Farmers' Rights, Registered Design Rights and Copyright.
14. EDM No. 904 tabled 27 March 1995.

Bibliography

Ad Hoc Group Immigration Document SN4821/92 (WGI 1281 AS145) 'Conclusions on Countries in Which There is Generally No Serious Risk of Persecution' (Internet: Statewatch).

Alford, R.R. and Friedland, R. (1985) *Powers of Theory: Capitalism, the State, and Democracy* (Cambridge: Cambridge University Press).

Allott, P. (1990) *Eunomia: New Order for a New World* (Oxford: Oxford University Press).

Amin, K., Fernandes, M. and Gordon, P. (1988) *Racism and Discrimination in Britain: A Select Bibliography 1984–87* (London: Runnymede Trust).

Anderson, B. (1991) *Imagined Communities* (London: Verso).

Anderson, M. (1989) *Policing the World: Interpol and the Politics of International Police Cooperation* (Oxford: Clarendon Press).

Andresen, S. (1993) 'The Effectiveness of the International Whaling Commission', 48(2) *Artic* 108.

Anker, D. (1987) 'Discretionary Asylum! A Protection remedy for Refugees under the Refugee Act of 1980', 25 *Virginia Journal of International Law* 1.

Appadurai, A. (1990) 'Disjuncture and Difference in the Global Cultural Economy' in M. Featherstone (ed.) *Global Culture* (London: Sage) reprinted from (1990) 7(2) *Theory, Culture and Society* .

Aristotle (1925) *Ethica Nichomachea V.3*, trans. W. Ross (Oxford: Oxford University Press).

Armstrong, P. and Armstrong, H. (1991) 'Limited Possibilities and Possible Limits for Pay Equity: Within and Beyond the Ontario Legislation', in J. Fudge and P. McDermott (eds) *Just Wages: A Feminist Assessment of Pay Equity* (Toronto: University of Toronto Press).

Atkins, S. and Hoggett, B. (1984) *Women and the Law* (Oxford: Blackwell).

Bacchi, C. (1990) *Same Difference: Feminism and Sexual Difference* (London: Allen and Unwin).

Bailey, S.H., Harris, D.J. and Jones, B.L. (1995) *Civil Liberties: Cases and Materials*, 4th edn (London: Butterworths).

Ball, S. (1995) 'Nuisance and Planning Permission', 7(2) *Journal of Environmental Law* 278.

Ball, S. and Bell, S. (1995) *Environmental Law*, 3rd edn (London: Blackwell).

Ballard, R. (ed.) (1994) *Desh Pardesh: The South Asian Presence in Britain* (London: Jurst & Co).

Ballard, R. and Virinder Singh Kalra (1993) *The Ethnic Dimensions of the 1991 Census: A Preliminary Report* (Manchester: Manchester University Press).

Banks, O. (1981) *Faces of Feminism* (Oxford: Martin Robertson).

Banton, M. (1988) *Racial Consciousness* (London: Longman).

Barrett, M. and Roberts, H. (1978) 'Doctors and Their Patients: the Social Control of Women in General Practice' in C. Smart and B. Smart (eds) *Women, Sexuality and Social Control* (London, Henley and Boston: Routledge).

Barrow, J., Deech, R., Larbie, J., Loomba, R and Smith, D. (1994) 'Equal Opportunities At The Inns of Court School of Law, Final Report of The Committee of Inquiry into Equal Opportunities on The Bar Vocational Course' (London: Council of Legal Education).

Bender, L. (1988) 'A Lawyer's Primer on Feminist Theory and Tort', 38 *Journal of Legal Education* 3.

Bender, L. (1990a) 'Changing the Values in Tort Law', 25 *Tulsa Law Journal* 759.

Bender, L. (1990b) 'Feminist (Re)torts: Thoughts on the Liability Crisis, Mass Torts, Power and Responsibilities', *Duke Law Journal* 848.

Bender, L. with Lawrence, P. (1993) 'Is Tort Law Male? Foreseeability Analysis and Property Manager's Liability for Third Party Rapes of Residents', 69 *Chicago-Kent Law Review* 313.

Benedict, R. (1983) *Race and Racism* (London: Routledge).

Benn, S. and Gaus, G. (1983) *Public and Private in Social Life* (London: Croom Helm).

Bergeron, J. (in press) 'An Even Whiter Myth: The Colonisation of Modernity in European Community Law' in J. Bergeron and R. Find (eds) *Nationalism, Modernity and the Language of Rights* (Aldershot: Dartmouth).

Berry, J.M. (1984) *The Interest Group Society* (Boston and Toronto: Little Brown and Co.).

Bhabha, H. (1994) *The Location of Culture* (London: Routledge).

Birnie, P.W. and Boyle, A.E. (1992) *International Law and the Environment* (Oxford: Clarendon Press).

Bistolfi, R. and Zabbal, F. (eds) (1995) *Islams d'Europe Intégration ou Insertion Communautaire?* (Paris: Éditions de l'Aube).

Blackstone, W. (1765) *Commentaries on the Laws of England* (Oxford: Clarendon Press).

Blom-Cooper, L. and Drabble, R. (1982) 'Police Perception of Crime: Brixton and the Operational Response', 22 *British Journal of Criminology* 184.

Blunden, J. and Curry, N. (1989) *A People's Charter* (London: Countryside Commission/HMSO).

Boothman, C. (1994) 'Race and racism – the missing dimensions in the Royal Commission on Criminal Justice' in M. McConville and L. Bridges (eds) *Criminal Justice in Crisis* (Aldershot: Edward Elgar).

Bork, R.H. (1989) 'The Limits of "International Law"', 18 *National Interest* 3.

Bork, R.H. (1990) *The Tempting of America: The Political Seduction of the Law* (New York: Free Press).

Box, S. (1983) *Power, Crime and Mystification* (London: Tavistock).

Bradney, A.W. (1993) *Religions, Rights and Laws* (Leicester: Leicester University Press).

Bramble, B.J. and Porter, G. (1992) 'Non Governmental Organisations and the Making of US Environmental Policy' in A. Hurrell and B. Kingsbury (eds) *The International Politics of the Environment: Actors, Interests and Institutions* (Oxford: Clarendon Press).

Bratton, W., McCahery, J., Picciotto, S. and Scott, C. (1996) *International Regulatory Competition and Coordination* (Oxford: Clarendon Press).

Bridges, L. and Forbes, D. (1990) *Making the Law Work on Racial Harassment: A LAG Special Report* (London: Legal Action Group).

Brittan, Y. (1984) *The Impact of Water Pollution Control on Industry: A Case Study of Fifty Dischargers* (Oxford: Centre for Socio-legal Studies).

Brownmiller, S. (1975) *Against Our Wills: Men, Women and Rape* (London: Pelican).

Burton, J. (1972) *World Society* (Cambridge: Cambridge University Press).

Cahn, N. (1992) 'The Looseness of Legal Language: The Reasonable Woman Standard in Theory and Practice', 77 *Cornell Law Review* 1398.

Cain, M. and Saddigh, S. (1982) 'Racism, the Police and Community Policing. A Comment on the Scarman Report', 9 *Journal of Law and Society* 1.

Cain, P. (1991) 'Feminist Jurisprudence: Grounding the Theories' in K. Barlett and R. Kennedy (eds) *Feminist Legal Theory* (Boulder: Westview).

Cane, P. (1987) *Atiyah's Accidents Compensation and the Law*, 4th edn (London: Weidenfeld & Nicolson).

Carlin, J. (1982), 'Significant Refugee Crises Since World War II and the response of the International Community', 3 *Transnational Legal Problems of Refugees, Michigan Yearbook of International Legal Studies* 12.

Carty, A. (1986) *The Decay of International Law: A Reappraisal of the Limits of Legal Imagination in International Affairs* (Manchester: Manchester University Press).

Carty, A. (1991) 'Critical International Law: Recent Trends in the Theory of International Law', 2 *European Journal of International Law* 66.

Cashmore, E.E. and Troyna, B. (1990) *Introduction to Race Relations,* 2nd edn (London: The Falmer Press).

Cassese, A. (1986) *International Law in a Divided World* (Oxford: Oxford University Press).

Cassese, A. (ed.) (1980) *The New Humanitarian Law of Armed Conflict* (Naples).

Central Statistical Office (1993) *New Earnings Survey* (London: HMSO, Central Statistical Office).

Chamberlain, M.E. (1974) *The Scramble for Africa* (London: Longman).

Charney, J.I. (1994) 'Progress in International Maritime Boundary Delimitation', 88 *American Journal of International Law* 227.

Chiba, M. (1986) *Asian Indigenous Law in Interaction with Received Law* (New York and London: KPI).

Chiba, M. (1989) *Legal Pluralism: Towards a General Theory Through Japanese Legal Culture* (Tokyo: Takai University Press).

Chomsky, N. (1994) *World Orders: Old and New* (London: Pluto Press).

Clapp, B. (1994) *An Environmental History of Britain since the Industrial Revolution* (London: Longman).

Clarkson, C. and Keating, H. (1994) *Criminal Law: Text and Materials* (London: Sweet and Maxwell).

Coase, R. (1960) 'The Problem of Social Cost', 3 *Journal of Law and Economics* 1.

Collier, A. (1994) 'Value, Rationality and the Environment', 66 *Radical Philosophy* 3.

Commoner, B. (1989) 'The Social Use and Misuse of Technology' in M. Allaby (ed.) Thinking Green: An Anthology of Essential Ecological Writing (London: Barrie and Jenkins).

Conaghan, J. (1995) 'Tort Law and the Feminist Critique of Reason' in A. Bottomley (ed.) *Gender Goes to the Core* (London: Cavendish).

Conaghan, J. (1996) 'Gendered Harms and the Law of Tort', 16(3) *Oxford Journal of Legal Studies* (407).

Conaghan, J. and Mansell, W. (1993) *The Wrongs of Tort* (London: Pluto Press).

Council of Legal Education (1993) 'The Administration of Justice in a Multi-Cultural Society' (The Kapila Fellowship Lecture).

Crenshaw, K. (1988) 'Race, Reform and Retrenchment: Transformation and Legitimation in Antidiscrimination Law', 101 *Harvard Law Review* 1331.

Crenshaw, K. (1991) 'Demarginalising the Intersection of Race and Sex: A Black Feminist Critique of Antidiscrimination Doctrine, Feminist Theory and Antiracist Politics' in K. Barlett and R. Kennedy (eds) *Feminist Legal Theory* (Boulder: Westview).

Crenson, M.A. (1971) *The Un-politics of Air Pollution: A Study of Non-Decision Making in the Cities* (Baltimore: Johns Hopkins University Press).

Dalton, K. (1991) *Once a Month* (London: Fontana).

Davies, V. (1991) *Abortion and Afterwards* (Bath: Ashgrove Press).

Davis, K. (1988) *Power Under the Microscope: Towards a Grounded Theory of Gender Relations in Medical Encounters* (Amsterdam: Foris Publications).

Derrida, J. (1992) *The Other Heading: Reflections on Today's Europe* (Bloomington: Indiana University Press).

Dezalay, Y. and Garth, B. (1995) 'Merchants of Law as Moral Entrepreneurs: Constructing International Justice from the Competition for Transnational Business Disputes', 29(1) *Law and Society Review* 27.

Dhabha, H. (1994) *The Location of Culture* (London: Routledge).

Dobash, R.E. and Dobash, R. (1992) *Women, Violence and Social Change* (London: Routledge).

Downs, A. (1957) *An Economic Theory of Democracy* (New York: Harper and Row).

Duroselle, J.B. (1990) *Europe: A History of Its Peoples* (London: Viking).

Easlea, B. (1981) *Science and Sexual Oppression* (London: Weidenfeld and Nicolson).

Eckersley, R. (1992) *Environmentalism and Political Theory* (Albany: SUNY Press).

Edwards, J. and Batley, R. (1978) *The Politics of Positive Discrimination: An Evaluation of the Urban Programme 1966–77* (London: Tavistock).

Edwards, S. (1988) 'Mad, Bad or Premenstrual?', 138 *New Law Journal* 456.

Edwards, S. (1989) *Policing Domestic Violence* (London: Sage).

Ehrenreich, B. and English, D. (1978) *For Her Own Good: 150 Years of the Experts' Advice to Women* (London: Pluto Press).

Eisenstein, Z. (1984) *The Radical Future of Liberal Feminism* (New York: Monthly Review Press).

Elshtain, J. (1981) *Public Man, Private Woman*: Women in Social and Political Thought (Oxford: Martin Robertson).

Engels, F. (1892) *Conditions of the Working Classes in England* (London: Sonnenschein).

Enloe, C.H. (1975) *The Politics of Pollution in a Comparative Perspective: Ecology and Power in Four Nations* (New York: David Macay Co.).

Enzenberger, H.M. (1974) 'A Critique of Political Ecology', 84 *New Left Review* 3.

Equal Opportunities Commission (EOC) (1995) *Equal Pay for Men and Women: Strengthening the Acts* (Manchester: EOC).

Equal Opportunities Review (1994) 'Equal Value Update', 58 *EOR* 11–30.

Evans, D. (1992) *A History of Nature Conservation in Britain* (London: Routledge).

Eyerman, R. and Jamison, A. (1989) 'Environmental Knowledge as an Organisational Weapon: the Case of Greenpeace', 28 *Social Science Information* 99.

Farber, D.A. (1992) 'Politics and Procedure in Environmental Law', 8(1) *Journal of Law, Economics and Organisation* 61.

Fekete, L (1994) 'Inside Racist Europe', in T. Bunyan (ed.) *State Watching the New Europe: A Handbook on the European State* (Nottingham: Statewatch).

Feller, E. (1989) 'Carrier Sanctions and International Law', 1 *International Journal of Refugee Law* 1.

Finley, L. (1989) 'A Break in the Silence: Including Women's Issues in a Torts Course', 1 *Yale Journal of Law and Feminism* 41.

Fitzgerald, M. (1993) *Ethnic Minorities and the Criminal Justice System* (London: HMSO).

Fitzpatrick, P. (1995) '"We Know What it is When You Do Not Ask Us" Nationalism as Racism' in P. Fitzpatrick (ed.) *Nationalism, Racism and the Rule of Law* (Aldershot: Dartmouth).

Forbes, D. (1988) *Action on Racial Harassment: Legal Remedies and Local Authorities* (London: LAG).

Forbes, D. (1995) *Action against Racial Harassment*, 2nd edn (London: LAG).

Forell, C. (1992) 'Reasonable Woman Standard of Care', 11 *University of Tasmania Law Review.* 1.

Foster, P. (1995) *Women and the Health Care Industry* (Buckingham: Open University Press).

Foucault, M. (1989) *Madness and Civilization: A History of Insanity in the Age of Reason* (London and New York: Tavistock and Routledge).

Franck, T.M. (1990) *The Power of Legitimacy Among Nations* (Oxford: Oxford University Press).

Fredman, S. (1994) 'Equal Pay and Justification', 23 *Industrial Law Journal* 37.

Friedman, L. and Karsh, E. (1992) *The Gulf Conflict 1990–1991: Diplomacy and War in the New World Order* (Princeton: Princeton University Press).

Frogaman, A. (1970) 'The Refugee: A Problem of Definition', 45 *Case Western Reserve Journal of International Law.*

Fudge, J. and McDermott, P. (1991) *Just Wages: A Feminist Assessment of Pay Equity* (Toronto: University of Toronto Press).

Fukuyama, F. (1992) *The End of History and the Last Man* (London: Hamish Hamilton).

Giddens, A. (1994) *Beyond Left and Right: The Future of Radical Politics* (Cambridge: Polity Press).

Gilligan, C. (1982) *In a Different Voice: Psychological Theory and Women's Development* (Cambridge, Mass.: Harvard University Press).

Gilroy, P. (1987) *'There Ain't No Black in the Union Jack': The Cultural Politics of Race and Nation* (London: Hutchinson).

Goldman, M. (1972) *The Spoils of Progress: Environmental Pollution in the Soviet Union* (Cambridge, Mass.: MIT Press).

Goldsmith, E. et al. (1972) *A Blueprint for Survival* (Harmondsworth: Penguin).

Goodwin-Gill, G. (1982) 'Entry and Exclusion of Refugees: The Obligations and Protective Functions of the United Nations High Commissioner for Refugees', 291 *Transnational Legal Problems of Refugees, Michigan Yearbook of International Legal Studies* 302.

Goodwin-Gill, G. (1983) *The Refugee in International Law* (Oxford: Clarendon Press).

Gordon, P. and Klug, F. (1984) *Racism and Discrimination in Britain: A Select Bibliography 1970–83* (London: Runnymede Trust).

Gordon, R.W. (1984) 'Critical Legal Histories', 36 *Stanford Law Review* 57.

Grahl-Madsen, A. (1966) *The Status of Refugee in International Law* (Leydon: A.W. Sijthoff).

Grant, C. (1994) *Inside the House that Jacques Built* (London: Nicholas Brealey).

Gray, J. (1994) 'Equitable Property', 47(2) *Current Legal Problems* 157.

Greenawalt, K. (1983) *Discrimination and Reverse Discrimination* (New York: Alfred A. Knopf).

Griffith, J. (1985) *The Politics of the Judiciary*, 3rd edn (London: Fontana).

Griffith, J. (1986) 'What is Legal Pluralism?', 24 *Journal of Legal Pluralism and Unofficial Law* 1.

Grigg-Spall, I. and Ireland, P. (eds) (1992) *The Critical Lawyers' Handbook* (London: Pluto Press).

Groom, A.J.R. and Taylor, P. (eds) (1990) *Frameworks for International Cooperation* (London: Pinter).

Grundmann, R. (1991) 'The Ecological Challenge to Marxism', 187 *New Left Review* 103.

Guild, E. (1993) 'Toward a European Asylum Law: Developments in the European Community', 7 *Immigration and Nationality Law and Practice* 3.

Haas, P.M. et al. (1992) Special Issue on 'Knowledge, Power and International Policy Coordination' 46 *International Organization* 1.

Habermas, J. (1976) 'Problems of Legitimation in Late Capitalism' in P. Connerton (ed.) *Critical Sociology* (London: Penguin).

Habermas, J. (1992) *The Theory of Communicative Action: The Critique of Functionalist Reason* (Cambridge: Polity Press).

Hall, P. (1988) *Cities of Tomorrow* (Oxford: Blackwell).

Halpern, D. (1994) *Entry into the Legal Professions. The Law Student Cohort Study Years 1 and 2* (London: The Law Society).

Hamilton, C. (1995) *Family, Law and Religion* (London: Sweet & Maxwell).

Hanmer, J. and Maynard, M. (1987) *Women, Violence and Social Control* (Basingstoke: Macmillan).

Hartshorne, C. (1974) 'The Environmental Results of Technology' in W.T. Blackstone, *Philosophy and Environmental Crisis* (Athens: University of Georgia Press).

Harvey, D. (1993) 'Class Relations, Social Justice and the Politics of Difference' in J. Squires (ed.) *Principled Positions* (London: Lawrence and Wishart).

Hathaway, J.C. (1990) 'A Reconsideration of the Underlying Premise of Refugee Law' 31 *Harvard International Law Journal* 129.

Hathaway, J.C. (1991) *The Law of Refugee Status* (Toronto: Butterworths).

Hawkins, K. (1984) *Environment and Enforcement: Regulation and the Social Definition of Pollution* (Oxford: Clarendon Press).

Hepple, B. and Matthews, M. (1991) *Tort: Cases and Materials*, 4th edn (London: Butterworths).

Hepple, B. and Szyszczak, E.M. (eds) (1992) *Discrimination: The Limits of law* (London: Mansell).

Herbert, A. (1936) *Uncommon Law* (London: Methuen).

Herman, D. (1993) 'Beyond the Rights Debate', 2 *Social and Legal Studies* 25.

Higgins, R. (1994) *Problems and Process: International Law and How to Use It* (Oxford: Oxford University Press).

Hindell, K. and Simms, M. (1971) *Abortion Law Reformed* (London: Peter Owen).

Hobsbawm, E.J. (1992a) 'Ethnicity and Nationalism in Europe', 8(1) *Anthropology Today* 3.

Hobsbawm, E.J. (1992b) *Nations and Nationalism since 1780* (Cambridge: Cambridge University Press).

Hocke, J. (1990) 'Beyond Humanitarianism: The Need for Political Will to Resolve Today's Refugee Problem' in G. Loescher and L. Monahan (eds) *Refugees and International Relations* (Oxford: Clarendon Press).

Holder, J. (1991) 'Regulating Green Advertising in the Motor Car Industry' 18(3) *Journal of Law and Society* 323.

Home Office (1989) *Home Office Statistical Bulletin, 5/89* (London: HMSO).

Hood, R. (1992a) 'A Question of Judgement' (London: Campaign for Racial Equality).

Hood, R. (1992b) *Race and Sentencing: A Study in the Crown Court* (Oxford: Clarendon Press).

Hooker, M.B. (1975) *Legal Pluralism* (Oxford: Clarendon Press).

House of Commons Committee of Public Accounts (1994) Session 1993–94, *Protecting and Managing Sites of Special Scientific Interest: Minutes of Evidence*, Monday 31 October 1994.

Howarth, W. (1994) 'Making Water Polluters Pay', 2(2) *Environmental Liability* 29.

Hudson, D. (1987) 'You Can't Commit Violence Against an Object: Women, Psychiatry and Psychosurgery' in J. Hanmer and M. Maynard (eds) *Women, Violence and Social Control* (Basingstoke: Macmillan).

Humana, C. (1992) *World Human Rights Guide*, 3rd edn (Oxford: Oxford University Press).

Hunt, A. (1990) 'Rights and Social Movements: Counter Hegemonic Strategies', 17 *Journal of Law and Society* 309.

Hunt, A. (1991) 'Marxism, Law, Legal Theory and Jurisprudence', in Peter Fitzpatrick (ed.), *Dangerous Supplements: Resistance and Renewal in Jurisprudence* (London: Pluto Press).

Illich, I. (1975) *Medical Nemesis: The Expropriation of Health* (London: Marion Boyars).

Immigration and Nationality Law and Practice (1994) 'Asylum Seekers: Exceptional Leave to Remain and Detention' (Quarterly Legal Update) vol 8, no 3.

Ingelhart R. (1977) *The Silent Revolution: Changing Values and Political Styles among Western Publics* (Princeton: Princeton University Press).

Jefferson, T. and Walker, M.A. (1992) 'Ethnic Minorities in the Criminal Justice System', *Criminal Law Review* 83.

Jenkins, R. (1986) *Racism and Recruitment* (Cambridge: Cambridge University Press).

Jessup, P. C. (1956) *Transnational Law* (Yale: Yale University Press).

Jones, T., Maclean, B. and Young, J. (1986) *The Islington Crime Survey* (London: Gower).

Jordan, A. (1993) 'Integrated Pollution Control and the Evolving Style and Structure of Environmental Regulation in the UK', 2 *Environmental Politics* 405.

Kane, P. (1991) *Women's Health: From Womb to Tomb* (London: Macmillan).

Karp, J.P. (1992–93) 'A Private Property Duty of Stewardship: Changing Our Land Ethic', 23 *Environmental Law* 735.

Kelman, M. (1987) *A Guide to Critical Legal Studies* (London: Harvard University Press).

Kennedy, D. (1986) 'Primitive Legal Scholarship', 27 *Harvard International Law Journal* 1.

Kennedy, H. (1993) *Eve was Framed* (London: Vintage).

Kennedy, I. (1985) *Treat Me Right: Essays in Medical Law and Ethics* (Oxford: Clarendon Press).

Keown, J. (1988) *Abortion, Doctors and the Law: Some Aspects of the Legal Regulation of Abortion in England from 1803 to 1982* (Cambridge: Cambridge University Press).

King, M. (ed.) (1995) *God's Law Versus State Law. The Construction of an Islamic Identity in Western Europe* (London: Grey Seal).

Kingdom, E. (1991) *What's Wrong with Rights?* (Edinburgh: Edinburgh University Press).

Kinnersley, D. (1988) *Troubled Water: Rivers, Politics and Pollution* (London: Hilary Shipman).

Kirby, A. (1982) *The Politics of Location* (London: Methuen).

Komarov, B.(1978) *The Destruction of Nature in the Soviet Economy* (London: Pluto Press).

Koskenniemi, M. (1988) 'From Apology to Utopia. The Structure of International Legal Argument', 31(1) *Harvard International Law Journal* 385.

Koskenniemi, M. (1990) 'The Politics of International Law', 1 *European Journal of International Law* 4.

Koskenniemi, M. (1991a) 'Theory: Implications for the Practitioner' in *Theory and International Law: An Introduction* (London: British Institute of International and Comparative Law).

Koskenniemi, M. (1991b) 'The Future of Statehood', 32 *Harvard International Law Journal* 397.

Koskenniemi, M. (1994) 'The Wonderful Artificiality of States', *American Society of International Law Proceedings* 22.

Kramer, L. (1991) 'Participation of Environmental Organisations in the Activities of the EEC' in M. Fuhr and G. Roller (eds) *Participation and Litigation of Environmental Associations in Europe* (Frankfurt am Main: Verlag Peter Lang).

Krasner, S.D. et al. (1982) 'International Regimes', 36(2) *International Organization* 185.

Krenz, F. (1966) 'The Refugee as a Subject of International Law', 15 *International Comparative Law Quarterly* 90.

Lacey, N. (1993) 'Theory into Practice? Pornography and the Public/Private Dichotomy', 20(1) *Journal of Law and Society* 93.

Lauterpacht, H. (1970) *International Law* (Cambridge: Cambridge University Press).

Law, S. (1984) 'Rethinking Sex and the Constitution', 132 *University of Pennsylvania Law Review* 955.

Law Society (1991) *Advice on Avoiding Racial Discrimination* (London: Law Society).

Law Society (1995) *New Anti-Discrimination Measures* (London: Law Society).

Lester, A. and Bindman, G. (1972) *Race and Law* (Harmondsworth: Penguin).

Lester, T. (1993) 'The Reasonable Woman Test in Sexual Harassment – Will It Really Make a Difference?', 26 *Indiana Law Review* 227.

Levy, M. A., Young, O.R. et al. (1995) 'The Study of International Regimes', 1(3) *European Journal of International Relations* 267.

Lipschutz, R. D. (1992) 'Reconstructing World Politics: The Emergence of Global Civil Society' 21(3) *Millennium* 389.

Littleton. C. (1981) 'Towards a Redefinition of Sexual Equality', 95 *Harvard Law Review* 487.

Lockton, D. (1993) *Employment Law* (London: Butterworths).

Lowe, P. and Goyder, J. (1983) *Environmental Groups in Politics* (London: George Allen & Unwin).

Lustgarten, L. (1980) *Legal Control of Racial Discrimination* (London: Macmillan).

Macdonald, I. (1969) *Race Relations and Immigration Law* (London: Butterworths).

Macdonald, I. and Blake, N. (1991) *Macdonald's Immigration Law and Practice* 3rd edn (London: Butterworths).

MacKinnon, C. (1979) *Sexual Harassment of Working Women* (New Haven and London: Yale University Press).

MacKinnon, C. (1983a) 'The Male Ideology of Privacy: A Feminist Perspective on the Right to Abortion', 17 *Radical America* 23.

MacKinnon, C. (1983b) 'Feminism, Marxism, Method and the State: Towards a Feminist Jurisprudence', 7 *Signs* 515.

MacKinnon, C. (1983c) 'Feminism, Marxism, Method and State: Towards Feminist Jurisprudence', 8 *Signs* 635.

MacKinnon, C. (1987) *Feminism Unmodified: Discourses on Life and Law* (Cambridge, Mass.: Harvard University Press).

MacKinnon, C. (1989) *Towards a Feminist Theory of the State* (Cambridge, Mass.: Harvard University Press).

MacKinnon, C. (1994) *Only Words* (London: HarperCollins).

Mann, C.R. (1993) *Unequal Justice: A Question of Color* (Bloomington and Indianapolis: Indiana University Press).

Mansell, W. (1991) 'Legal Aspects of International Debt', 18 *Journal of Law and Society* 381.

Mansell, W., Meteyard, B. and Thomson, A. (1995) *A Critical Introduction to Law* (London: Cavendish).

Mansell, W., and Scott, J. (1994) 'Why Bother About a Right to Development?', 21 *Journal of Law and Society* 171.

Marcuse, H. (1968) *One Dimensional Man* (London: Sphere).

Marcuse, H. (1969) 'Repressive Tolerance' in Wolff, R.B., Moore, Barrington Jr, and Marcuse, H. *A Critique of Pure Tolerance* (London: Jonathan Cape).

Marcuse, H. (1972) *An Essay on Liberation* (Harmondsworth: Pelican).

Martin, E. (1987) *The Woman in the Body: A Cultural Analysis of Reproduction* (Milton Keynes: Open University Press).

Martin, R. (1994) 'A Feminist View of the Reasonable Man', 23(1) *Anglo-American Law Review* 334.

Marx, K. (1993) *Grundrisse, Foundations of the Critique of Political Economy* (London: Penguin).

Mason, D. (1995) *Race and Ethnicity in Modern Britain* (Oxford: Oxford University Press).

Mason, J.K. and McCall Smith, R.A. (1987) *Law and Medical Ethics*, 2nd edn (London: Butterworths).

Mazey, S.P. and Richardson, J.J. (1992) 'British Pressure Groups in the European Community: The Challenge of Brussels', 45(1) *Parliamentary Affairs* 92.

Mbuyi, B. (1993) *Refugees and International Law* (Toronto: Carswell).

McAuslan, P. (1980) *The Ideologies of Planning Law* (Oxford: Pergamon Press).

McColgan, A. (1993a) 'In Defence of Battered Women who Kill', 13 *Oxford Journal of Legal Studies* 508.

McColgan, A. (1993b) *Pay Equity – Just Wages for Women?* (London: Institute of Employment Rights).

McCrudden, C. (1986) 'Rethinking Positive Action', 15 *Industrial Law Journal* 218.

McCrudden, C., Smith, C.J.D. and Brown, C. (1991) *Racial Justice at Work: The Enforcement of the Race Relations Act 1976 in Employment* (London: Policy Studies Institute).

Meadows, D.H. et al. (1972) *The Limits to Growth* (London: Earth Island).

Menski, W.F. (1987) 'Legal Pluralism in the Hindu Marriage' in R. Burghart (ed.) *Hinduism in Great Britain* (London: Tavistock).

Menski, W.F. (1993) 'Asians in Britain and the Question of Adaptation to a New Legal Order: Asian Laws in Britain?' in Israel, Milton and Wagle (eds) *Ethnicity, Identity, Migration: The South Asian Context* (Toronto: University of Toronto Press).

Miles, R. (1989) *Racism: Key ideas* (London: Routledge).

Mill, J.S. [1869] (1985) *The Subjection of Women* (London: J.M. Dent).

Millns, S. (1995) 'Making "Social Judgments that go Beyond the Purely Medical": The Reproductive Revolution and Access to Fertility Treatment

Services', in J. Bridgeman and S. Millns (eds) *Law and Body Politics* (Aldershot: Dartmouth).

Milner, D. (1981) 'The Education of the Black Child in Britain', 9(2) *New Community* 289.

Modood, T. (1993) 'Muslim Views on Religious Identity and Racial Equality', 19(3) *New Community* 513.

Modood, T. (1992) *Not Easy Being British: Colour, Culture and Citizenship* (Stoke-on-Trent: Trentham).

Modood, T. and Shiner, D. (1994) *Ethnic Minorities in Higher Education: Why Are There Different Rates of Entry?* (London: PSI).

Montgomery, J. (1989) 'Medicine, Accountability, and Professionalism', 16 *Journal of Law and Society* 319.

Mossman, M. (1986) 'Feminism and Legal Method: the Difference it Makes', 28 *Australian Journal of Law and Society* 30.

Moxon, D. (1988) 'Sentencing Practice in the Crown Court', Home Office Research Study 103 (London: HMSO).

Moynihan, D.P. (1990) *On the Law of Nations* (Harvard: Harvard University Press).

Mumma, A. (1992) 'Protection of the Water Environment Through Private Court Action', 3(2) *Water Law* 51.

Nash, R. (1982) *Wilderness and the American Mind* (New Haven and London: Yale University Press).

National Rivers Authority (1993) *Water Pollution Incidents in England and Wales – 1992* (Newcastle: National Rivers Authority).

Neustatter, A. and Newson, G. (1986) *Mixed Feelings: The Experience of Abortion* (London, Sydney and New Hampshire: Pluto Press).

Nicolson, D. (1995) 'Telling Tales: Gender Discrimination, Gender Construction and Women Who Kill', 3(2) *Feminist Legal Studies* 185.

Nicolson, D. and Sanghvi, R. (1993) 'Battered Women and Provocation: the Implications of *R* v. *Ahluwalia*', *Criminal Law Review* 728.

O'Donovan, K. (1985) *Sexual Divisions in Law* (London: Weidenfeld and Nicolson).

O'Donovan, K. (1991) 'Defences for Battered Women who Kill', 18(2) *Journal of Law and Society* 219.

O'Donovan, K. (1993) 'Law's Knowledge: the Judge, the Expert, the Battered Woman and her Syndrome', 20(4) *Journal of Law and Society* 427.

OECD (1987) *Minimizing Conflicting Requirements* (Paris: OECD).

Olson, M. 'The Logic of Collective Action' (Cambridge, Mass.: Harvard University Press, 2nd edn, 1971) reprinted in part in J.J. Richardson (1993) *Pressure Groups* (Oxford: Oxford University Press).

Paliwala, A. (1995) 'Law and the Constitution of the "Immigrant" in Europe: A UK Policy Perspective' in P. Fitzpatrick (ed.) *Nationalism, Racism and the Rule of Law* (Aldershot: Dartmouth).

Pallaemerts, M. (1993) 'International Environmental Law from Stockholm to Rio: Back to the Future?' in P. Sands (ed.) *Greening International Law* (London: Earthscan).

Palmer, C. (1992) *Discrimination at Work: The Law on Sex and Race Discrimination*, 2nd edn (London: LAG).

Palmer, G. (1989) 'Settlement of International Disputes: the "Rainbow Warrior" affair', *Commonwealth Law Bulletin* 585.

Pannick, D. (1993) Employment Lawyers' Association Annual Lecture 137 *Solicitors Journal*, 12 November.

Pascal, A.H. (ed.) (1972) *Racial Discrimination in Economic Life* (Lexington: Lexington Books).

Pateman, T. (ed.) (1972) *Counter Course: A Handbook for Course Criticism* (London: Penguin Books).

Pearce, D.W. and Turner, R.K. (1990) *Economics of Natural Resources and the Environment* (Hemel Hempstead: Harvester Wheatsheaf).

Pearce, D., Markandya, A. and Barbier, E. (1989) *Blueprint for a Green Economy* (London: Earthscan).

Pearce, F. (1993) 'Road to Ruin for Britain's Wildlife', *New Scientist*, 11 September 1993, 35.

Pearl, D. (1986) *Family Law and the Immigrant Communities* (Bristol: Jordan & Sons).

Picciotto, S. (1983) 'Jurisdictional Conflicts, International Law and the International State System', 11 *International Journal of the Sociology of Law* 11.

Pieterse, J.N. (1991) 'Fictions of Europe', 32 *Race and Class* 3.

Pollard, D. and Ross, M. (1994) *European Community Law: Texts and Materials* (London: Butterworths).

Porras, I.M. (1993) 'The Rio Declaration: A New Basis for International Cooperation' in P. Sands (ed.) *Greening International Law* (London: Earthscan).

Poulter, S.M. (1986) *English Law and Ethnic Minority Customs* (London: Butterworths).

Poulter, S.M. (1990) 'Cultural Pluralism and its limits: A Legal Perspective' in 'Britain: A plural society. Report of a seminar' (London: Campaign for Racial Equality).

Poulter, S.M. (1994) 'Minority rights' in C. McCrudden and G. Chambers (eds) *Individual Rights and the Law in Britain* (Oxford: Clarendon Press).

Prince, T. and Finger, M. (1994) *Environmental NGOs in World Politics: Linking the Local and the Global* (London: Routledge).

Rex, J. (1983) *Race Relations in Sociological theory*, 2nd edn (London: Routledge and Kegan Paul).

Ridgeway, J. (1971) *The Politics of Ecology* (New York: Dutton).

Rimmer, M. (1972) *Race and Industrial Conflict. A Study in a Group of Midland Foundries* (London: Heinemann Educational Books).

Roberts, H. (1985) *The Patient Patients: Women and Their Doctors* (London, Boston, Melbourne and Henley: Pandora Press).

Robilliard, St J.A. (1983) 'Sikhs, Religion and the Race Relations Act 1976', *Public Law* 348.

Rose, E.J.B. (1969) *Colour and Citizenship: A Report on British Race Relations* (Oxford: Oxford University Press).

Rosenberg, J. (1994) *The Empire of Civil Society. A Critique of the Realist Theory of International Relations* (London: Verso).

Rosenfeld, M. (1991) *Affirmative Action and Justice* (New Haven: Yale University Press).

Royal Commission on Pollution of Rivers (1872) 4th Report, C. 603.

Ruddick, S. (1989) *Maternal Thinking* (London: The Women's Press).

Ruggie, J.G. (1993) 'Territoriality and Beyond: Problematizing Modernity in International Relations', 4(1) *International Organization* 139.

Sachs, A. and Hoff Wilson, J. (1978) *Sexism and the Law: A Study of Male Beliefs and Legal Bias in Britain and the USA* (Oxford: Martin Robertson).

Sagoff, M. (1988) *The Economy of the Earth: Philosophy, Law and the Environment* (Cambridge: Cambridge University Press).

Scarman, Lord (1981) 'The Brixton Disorders', Cmnd. 8427 (London: HMSO).

Scarrow, H.A. (1972) 'The Impact of British Domestic Air Pollution Legislation', 2(3) *British Journal of Political Science* 282.

Schepel, H. (1995) 'Legal Pluralism in the European Union', paper given at the conference Contested Communities: Critical Legal Perspectives, University of Edinburgh September 1995.

Schepel, H. and Wesseling, R. (1995) 'The Legal Community: Judges, Lawyers, Officials and Clerks in the Writing of Europe', Draft (Florence: European University Institute).

Schneider, E. (1991) 'The Dialectic of Rights and Politics: Perspectives from the Women's Movement' in K. Barlett and R. Kennedy (eds) *Feminist Legal Theory* (Boulder: Westview).

Schumacher, E.F. (1974) *Small is Beautiful: A Study of Economics as if People Mattered* (London: Sphere Books).

Scott, J. (1988) 'Deconstructing Equality-versus-Difference: or the uses of Poststructural Theory for Feminism', 14(1) *Feminist Studies* 33.

Scully, D. (1980) *Men Who Control Women's Health: The Miseducation of Obstetrician-Gynecologists* (Boston: Houghton Mifflin Company).

Segal, L. (1991) 'Whose Left?: Socialism, Feminism and the Future', 185 *New Left Review* 81.

Seton-Watson, H. (1985) 'What is Europe, Where is Europe?', 65(2) *Encounter* 9.

Shaw, M. (1991) *International Law* (Cambridge: Grotius).

Sheldon, S. (1993) '"Who is the Mother to Make the Judgment?": the Constructions of Woman in English Abortion Law', 1 *Feminist Legal Studies* 3.

Sheldon, S. (1995) 'The Law of Abortion and the Politics of Medicalisation' in J. Bridgeman and S. Millns (eds) *Law and Body Politics* (Aldershot: Dartmouth).

Shore, C. (1993) 'Inventing the "People's Europe": Critical Approaches to European Community "Cultural Policy"', 28(4) *Man* 779.

Shore, C. (1995) 'Transcending the Nation-State? The European Commission and the (Re)-Discovery of Europe', paper given at the conference 'Reappraising the Force of Tradition', University of Kent, April 1995.

Shore, C. and Black, A. (1994) 'Citizens' Europe and the Construction of European Identity' in V. Goddard et al. (eds) *The Anthropology of Europe: Identity and Boundaries in Conflict* (Oxford: Berg).

Showalter, E. (1987) *The Female Malady: Women, Madness and English Culture, 1830–1980* (London: Virago).

Simon, H. (1975) *Administrative Behaviour: A Study of Decision-making Processes in Administrative Organisations* (New York: Free Press).

Skogan, W.G. (1990) 'The Police and Public in England and Wales', Home Office Research Study 117 (London: HMSO).

Sklair, L. (1991) *Sociology of the Global System* (Hemel Hempstead: Harvester Wheatsheaf).

Smart, C. (1989) *Feminism and the Power of the Law* (London: Routledge).

Smart, C. (1992) 'The Woman of Legal Discourse', 1 *Social and Legal Studies* 29.

Smart, C. (1995) *Law, Crime and Sexuality* (London: Sage).

Smets, H. (1994) 'The Polluter Pays Principle in the Early 1990s' in L. Campiglio, L. Pineschi, D. Siniscalco and T. Treves, *The Environment after Rio* (London: Graham and Trotman).

Smith, D.J. (1977) *Racial Disadvantage in Britain. The PEP Report* (Harmondsworth: Penguin).

Smith, D.J. (1983) 'Police and People in London' (London: Policy Studies Institute).

Solomos, J. (1993) *Race and Racism in Britain* (Basingstoke: Macmillan).

Spencer, S. (ed.) (1994) *Strangers & Citizens. A Positive Approach to Migrants and Refugees* (London: IPPR and Rivers Oram Press).

Spijkerboer, T. (1993) *A Bird's Eye View of Asylum Laws in Eight European Countries* (Amsterdam: Dutch Refugee Council).

Stair, K. and Taylor, P. (1992) 'Non Governmental Organisations and the Legal Protection of the Oceans' in A. Hurrell and B. Kingsby, *The International Politics of the Environment: Actors, Interests and Institutions* (Oxford: Clarendon Press).

Stanfield, J.H. (ed.) (1993) *A History of Race Relations Research. First Generation Recollections* (London: Sage).

Stetson, D. (1982) *A Woman's Issue: The Politics of Family Law Reform in England* (Westport: Greenwood Press).

Stigler, G.J. (1971) 'The Theory of Economic Regulation', 2(1) *Bell Journal of Economics and Management* 3.

Stolcke, V. (1995) 'Talking Culture: New Boundaries, New Rhetorics of Exclusion in Europe', 36(1) *Current Anthropology* 1.

Strachey, R. (1978) *The Cause: A Short History of the Women's Movement in Great Britain* (London: Virago).

Tarn, J. (1980) 'Housing Reform and the Emergence of Town Planning in Britain before 1914' in A. Sutcliffe (ed.), *The Rise of Modern Urban Planning 1800–1914* (London: Mansell).

Taylor, P. (1986) *Respect for Nature* (Oxford: Princeton University Press).

Thomas, H. (1985) 'The Medical Construction of the Contraceptive Career' in H. Homans (ed.) *The Sexual Politics of Reproduction* (Aldershot: Gower).

Thompson, E.P (1985) *Whigs and Hunters* (London: Penguin).

Thomson, J.E. and Krasner S.D., (1989) 'Global Transactions and the Consolidation of Sovereignty' in E.O. Czempiel and J.N. Rosenau (eds) *Global Changes and Theoretical Challenges* (Lexington, Mass.: Lexington Books).

Thomson, M. (1995) 'Woman, Medicine and Abortion in the Nineteenth Century' 3(2) *Feminist Legal Studies* 159.

Thornton, M. (1991) 'The Public/Private Dichotomy: Gendered and Discriminatory', 18 *Journal of Law and Society* 448.

Tong, R. (1992) *Feminist Thought* (London: Routledge).

Townsend-Smith, R. (1990) 'The Role of Affirmative Action Officers in North American Universities', 19 *Anglo-American Law Review* 325.

Tromans, S. (1995) 'High Talk and Low Cunning: Putting Environmental Law Principles into Legal Practice', *Journal of Environment and Planning Law,* September 1995, 779.

Trubek, D.M., Dezalay, Y., Buchanan, R. (1994) 'Global Restructuring and the Law: Studies of the Internationalization of Legal Fields and the Creation of Transnational Arenas', 44(2) *Case Western Reserve Law Review* 407.

Tucker, W. (1980) 'Environmentalism, the Newest Toryism' *Policy Review,* fall issue, 141.

Tuitt, P. (1995) *False Images* (London: Pluto Press).

Tulloch, G. (1989) *Mill and Sexual Equality* (Hemel Hempstead: Harvester Wheatsheaf).

Turner, B.S. (1987) *Medical Power and Social Knowledge* (London: Sage).

Turner, R.K. and Pearce, D.W. (1990) *The Economics of Natural Resource Management* (Hemel Hempstead: Harvester Wheatsheaf).

United Nations High Commission for Refugees (1979) *Handbook on Criteria for Determining Refugee Status* (Geneva: UNCHR).

Ussher, J. (1989) *Women's Madness: Misogyny or Mental Illness?* (London: Harvester Wheatsheaf).

Walker, M.A. (1990) 'The Court Disposal and Remands of White, Afro-Caribbean and Asian Men', 29(4) *British Journal of Criminology* 353.

Weale, A. (1992) *The New Politics of Pollution* (Manchester: Manchester University Press).

Weale, A. and Williams, A. (1993) 'Between Economy and Ecology? The Single Market and the Integration of Environmental Policy' in D. Judge (ed.), *A Green Dimension to the European Community: Political Issues and Processes* (London: Frank Cass).

Westen, P. (1982) 'The Empty Idea of Equality', 95 *Harvard Law Review* 537.

Wilkes, A. (1995) 'Boom Time', 648 *Water Bulletin* 8.

Williams, P. (1991) *The Alchemy of Race and Rights* (Cambridge, Mass.: Harvard University Press).

Williams, W. (1982) 'The Crisis in Equality Theory', 7 *Women's Rights Reporter* 1.

Williams, W. (1984) 'Pregnancy and the Equal Treatment/Special Treatment Debate', 13 *New York University Review of Law and Social Change* 325.

Williams, W. (1991) 'The Equality Crisis: Some Reflections on Culture, Courts and Feminism' in K. Barlet and R. Kennedy (eds) *Feminist Legal Theory* (Boulder: Westview).

Winn, D. (1988) *Experiences of Abortion* (London: Macdonald Optima).

Wolgast, E. (1980) *Equality and the Rights of Women* (Ithaca: Cornell University Press).

Wollstonecraft, M. [1792] (1985) *A Vindication of the Rights of Woman* (London: J.M. Dent).

Wood, E.M. (1991) *The Pristine Culture of Capitalism* (London: Verso).

Wood, E.M. (1995) *Democracy Against Capitalism* (Cambridge: Cambridge University Press).

Woodman, G. (1983) 'The Limits of "The Limits of Law"', 21 *Journal of Legal Pluralism and Unofficial Law* 129.

World Commission on Environment and Development (1987) *Our Common Future* ('The Bruntland Report') (Oxford: Oxford University Press).

Zola, I.R. (1977) 'Healthism and Disabling Medicalization' in I. Illich (ed.) *Disabling Professions* (London: Marion Boyars).

Index

212